SECRET LIVES OF THE CIVIL WAR

WHAT YOUR TEACHERS NEVER TOLD YOU ABOUT THE WAR BETWEEN THE STATES

BY CORMAC O'BRIEN

PORTRAITS BY MONIKA SUTESKI

QUIRK BOOKS

PHILADELPHIA

Library of Congress Cataloging in Publication Number: 2007920527

ISBN: 978-1-59474-138-8

Printed in China

Typeset in Caecilia, Grotesque MT, Snell Roundhand

Designed by Jon Barthmus @ Skidmutro Creative + Layout
Illustrations by Monika Suteski
Map on pages 14–15 by Robert Romagnoli

Distributed in North America by Chronicle Books
680 Second Street
San Francisco, CA 94107

10 9 8 7 6 5 4 3 2

Quirk Books
215 Church Street
Philadelphia, PA 19106
www.quirkbooks.com

CONTENTS

PREFACE

Some 620,000 people died in the United States's costliest war, all of them Americans killed by other Americans. For the first time anywhere, populations preyed on each other with industrialized efficiency, attracting the attention of a world keen on witnessing the birth of modern slaughter. At stake were issues of profound importance: basic human freedom, sovereignty, the definition of self-government, and the limits of revolution, to name a few. It was—is—the defining watershed in the nation's history. No wonder we're preoccupied with it.

But our fascination goes beyond that. In addition to being the crucible in which America was reshaped, the Civil War was an enthralling drama. Its scale and ferocity were Homeric, its tragedies Shakespearean. And its endlessly varied characters seem to have walked off the pages of literature's most imaginative fiction.

Dan Sickles, for instance, was one of the nineteenth century's most notorious rogues. But he went on to become a political general whose performance in the war's greatest battle produced controversy equal to his outrageous behavior in civilian life. Thomas Jackson, by contrast, would have disappeared beneath the pages of posterity as a backwoods eccentric, middling teacher, and religious zealot. War, however, afforded his bizarre suite of abilities an opportunity to make military history, vaulting this humorless oddball into the pantheon of hallowed warlords—an unlikely fate indeed, given the material of which he was made. Such sensational lives are a dime a dozen in the War Between the States, presenting a panoply of weakness, heroism, triumph, waste, irony, idiocy, and even romance. Their stories are inherently irresistible, and not always because they performed a tremendous deed or won a crucial battle. Sometimes they wore carpet slippers into combat, blew off the president with astounding impropriety, had a nervous breakdown, or carried a hambone in their pocket. "Fascinating" wears all sorts of faces.

From the great and famous whose names have become household phrases to the numberless and forgotten whose lives require more effort to reveal, the players in this greatest of American struggles were human beings—flawed, awkward, spontaneous, strange, earnest, neurotic, and often quite smelly. No amount of eulogizing or monument-building can erase this salient fact. And that is as it should be.

INTRODUCTION

On December 2, 1859, Charles Town, Virginia, had a hanging. The condemned was a man named John Brown, whose recent "invasion" of Virginia had polarized a nation already quaking with ideological friction. Seven weeks before, he had descended with a small band of armed partisans on Harpers Ferry with the intention of capturing the armory there and igniting a slave revolt, hoping to precipitate a crusade to destroy the South's "peculiar institution." The adventure, unrealistic and poorly planned, failed miserably. Though the armory and arsenal were taken, Brown and his men were eventually surrounded in the town's fire engine house. Marines commanded by Robert E. Lee stormed the place, killing and capturing most of the defenders. Brown was tried for treason against the Commonwealth of Virginia and found guilty.

Though his mission had been foiled, the nature of Brown's fate was anything but disagreeable to him: the gallows would be as close to a national pulpit as he was ever going to get. He had been committed to the complete annihilation of slavery for years, at any cost, personifying a furious contempt for compromise that was increasingly claiming both sides of the slavery debate. In Kansas, during the grisly guerrilla conflicts that soaked that state in blood during the 1850s, Brown and his sons had hacked five pro-slavery men to death in retaliation for a notorious raid on the community of Lawrence. For Brown, such crude justice was nothing compared to the gargantuan collective sin of human bondage.

His hanging was by invitation only, and most of the honored spectators were soldiers. Nevertheless, the eyes of the world were on the doomed man, and he made the most of circumstances in the oddly punctuated note he left to his jailers. "I John Brown am now quite certain that the crimes of this guilty, land: will never be purged away; but with Blood," he wrote like a prophet.

And so he was. Two years later, in the midst of a terrible war, soldiers put Harpers Ferry to the torch. But the fire engine house where Brown had made his stand remained intact and defiant amongst the smoking rubble, a chilling reminder of the firebrand who foresaw a nation's self-mutilation.

Whether you viewed Brown as a traitor, a hero, a fool, a messiah, or a homicidal maniac depended on where you lived and how you felt about the slave issue that had driven him to act. The schism between free and slave states had existed since the previous century. Having failed to deal with it for the sake of sectional harmony, the founding fathers in effect passed the buck to future generations. For more than half a century, the United States carried the controversy westward as new territories were added to the republic. Each became a pawn in the ongoing debate, adding votes in Congress for the side that claimed it. Political bargains—particularly the Missouri Compromise (1820), the Compromise of 1850, and the Kansas-Nebraska Act (1854)—were arranged with the intention of balancing the relative territory and power of slave and free factions, but usually pleased neither. With the passage of time, abolitionist circles became more vocal, more determined against concessions, and more brazen in their extralegal efforts to aid runaway slaves. Incensed by their activities and seeing a growing immigrant North as a threat to the balance of power (by the advent of the Civil War there were four more free states than slave states) and hence to its slave-based economy and culture, the agrarian South cultivated secession from the Union as an increasingly likely option.

It is easy to oversimplify, of course. There were plenty of those in the free North who believed that interfering with the slave laws of Southern states was constitutionally unacceptable. And in areas of the South, some of them quite large, breaking away from the sovereign United States was treasonous, whatever the reason. But these were the exceptions in a mounting tale of angry discord. An immense impasse had been reached between two divergent, irreconcilable, self-righteous cultures.

Abraham Lincoln's election to the highest office in the land brought it all to a head. Representing the relatively new Republican Party, Lincoln—though a moderate—was a known critic of the spread of slavery. His victory was a model worst-case scenario for fretting Southern secessionists, representing all the requisite horrors: A free state candidate from the party of abolitionists had acquired the very pinnacle of political power. The long years of compromise were over.

South Carolina severed its connection to the greater United States on December 20, 1860, just a month and a half after Lincoln's electoral victory. Its future Confederate fellows would take a little longer, not least because so many Southerners blanched at the prospect. But by February of the following year, the Palmetto State had been joined by Mississippi, Florida, Alabama, Georgia, Louisiana, and Texas (in that order). Meeting in Montgomery, Alabama, delegates from each of them except Texas organized the Confederate States of America with a constitution based closely on that of the United States. In April, Confederate forces fired on Fort Sumter in Charleston Harbor, which worked as a catalyst for four of the remaining slave states to secede: Virginia, Arkansas, North Carolina, and Tennessee. Two American nations now existed in fact as well as in theory, and they had already come to blows.

The Confederacy had a couple of distinct advantages in the war that followed. For one, it was the world's largest producer of cotton, which Europe's mills—particularly those in the United Kingdom and France—consumed hungrily, making foreign intervention on its behalf a real possibility. And most important, it could take advantage of the defensive: the Union had to come after the Confederacy, not the reverse.

While all the South had to do was not lose, the North had to conquer to achieve its aims. For Lincoln, secession was a mighty test that his civilization must not fail. Should it do so, America was nothing more than a collection of autonomous polities that could cancel their membership when it suited them. The great democratic experiment would be a farce. To coerce the Rebels back into the Union, Lincoln's forces could draw on advantages that would eventually trump those possessed by the South: a navy, which was to strangle the Confederacy in a blockade; a much larger population; and an overwhelming superiority in arms, factories, railroads, and all the other industrial requirements of war.

Nevertheless, finding the right generals to exploit these assets would prove difficult for the Federal cause, particularly in the eastern theater. There, after the Confederate government was moved to Richmond in May 1861, the two capitals frowned at each other across less than 100 miles of Virginia real estate, coaxing many on both sides into thinking that the war could be won with one bold charge. In July, bowing to pressure from the masses to do something decisive, Union general in chief Winfield Scott sent Irvin McDowell south to rout P. G. T. Beauregard's Rebels along a creek called Bull Run. Reinforced by an army under Joseph Johnston, it was the Confederates who did the routing, sending McDowell and most of his green soldiers scurrying back to Washington in a state of unbridled panic. So much for McDowell.

His replacement was George McClellan, who would turn the victims of Bull Run and their reinforcements into a force to be reckoned with through ceaseless drilling and shrewd organization. Sadly, he would take forever to do this. He finally got moving in April 1862, when he landed the Army of the Potomac on the Peninsula between the York and James Rivers with the intention of marching on Richmond. It was a bold stroke, and it should have ended the war. But the Rebel forces were beginning to display a level of resourcefulness and cunning that men like McClellan were unprepared to deal with. By the time of McClellan's Peninsula campaign, for instance, a former Virginia Military Institute professor named Thomas "Stonewall" Jackson was causing sheer havoc in the Shenandoah Valley against superior numbers. Men like Jackson were to prove the undoing of McClellan, especially Robert E. Lee, who ended up assuming command of the Southern forces around Richmond after the Battle of Seven Pines at the end of May. By that time the Army of the Potomac had approached close enough to the Confederate capital to see its church spires. It would get no further. In a series of counterstrokes called the Seven Days' Battles, Lee's numerically inferior Confederates maneuvered, pushed, and levered their Northern foes back from the approaches of Richmond toward the ocean and eventual evacuation. The Confederacy had been saved.

It would be saved again. In August, John Pope—yet another general in which the Union cause would invest a forlorn hope—went out to meet Lee and Jackson at the Second Battle of Bull Run and was roundly defeated. Nearly defenseless, Washington quaked with fear and turned once again to McClellan, who managed to catch the sort of break that every commanding general prays for: Through sheer luck, he came to possess his enemy's plans. Armed with an intelligence coup of the first order, he marched into Maryland to thwart Lee's invasion of that state and, perhaps, bag the whole Army of Northern Virginia. On September 17, the bloodiest day in American history, the two forces clashed at Antietam Creek. Though offered the first opportunity to destroy Lee utterly, the best McClellan could manage was a draw.

It wasn't much of a military achievement for the Union. But Antietam marked a turn in American history of enormous significance. Lincoln, having penned the Emancipation Proclamation, was waiting for a shift in the military wind to make it public. Antietam was it: Though Lee hadn't been destroyed, he had been checked and pushed out of Northern territory. The preliminary proclamation was issued. As of January 1, 1863, all slaves in areas rebelling against the United States that were not already occupied by Federal forces would be considered free. The government in Washington had made official what plenty of Americans already knew: this was to be a war for freedom as well as for the Union.

Of course, the Emancipation Proclamation evoked an indignant uproar throughout the Confederacy. But it also pissed off no small number of Northerners—McClellan, ironically, chief among them—who saw Lincoln's gambit as a reckless perversion of a just constitutional crusade against secessionists. For them this was supposed to be a fight on behalf of the Union, not black slaves. Nevertheless, the two issues—freedom or slavery, states' rights or federal sovereignty—had become inextricably intertwined by Lincoln's visionary document. The proclamation was also a crucial war measure, not least because it attached the Union cause with abolition. To foreign powers, supporting the Confederacy now meant supporting a nation whose economy was founded on a racist institution that they had abolished in their own empires long ago. With a stroke, Lincoln had eliminated the international question.

The Confederacy, then, was on its own. And for the moment, that was more than enough. In December 1862, Lee happily went on the defensive to receive a disastrous Union attack at Fredericksburg. The following May, another Union thrust in Virginia fell to pieces at

Chancellorsville, where Lee proved to be more than the sum of his oppo-nents' parts. The Confederate Army of Northern Virginia had become more than a match for anything the North could throw at it, and Lee decided to take it on the offensive once again as he had done the previ-ous year in Maryland. Seizing the initiative and forcing his disoriented enemy to react to his actions was sound thinking, but it ended in disaster. At the town of Gettysburg, Pennsylvania, the Army of Northern Virginia and the Army of the Potomac essentially bumped into each other in July 1863. The result was the greatest clash of arms in the history of the western hemisphere and a decisive Union victory. Lee had made his grandest gamble and lost.

Gettysburg was enough of a victory to buoy Union morale. But it came at virtually the same moment as another Federal triumph nearly a thousand miles to the southwest: Vicksburg. Extending from the western slope of the Appalachians to the Mississippi River, the western theater was far vaster than its eastern counterpart and, despite its distance from the capitals, at least as significant strategically. The prizes to be had were Tennessee, which controlled access to the heart of the Confederacy, and the great Mississippi River itself, which—depending on who controlled it—either united or bifurcated the South. Here things had gone mostly the North's way, beginning in February 1862 when troops under Ulysses Grant captured Forts Henry and Donelson, seizing control of western Tennessee. He nearly lost the gains he had made at the furious and extremely bloody Battle of Shiloh in April, but managed to rescue success from disaster on the second day of the fight. That same month the critical port of New Orleans fell to Flag Officer David Farragut, putting in place all the elements needed to begin an advance on the Mississippi from both directions. A Confederate offensive in Mississippi came to nothing and Rebel general Braxton Bragg's autumn invasion of Kentucky was turned back at Perryville, then further mauled at Murfreesboro, Tennessee, in the new year.

For Union forces in the West, 1862 had been a good year. But the winter offensive against Vicksburg itself—the city whose lofty bluffs, bristling with guns, continued to command the Mississippi—had failed. It wouldn't be until the summer of 1863 that Grant, employing daring and unorthodox tactics, was able to invest Vicksburg and pummel it into submission. The city surrendered on July 4, essentially completing the Union conquest of the continent's greatest waterway and cutting the South in two.

The twin victories of Gettysburg and Vicksburg were joined that summer by the capture of Chattanooga, a Northern success that Bragg, with James Longstreet's help, nearly reversed at the epic Battle of Chickamauga and the siege of Chattanooga that followed. But the vital Tennessee rail center remained in Federal hands, further hindering the Confederacy's ability to maneuver troops where they were most needed throughout its embattled territory. The war was now indisputably going poorly for the South, narrowing its hopes down to one month: November 1864, the date of the North's presidential election. Should Lincoln lose, his successor might well be willing to offer peace. All the Confederate armies had to do was hold on until then—and make their enemy pay dearly for every inch of ground, pouring fuel on the glowing embers of Northern antiwar sentiment.

It may seem in hindsight that Dixie was doomed. But the Army of Northern Virginia had long since proven itself to be a tough and enterprising adversary, even in the most dire of situations. And the Confederacy was still a seriously big place; lancing its innards with great thrusting columns was a lot easier said than done.

Nevertheless, that is what the newly appointed lieutenant general Ulysses Grant intended to do. With so much riding on the clock, 1864 was slated to be the year of final victory. The two principal instruments of that victory were to be the Army of the Potomac, ostensibly commanded by George Meade, and the combined armies of the west, under William T. Sherman. Commander in Chief Grant, in charge of all the Union armies, would ride with Meade. There were other weapons in Grant's arsenal: Benjamin Butler coming up from the Virginia coast, Franz Sigel in the Shenandoah Valley, and others. But Meade and Sherman were to be the principal pincers in a conclusive squeeze play meant to crush the Rebel armies and their supply depots from north and west.

Grant bore down on Lee like the relentless hammer he was hired to be. In his unsparing Overland campaign through Virginia, his troops grappled with the enemy in battles that continue to signify violent excess: The Wilderness, Spotsylvania Court House, Cold Harbor. Until then, Lee had been able to dazzle his enemy, then regroup while the other side came back to its senses. Grant, by contrast, was something new: Matching Lee's movements, he held on to the enemy and kept coming at him, thrashing and maiming until his tireless wrath took its toll. The cost in lives was appalling. It was a brave new war, and Lee knew it. In a series of controlled retreats, he retired into the defenses of Petersburg, drawing the Army of the Potomac into a siege replete with trenches, enormous siege guns, snipers, and—above all—stalemate.

Sherman, out in the northwest corner of Georgia, had his own version of total war, advancing toward Atlanta through the summer. When his columns stalled before the defenses of Atlanta just as surely as Grant's had halted at Petersburg, it seemed as if the Confederacy's plan of deciding the November election bore hope. Despite an overwhelming superiority in troops and matériel, the North sank into a slough of despond even as ultimate victory seemed closer than ever.

Then, on September 3, Washington received a wire from Sherman: "Atlanta is ours, and fairly won." Like a lightning bolt, Lincoln's reelection campaign was reinvigorated. Two months later Sherman left Atlanta for his famous "march to the sea" and Honest Abe was securely back in the saddle.

With Lee's army anchored at Petersburg to defend Richmond, and Federal offensives in Alabama and the Carolinas, the Confederacy had embarked upon its final days. Lee, having made desperate and futile attacks against Grant's besieging army, abandoned Petersburg on April 2, leaving Richmond to the enemy. By that time Sherman had marched his army up into North Carolina, leaving what was left of the Army of Northern Virginia no choice but to flee west. It didn't get far. On April 9, 1865, Lee surrendered his weary forces to Grant at Appomattox Court House. The remaining Confederate forces would end up surrendering over the ensuing two months.

Lincoln would never receive word of them. On April 14, he was shot in the head while watching a play at Ford's Theatre in Washington and died the next morning. The man had skulked into the White House with the hope of preserving the Union as it was; he died having changed it beyond recognition. On December 6, 1865, the Thirteenth Amendment was ratified, abolishing slavery.

The war cost 620,000 lives. And the era of Reconstruction that followed would be one of the most contentious and unstable periods in American history. But in addition to abolishing legal slavery throughout the country, the war had begun to forge a centralized nation that was impossible before—the United States had become more "United" and less "States." Perhaps the unfinished business of the founding fathers was at last complete.

THE UNION

1 ABRAHAM
LINCOLN

February 12, 1809–April 15, 1865

HIGHEST RANK:

American President

ASTROLOGICAL SIGN:

Aquarius

NICKNAMES:

Honest Abe, the Rail-splitter, Father Abraham, the Great Emancipator

WORDS TO REMEMBER:

"Doesn't it strike you as queer that I, who couldn't cut the head off of a chicken, and who was sick at the sight of blood, should be cast into the middle of a great war, with blood flowing all about me?"

The election of 1860 was a strange one. To begin with, the Democrats coughed up two candidates. Divided like the rest of the country over slavery, the party of Andrew Jackson and Martin Van Buren—the political juggernaut that had dominated the national scene for years—simply blew apart. Senator Stephen Douglas was the natural front-runner, but he had infuriated many Southern Democrats for views that were hostile to the spread of slavery into the territories. Mostly (though not exclusively) from Dixie, these disillusioned Dems favored an aggressive, national pro-slavery platform. At their own little get-together, they nominated Vice President John Breckinridge as an alternative candidate. The Constitutional Union Party, which went out of its

> When Abraham Lincoln was called out to a duel by state auditor James Shields, the future president agreed to the challenge—and chose broadswords as the weapon of choice.

way to say nothing of substance on the slavery issue, threw a former senator from Tennessee named John Bell into the race, with no real chance of victory.

Taking them all on was the Republican Party, which specifically opposed the spread of slavery in its platform. The 1860 contest was immensely important for them, as it marked a genuine opportunity to put a man in the Executive Mansion. Consequently, their cleanup hitters— William Seward and Salmon Chase—came out swinging. Unfortunately for them, they were swinging too hard. Considered too radical for the Republican rank and file, neither of these very esteemed and capable politicians ended up getting on the ballot. The man who did was a typical dark horse, chosen for his moderate views and capacity to appease. His name was Abraham Lincoln, an Illinois attorney and politician known for his eloquent speeches against slavery, sinewy frontier strength, earthy humor, and ill-fitting clothes. In the election that followed, his name did not even appear on most Southern ballots, so extraordinary was the hatred for him and his party in that part of the country. But he would win forty percent of the popular vote and a clean majority in the electoral college. A gawky, self-educated depressive, he was now president of a vast republic teetering on the edge of calamity.

It soon stopped teetering and plunged right in—not in spite of Lincoln's election, but because of it. He was an unlikely figure to bring the world's foremost democratic civilization to its knees. Born to a poor backwoods family in 1809, he grew up in the wilds of Kentucky and Indiana. Lincoln hardly knew his mother, who died before his tenth year, and came to fear his father, whose bad luck, large family, and lack of resources compelled him to lease Abe out as a laborer for extra money. Abe loved his adoring stepmother, however, and came to love words just as much—reading them, writing them, memorizing them. Though he acquired less than a year's worth of formal education, he discovered a fascination for the intellectual life that was totally at odds with his manual, impoverished, frontier situation. He absorbed *The Life of George Washington* and *Aesop's Fables* and tried his own hand at prose and poetry when he was able. Determined to better himself, he became practiced at writing, a skill that was hard to come by in the forests of the Old Northwest. As a boy he was transcribing the correspondence of neighbors.

In 1830, the Lincolns moved to Illinois. A precocious young man who could entertain an audience for hours from a soapbox or a pickle barrel, Abe was desperate to get out from under his father and do something on his own. Though unusually well read for his environment, Abe's most obvious asset was his six-foot-four-inch frame. He could wield an ax like nobody's business, and local thugs learned to fear his ability to wrestle and to throw a devastating haymaker. To his dying day, Lincoln would remain a formidable physical specimen, despite the toll on his health that the war would take. Most have never stopped to think about it, but it bears consideration that the sixteenth president—that hallowed sage who penned the Gettysburg Address—was more able than most of his contemporaries to defend himself in a tight spot. Nevertheless, Lincoln's gnarly frame was just a last resort and nothing more. He hated physical labor, which goes a long way toward explaining his need to escape the family and do something . . . different.

Lincoln became a storekeeper, a militia captain during the Black Hawk War, a surveyor, and a postmaster, among other things. Whatever he did, he exuded an attractive capacity for humor and intelligence. He made people think and laugh and connect without burdening them with the knowledge that they were doing so. In short, he was becoming a damn good politician. Elected to four consecutive terms in the state legislature, he spent much of his time studying law—intensely. He was to pass the bar and become one of Illinois's most celebrated circuit lawyers; and it was all made possible by his own instruction. Licensed to practice from 1836, Lincoln entered a series of law partnerships that built his reputation as "Honest Abe"—a lawyer of better than average ability whose closings were always entertaining and who never lied or trucked with liars. He would eventually snag clients as big and lucrative as the Illinois Central Railroad.

In 1846, he was elected to a single term in the U.S. House of Representatives, attracting some attention as a cunning opponent of the war with Mexico. But his most significant performance on the national stage came with defeat. After leaving his Whig origins behind, Lincoln became the most famous Republican in Illinois. He ran for the United States Senate in 1858 against the pugnacious, diminutive Stephen Douglas and lost. His debates with the "little giant," however, were among the most substantive and sensational in the country, pitting two extraordinary public debaters against each other over the toughest issue of the day: the nature and fate of slavery. Douglas went to Washington; but his opponent had left a lasting impression.

Especially in the minds of his fellow Republicans, who liked him as a candidate. Not only was Lincoln persuasive and well liked, he was also easier to sell to the people than some wild-eyed abolitionist bent on the destruction of slavery everywhere immediately. He did not have the national stature of a Chase or a Seward. But he was a safe choice for a new party with a bold agenda.

The party's choice paid off, precipitating the country's most disastrous crisis. This rough cornstalk of a man, hailing from the rutted wilds of America's interior, with virtually no real schooling, had become the most powerful figure in the nation and a casus belli. Now what? To begin with, Lincoln formed a cabinet that was everything he wasn't: polished, highly educated, and confrontational. Salmon Chase became secretary of the treasury, for instance, and William Seward was made secretary of state. That Lincoln ended up controlling and ultimately winning over these men—some of whom coveted his job and thought him unworthy of it—was a measure of his inner strength and ability. But he was unable to control events with nearly as much success. When Rebel batteries fired on Fort Sumter, which South Carolina claimed as Confederate property and Lincoln chose to supply and defend, it began an escalation of violence for which the new president was ill prepared. He called up 75,000 militiamen from the states to serve for ninety days. Needless to say, he would end up needing a lot more.

He would need something else, too: power. Lincoln said that his intention was to maintain the union of the states, and he meant it. The dissolution of that union presented an emergency dire enough, in his eyes, to test the limits of the constitution that governed it. He wasn't just a wartime president; he was president of a nation that had temporarily ceased to exist in its conventional sense, leaving him a uniquely wide berth when it came to executive authority. Congress obliged by awarding him liberal war powers. James Buchanan, his predecessor, had balked at using force to coerce secessionists back to the fold for the same reason, ironically, that he hated secessionists: it was unconstitutional. It is to Lincoln's credit that he forced a way out of that circuitous thinking.

Nevertheless, it was a terrific risk. Suspending the writ of habeas corpus, declaring martial law in the border states, and arresting writers and editors hostile to the administration hardly endeared the president to many of his fellow Americans. But one group in the North took particular issue with the president's performance: the abolitionists. When several of his leading generals began freeing slaves in occupied territory on their own authority, he was quick to reverse their decisions. It is one of those intriguing ironies of history that the thing about Lincoln that caused the South to secede when he was elected—a direct hostility to slavery—was the same thing that he was willing to suspend in order to mend the mess that his election had created. In other words, he ended up pleasing no one: not the slaveholders whose human property, they believed, he was out to set loose, and not the abolitionists, whose agenda he seemed entirely willing to trash in the name of the Union.

Lincoln was many things, and not all of them flattering. But one of his greatest qualities was a capacity to learn and grow—fast. It became apparent to him that a war of radical dangers required radical action to win. He had always had a revulsion toward slavery, a fact that abolitionists like Frederick Douglass took pains to remind him of. And as the war crept into its second nightmarish year, proving that all bets were off, Lincoln was compelled to understand the role that his revulsion had in the fight for union. The Emancipation Proclamation was a brilliant way of blending the abolitionist agenda with a practical war measure: affecting only those slaves in Rebel states (as opposed to those slave states like Maryland and Kentucky that remained loyal to the Union), it fell under Lincoln's jurisdiction as commander in chief. With stealth and conviction, the president had broadened the scope and purpose of the war. It would prove decisive as well as historic.

ABRAHAM LINCOLN

Of course, to be truly decisive he needed to win a military conflict. A really big military conflict. But pushing a few rowdies around as a militia "captain" in his youth didn't make him an Alexander the Great. The quintessential self-taught man, Lincoln studied up on tactics and did his best to understand the basics. But that took a while. In the meantime, he trusted in men who took advantage of his expansive nature or even thwarted his true objectives. George McClellan was a perfect example, but only the most sensational. There were plenty of others. Lincoln needed victories; but not really knowing precisely what it was that brought them about, he relied on the advice of those of mediocre ability. The Federal war machine staggered forward, honing its effectiveness at a dreadfully slow and costly rate. This was Lincoln's burden: to maintain his intensity of purpose and never lose sight of the ultimate prize in the face of unprecedented death and destruction—a relentless harvest of lives that could conceivably be laid at his feet. "I expect to maintain this contest until successful, or till I die," he once said. Lesser men would've disappeared beneath the pressure.

If he was to have constant trouble on the military front, the president handled his political battles with much more confidence and felicity. This was fortunate for him and the country, as Lincoln had serious trouble from his own cabinet members right from the beginning. One of them, Secretary of War Simon Cameron, was a political appointee whose ham-handed management made it easy for the president to sack and banish him abroad as minister to Russia. He was replaced with the eminently capable Edwin Stanton. But when it came to Secretaries Seward and Chase, Lincoln was dealing with men who—though covetous of his power—were necessary to the war effort. He was deeply irritated by them, but smart enough to appreciate their abilities. Just as bad were the Republican hotheads in Congress who hounded the administration for every error. Lincoln's genius was to play all these self-important men off each other, manipulating their egos and maneuvering them into positions of agreement that were of use to him. Those who saw what was happening were usually too late to alter the president's manipulations, and often merely felt more respect for him afterward.

28

(In reference to the balance he had acquired in his cabinet between Chase and Seward, Lincoln once likened himself to a farmer riding to market on a horse whose load had been evened out by a pumpkin in each saddlebag.) It wasn't long before enemies who originally dismissed him as a frontier yokel were singing a very different tune. This guy was not to be trifled with.

It was a lot to deal with, to be sure. And Lincoln had also to cope with an increasingly hysterical wife and the death of his son Willie in 1862. Through such nightmares, Lincoln had always expressed two reactions that were seemingly inseparable: deep melancholy and colorful humor. Having long ago honed the latter in order to dull the edge of the former, the president waded through the unending litany of wartime setbacks with both writ plainly on his face. He became the funniest and most depressed man many in Washington ever met. And, perhaps, the most sensitive. As a child he had shot a turkey and been mortified by it, becoming acutely distressed by the sight of suffering in any form. Now he was the chief player in a great national evisceration—one of the few who could possibly bring it all to an end, but who was compelled instead to keep it going toward a goal that seemed farther and farther away with every bloodletting. And yet he chased his children like a carefree youngster, told coarse frontier tales that made people blush, kept his office door open to office-seekers and quacks, and indulged a parade of inventors peddling the next war-winning weapon (one of which, a kind of grenade, became a fixture on Lincoln's desk as a paperweight). It wasn't the life that many would've preferred for a stern wartime president, but Lincoln always did things his own way, and—whenever possible— emphasized forbearance. "Let me tell you a story," he once said to an assistant secretary of war who had come to tell Lincoln that the infamous Confederate agent Jacob Thompson was reportedly fleeing Portland, Maine. "There was an Irish soldier here last summer who wanted something to drink stronger than water, and stopped at a drug shop where he espied a soda fountain. 'Mr. Doctor,' said he, 'give me, please, a glass of soda water, an' if yez can put in a few drops of whiskey, unbeknown to anyone, I'll be obliged.' Now, if Jake Thompson is permitted to go through Maine 'unbeknown to anyone,' what's the harm?"

He could be profound as well as endearing—Lincoln contributed to posterity some of the most outstanding speeches ever spoken in English. But not everyone was listening to what he was saying. To people who stood at the culmination of generations of racist indoctrination, Lincoln was an incredibly dangerous fool. He himself was unsure as to how the country would cope with its African freedmen and Confederate defeated, but he was forming ideas that reflected his optimism and forgiveness. The world would never see them put into action. John Wilkes Booth, a middling actor and passionately pro-Southern malefactor, wasn't the most famous or interesting man to hate the president. But he was base enough to consider kidnapping him—a pet project Booth had been working on since 1861. Confederate defeat spurred him to up the stakes, and he decided to get rid of his target altogether. On April 14, 1865, the actor snuck up behind Lincoln during a performance of a comedy called *Our American Cousin* in Ford's Theatre, and shot him in the back of the head. "Father Abraham" was dead the next morning.

He lived long enough to see the surrender of Lee, which had become the purpose of all that he endured and worked for. In essence, Lincoln *was* the Civil War: his election had sparked it, his reelection had decided it, and his death marked its close. Fortunately for us, he showed as great a capacity for metamorphosis as the nation he gave his life to save.

MISCHIEF

Lincoln had an overdeveloped sense of humor that became one of his hallmarks. In 1829 he and some fellow jokesters targeted the Grigsby family, into which Lincoln's sister Sarah had married before her death in childbirth. When a double wedding was thrown for two of Reuben Grigsby's sons, Abe—who was not invited—devoted his efforts to wreaking havoc with the wedding night festivities. He had a conspirator lead the grooms that night to the wrong brides, creating a flurry of embarrassment. Lincoln, who always blamed the Grigsbys for his sister's death, immortalized the silly little escapade in "The

Chronicles of Reuben," a lyrical bit of satire that people in southern Indiana were still reciting long after its author had moved to Illinois and greater glory.

LITERARY LICENSE

During the early 1840s, Lincoln and his soon-to-be bride, Mary Todd, weren't exactly hitting it off. Jealousies had gotten the better of both of them and the relationship was truly in trouble. But as David Herbert Donald recounts in *Lincoln*, fate intervened in the form of . . . economics. When the State Bank of Illinois failed, Lincoln and other Whigs took it as an opportunity to attack the Democratic leadership of the state. For his part, Abe wrote a series of scathing letters to the editor of a local paper against the state auditor James Shields using the pseudonym "Rebecca." Though Abe's jabs were more than enough, Mary Todd and a friend took up Lincoln's lead and joined the fun, contributing their own letter to the series under the same alias. Shields finally reached his limit of tolerance and pressed the newspaper editor to divulge the identity of "Rebecca." Abe did the gentlemanly thing and owned up to it all, sparing any mention whatsoever of his female co-conspirators. But the excitable object of his published barbs was demanding satisfaction. On September 22, 1842, Lincoln and Shields met on the field of honor—in Missouri, as dueling was quite illegal in Illinois. Abe, as the challenged party, had his choice of weapons. Taking his height and strength into consideration, he chose broadswords. (Yikes!) "If it had been necessary," said Lincoln, "I could have split him from the crown of his head to the end of his backbone."

Fortunately, it didn't come to that. The duelists' seconds got the two to agree that the whole mixup had been a symptom of political passion, and everyone ended up shaking hands. The affair may not have given Abe an opportunity to show off his filleting skills, but it did do something just as significant (and a lot less bloody): Impressed by Lincoln's chivalry in protecting her identity, Mary Todd came around and the troubled lovebirds were back on track. They would be married by the end of the year.

Facing Facts

Lincoln wasn't exactly a dashing young figure. His fellow Republicans had their concerns during the 1860 election campaign that voters might be less than smitten by photographs of the wiry lawyer from Illinois. They ended up getting a solution from the unlikeliest of sources. Her name was Grace Bedell, she was eleven years old, and she lived in Westfield, New York. Grace wrote a letter to the Republican candidate suggesting that he grow a beard: "You would look a great deal better for your face is so thin." Though Lincoln joked about the matter at first, he was soon sporting whiskers and would never return to the smooth-shaven look. Thanks to Ms. Bedell, Abraham Lincoln would be the first American president to wear a beard.

WHAT A GUY

When Lincoln assumed office as president, he seemed a little over-whelmed. After all, he had never had a position of supreme executive authority before, and he had trouble delineating the boundaries. One of the most conspicuous examples involved office seekers. Patronage was the bane of nineteenth-century White House life, as everyone wanted a job or a posting or a commission from the new big cheese. But Lincoln, far from turning most of them away, insisted on letting them have their say—in person. From early in the morning until well past sundown, the president's office was open to all comers, who often lined up outside his door and wound all the way downstairs. Few were rewarded with what they came for, but nearly everyone got a frontier tale to ease their rejection—Lincoln was usually the most amused by his own stories and jokes, shamelessly slapping his knee and bending over in laughter. When he returned to Washington after delivering his Gettysburg Address in 1863, the president became ill and was diagnosed with a minor form of smallpox. "Now I have something I can give everybody," he quipped.

2 MARY TODD
LINCOLN

December 13, 1818–July 16, 1882

HIGHEST RANK:

American First Lady

ASTROLOGICAL SIGN:

Sagittarius

NICKNAMES:

Molly, Mother, the Hellcat, Her Satanic Majesty, La Reine

WORDS TO REMEMBER:

"My husband—became distinguished above all. And yet owing to that fact, I firmly believe he lost his life and I am bowed to the earth with sorrow."

"Get down, you fool!" cried a young Captain Oliver Wendell Holmes Jr. to the commander in chief. It was July 1864, and Holmes was accompanying the president and his wife on a tour of the defenses of Washington. Jubal Early's Confederate army had made its surprising appearance outside the capital, and Mr. Lincoln, wanting to get a good view of the action, had peered out from the earthworks of Fort Stevens, presenting Rebel sharpshooters with a conspicuous target in the shape of a stovepipe hat. Allegedly, Captain Holmes's impertinent command did the trick, and a chastened Lincoln ducked for cover. His wife, standing nearby on safer ground, noted the episode with some alarm: The following day, while her husband was laughing about poor Holmes and his embarrassment over the incident, a stern-faced Mrs. Lincoln was telling Secretary of War Edwin Stanton that Washington's defenses were totally unsatisfactory.

Giving direct opinions to the secretary of war on matters of military engineering was definitely not your typical errand for a first lady. But Mary Lincoln was hardly typical. She was born in Lexington, Kentucky, to Eliza and Robert Smith Todd, head of one of the state's leading families. It was also one of the biggest—by the time Robert stopped breeding, he had blessed some sixteen children with life: seven with Eliza, his first wife and Mary's mother, and nine with his second wife, Elizabeth Humphreys. Often called "Molly,"

Mary Todd lived in a world of western American aristocracy that expected little more from its women than humility, poise, piety, constraint, some knowledge of books, and dancing. She learned a lot about these things at Shelby Female Academy in Lexington and Madame Mentelle's, acquiring from an early age an appreciation for refinement that distinguished her class.

She stood out as a young lady, but not always flatteringly. Mary had a couple of things she did quite naturally: engage in debate, a habit that proper belles were not supposed to cultivate, being the province of men; and mimicry, which most people thought was entertaining until they were the one being mimicked. Both were a sign of keen intelligence, however, as were her mastery of French, her ready wit, and her desire to plumb the depths of the era's toughest issues. Considered quite pretty in an unusual way, she had no shortage of beaux and found that she liked playing them off each other. But she ended up giving her heart to only one.

His name, of course, was Abraham Lincoln. Mary met him after moving in with her sister's family in Springfield, Illinois, and saw in the self-taught lawyer a man who was charming, eloquent, goofy, and careless by turns. He was clearly brilliant, however, and this was crucial; Mary had decided she needed a mate to match her own cerebral energies, one who could take her far. Lincoln had great expectations, even if he did look like an orangutan that had been kidnapped from Borneo, shaved, and dressed for display in P. T. Barnum's freak show. By 1840, they were engaged.

Mary Todd Lincoln claimed that she was frequently visited by ghosts while living in the White House; on several occasions, these spectral visitors even delivered top secret Confederate military plans.

It nearly didn't come off, owing to miscommunication by both parties. "Old Abe," as he was familiarly known to everyone but Mary (who never called him Abe), wasn't exactly smooth. He scratched, quipped, hooted, and guffawed when he wasn't really supposed to, which grated on her polished sensibilities.

Unimpressed with his attentions (he was also notoriously aloof and unobser-vant), Mary allowed the impression that other courtiers were still in the picture, and Lincoln oafishly replied with abject depression. It all got sorted out in time with the help of mutual friends, but clearly these two had some issues.

After marrying in 1842, the couple settled in Springfield, holing up at the Globe Tavern until 1844, when Abraham bought a handsome, spacious house at the corner of Eighth and Jackson Streets for them and their new son, Robert. The new Mrs. Lincoln looked forward to having a family—she would bear three more sons—but she looked forward to her husband's suc-cess just as much. After his public career stalled following his stint in the U.S. House of Representatives, nobody wanted him back in the thick of things more than she did. Lincoln was more than just an admirable figure and the love of her life; he was also equitable and self-confident enough to rely on her in ways that many nineteenth-century men would not have. He welcomed her opinion and wisdom, grew from her education, and relied on her support. She became an invaluable asset in his career, and she came to know it. A pleasant bonus came when Stephen Douglas, once a competitor for Mary's affections, emerged as Lincoln's principal antagonist. Though Douglas won the Senate contest in 1858, Honest Abe had secured his place on the national stage. Great things beckoned, and Mary was loving it.

Lincoln's presidential victory in 1860 was bittersweet, and not only because South Carolina led a parade of states out of the Union as a result. Having been surrounded by supporters for so long through the campaign, Mary was stunned in 1861 to discover crowds of angry protesters in Maryland who wanted nothing so much as to get their hands on her husband's neck before it arrived at the White House. Security considerations required that the president-elect sneak into Washington on a stealth train, while Mary covered the last leg of the trip without him. It wasn't how she'd dreamt of entering the capital as the president's spouse.

While pro-South agitators wanted to kill the president, the Unionists of Washington didn't exactly welcome his wife with open arms. Their com-plaints were many and varied. To begin with, her reputation as a smart-aleck woman who meddled in politics preceded her to the nation's capital. In another age, Mrs. Lincoln would've been considered an experienced advisor to her husband, but not by most ordinary folks in 1861. Then there was the fact that Mary Lincoln was a true Kentucky belle, complete with western mannerisms and a drawl—qualities that endeared her to the crowds of people that came out to welcome the Lincolns on the electoral train, but that Washington's pro-North sophisticates dismissed as simple and a little irritating. Stuff like this could be written off as the usual chatter of small-minded mouths. Much harder to ignore, on the other hand, was the fact that the new first lady's relations were unabashed, Lincoln-hating secessionists—hardly a small matter for the wife of a commander in chief whose young countrymen would soon be called upon to wade into sheets of Confederate fire. Indeed, Mary was the very personification of the war's conflicted tragedy. Ultimately she would have nothing less than one full brother, three half brothers, and three brothers-in-law fighting against her husband's armies. Such facts help to explain why so many loyal Unionists had a habit of cursing the White House after reading casualty lists that grew longer with every month.

Mary set about trying to win over some supporters with the usual tactics. She reviewed the troops in Washington along with her husband, making herself a noted fan of the military pageantry that gripped the city. And she visited local hospitals, where she brought food to wounded soldiers and wrote letters home for them. But her principal project involved the refurbishing of her new digs. The White House immediately became the project on which, she decided, her first ladyship would be either made or broken. Having Abraham elected president was like being given the key to the candy store, and Mary wasted no time gobbling up the goodies that awaited her.

And they awaited her principally in New York and Philadelphia. From celebrated merchants like E. V. Haughwout and Alexander Stewart, she purchased the finest porcelain, damask curtains and carpets, and wallpaper from France that cost nearly $7,000. Her buying habits were marked and voracious—accompanied by William Wood, commissioner of public buildings, she sometimes left her favorite emporiums carrying the goods herself like an addict who couldn't wait to get her fix. The president signed off on everything, his mind too busy with martial difficulties to keep a tally of his wife's reckless expenditures. She had always kept house back in Illinois, why should things be different in Washington?

Because she was out of control, that's why. In very little time at all, the first lady made the $20,000 congressional appropriation for White House refurbishing magically go away—a sum that was supposed to cover the entire four-year term. Even a $6,000 repair appropriation had been ... uh, appropriated. So serious was the situation that the secretary of the interior bothered to pay the president a visit in person to find out what in God's name was going on. Lincoln, feeling as if he'd been taken advantage of, lost his temper and laid into Mary like he wished his generals would lay into the Confederates. To help pay off the debts, Mrs. Lincoln did everything from sell off White House furniture to fire the mansion's steward. But it fell on someone else's shoulders to really sort it all out. His name was Benjamin French, and he was the new commissioner of public buildings (William Wood's appointment was never approved by the Senate). Playing a sort of shell game with government funds (as if nobody had ever done that before), French ended up paying for the first lady's new "flubdubs," as the president called them, with money slated for other public projects. Such was the state of bureaucratic cynicism in Washington at the time that nobody really gave a damn.

As for Mary, she never learned. Determined to plan and host the administration's first state dinner for the diplomatic corps, an honor traditionally given to the secretary of state, Mary went head-to-head with Secretary Seward to co-opt the occasion. In the end she won, and hired one of the most expensive caterers in the country to make sure everything was right. She promptly sent the bill right over to Seward.

It was as if the dream that this well-bred woman had longed for her whole life had turned out to be harder—much harder—than she had anticipated. She had no idea. Willie, her third and, most agreed, favorite son died on February 20, 1862. Though no one could truly know it at the time, the eleven-year-old was a casualty of war as surely as any soldier at the front. With the influx of troops from all over the North turning the capital into a giant military camp, the Potomac—from which the first family drew its water—had become contaminated with filth. Willie's typhoid was a direct result.

Though she had lost a son before (four-year-old Edward died in 1850), Mary was undone by Willie's death and entered a new stage of her life: one shaped by death and a preoccupation with its ramifications. She was in good company—after all, she was first lady through the four bloodiest years of the nation's history, stumbling like everyone else through a fugue of casualty lists, military hospitals, and photographs of mutilated men. It was a propitious time for mourning. And nobody did it as well as Mrs. Lincoln. Irritable and paranoid, she wore her heart on her sleeve, drove everyone in the household a little batty with bursts of incendiary anger, and turned to spiritualist séances to reach Willie's soul.

Apparently, she succeeded. Willie even appeared to her in the first lady's bedroom on occasion. Such visits went a long way toward assuaging Mary's grief, but they didn't prepare her for the horror of 1865. Not that she didn't see it coming: not long after Lincoln's reelection, she bought hundreds of dollars worth of mourning clothes, just in case her premonitions were true.

They were. Her husband's assassination sent Mary Lincoln into a pit of ungovernable despair, complete with moaning, hysterics, and physical illness that laid her up for weeks. Indeed, so impenetrable and ruinous was her writhing grief that people began to worry that she might soon join Abraham. If Mary, volatile and wronged, ever had a chance of living out a healthy life, it went away with her husband's corpse. Never again would she wear anything but black—an epic mourning jag that lasted seventeen years. She spent much of that time traveling in Europe and Canada, easing her ills at spa towns and trying to purge her memory of the past. Her frequent traveling companion was Tad, youngest of the Lincoln children. He died in Chicago in 1871, giving Mary a genuine complex. Her life had become as black as her clothes.

Incredibly, it would get worse. Stalked by death, adrift in financially chaotic circumstances that were a far cry from the comforts of Springfield and

Washington, Mary fell into a spiral of erratic behavior, from selling her husband's purported possessions to taking large doses of sedatives to raving about a fear of being alone to buying things she neither needed nor could afford. Her eldest and only surviving son, Robert, increasingly estranged, finally acted by having her taken to court to defend her own sanity. In a trial atmosphere that didn't really give her a chance, a slew of witnesses—including Robert—convinced a jury that she was not fit to be left to her own devices. She was committed to an institution called Bellevue Place in Batavia, Illinois.

With some very good legal help, Mary ultimately got the decision reversed in another trial, then ran off to Europe a scorned, emotionally bashed-up woman. By 1882 she was suffering from near blindness, diabetes, spinal trouble, and a few other unpleasant things. She died in her sister's house, in a darkened room she had been living (dying?) in for months.

It's unfortunate that Mary Todd Lincoln has become one of the tragicomic witches of American history. Though neurotic (at least) and emotionally fragile, she was a remarkable person in her own right, with an expansive and sophisticated personality. Her great doom was to fall for a man who became the nation's savior and sacrifice, a job that would've tested the hardiest of women. Withering under the intense light of public scrutiny and the loss of those dear to her, she succumbed to her weaknesses and became almost a parody of herself—a casualty of the war that stole from her the only source of love and stability she had ever known. Who wouldn't go a little crazy after that?

SPOOKED

Mary Lincoln's dear friend Elizabeth Keckley, former slave and seamstress par excellence, is supposed to have introduced the first lady to the world of spiritualism. Mrs. Lincoln responded to the occult as if it were the answer to her prayers—which it was. Not long after Willie's death, she began hanging out at the home of the Lauries, Georgetown's most celebrated spiritualists. There she met and befriended Nettie Colburn, the medium who became

Mary's primary conduit to her son's ghost. Colburn's skills were allegedly once put to the test in the White House when she was asked to identify a man who walked into the room disguised by a mask and heavy cloak. Assuming the identity of "Pinkie," a Native American spirit who supposedly inhabited Nettie on occasion, she answered "Crooked Knife." When the man turned out to be familiar Lincoln friend General Daniel Sickles, everyone agreed that Nettie (and Pinkie) had scored, as a "sickle" could be construed as a sort of crooked knife. (OK, it's a stretch. But these folks were open to suggestion anyway.)

The president, a skeptic, indulged his wife's eccentric beliefs for the obvious reason that they gave her emotional relief. But contacting Willie was one thing; bringing scandal into the White House was quite another. On those occasions when her son wasn't . . . er, picking up the spiritual phone, as it were, Mary and her fellow séance-sitters had no problem establishing contact with whomever was feeling chatty that day in the beyond. Mary often charged into her husband's office with Confederate military plans that had been provided by sources that were, to say the least, extraordinary. Not surprisingly, stuff like this began to wear on Old Abe's patience. But it was nothing compared with the time Mary invited Charles Colchester, an English noble (not really) and medium of great renown, to come ply his creepy trade in the Executive Mansion. There, in the stygian gloom of the heavily draped Red Room, the "lord" summoned a spirit through the veil that began making quite a noise. Refusing to be fooled, one of the sitters broke the circle to reach for the source of the sound and discovered the very corporeal hand of Colchester himself shamelessly beating a drum. Journalist Noah Brooks, a friend of the Lincolns', persuaded the humiliated Colchester to get the hell out of town. The charlatan soon pulled off a disappearing act that put his spirit shtick to shame.

BLUE BY YOU

Mrs. Lincoln took all kinds of guff during her stint as first lady. She was railed as extravagant, insensitive, erratic, superstitious, reckless. Interestingly, she was also criticized for being unfaithful to her belabored husband. One of Mary's greatest challenges upon entering the White House was coping with the fact that her husband, whose career she had actively helped to shape, was no longer unconditionally available to her. As president, he was constantly surrounded by officious, unsmiling men with business and bad news to heap on his shoulders. She felt (as so many in her select sorority would feel through the years) as if she'd been abandoned. Craving intellectual stimulation and ingratiating company, she ended up creating her very own salon in the mansion's Blue Room. There, Mrs. Lincoln held after-dinner court with her favorite sycophants, nearly all of whom were men—and men considered socially dangerous by Washington's priggish elite. This, as well as the fact that wives were rarely included, led a few interested parties to send warnings to Mary to stop her scandalous meetings. She disregarded them, reveling in her arranged conversations about literature, war, romance, history, and other heady topics.

Among the esteemed regulars were Oliver Halsted, scion of a prominent New Jersey family and unscrupulous arms dealer, and Dan Sickles, corrupt political general and killer of his wife's lover. But the most famous of Mary's "beau monde friends" may have been Henry Wikoff, whose arrival in America had been preceded by a stint as an English spy. A worldly and mysterious figure, he had spent time in an Italian prison for seducing and kidnapping his fiancée. Though welcomed into the first lady's circle, Mr. Wikoff had other things in mind besides Mary's company—specifically, the president's 1861 message to Congress, which he stole for printing by his employer, the *New York Herald*. Briefly imprisoned for his crime, the "Chevalier" Wikoff ultimately made his way back to Europe, where he offered his services to the French emperor.

DYSFUNCTIONAL FAMILY

It wasn't easy for Mary Lincoln to have three half brothers die for the Rebel cause. Indeed, one of them, David Todd, was purported to have tortured Yankee prisoners of war before being wounded at Vicksburg. As wife of Abraham Lincoln, this was the stuff of nightmares. But as difficult as her brothers were, Mary seems to have suffered more at the hands of her half sisters. Martha Todd White, who had married an Alabama man, appealed to Mary's sense of family to give her a White House pass with which she could travel north for valuable supplies. President Lincoln, stupidly generous, obliged. Martha soon appeared in Washington with trunks that everyone assumed were going to be filled with goods for the Confederate black market. A disgraced Mary Lincoln did what she could to distance herself from her pro-secessionist half sister, but Martha loved to blather on and on about her blood ties to the White House before returning to the South. Then there was Emilie Todd Helm, whose husband was killed at Chickamauga. By the winter of 1863, Emilie was living temporarily in the Executive Mansion, having been given a pass to do so by Lincoln despite her adamant refusal to take an oath of allegiance to the United States government. What ensued was one of the strangest episodes in the annals of presidential history: the half sister of the president's wife, widow of a man who'd given his life for the cause Lincoln was sworn to destroy, did her mourning in the Union capital—indeed, she ate nightly with the president and his family. Abraham called her "little sister" and allowed her and Mary to immerse themselves in the business of missing their dead while he went about his official duties. Hatefully, Emilie wrote a letter to the president after she'd returned to the Confederacy, forgetting his hospitality and reminding him of the crimes he was perpetrating on the South. Mary was incensed and never spoke to Emilie again.

3 HENRY WAGER HALLECK

January 16, 1815–January 9, 1872

HIGHEST RANK:

Union General

ASTROLOGICAL SIGN:

Capricorn

NICKNAMES:

Old Brains, Old Woodenhead

WORDS TO REMEMBER:

"War, on the smallest scale, is not without its horrors; and even in this by-place of the earth, many a suffering female and helpless orphan live to call down the vengeance of heaven upon the heads of profligate statesmen who involve nations in useless and unnecessary wars." (in La Paz, California, during the Mexican War)

In March 1865, four very powerful men met on a vessel moored off City Point, Virginia, to discuss how best to expedite the collapse of the rebellion. They were Abraham Lincoln, Admiral David Porter, Lieutenant General Ulysses Grant, and Major General William T. Sherman. One particular officer was conspicuous for his absence: Henry Halleck. He was chief of staff and, before that, general in chief, two titles that have "Gosh, I'm important!" written all over them. So why were the president and his military chiefs treating him like the unhygienic guy who never gets invited anywhere?

As the Civil War raged on, Union general Henry Halleck found the time to translate and publish a French military text. No wonder so many of his colleagues despised him.

The short answer, perhaps, is that he simply wasn't needed. Halleck had long since developed a rare and peculiar talent for accreting significance while simultaneously reducing accountability, a process that made

him a fixture of the Lincoln administration who was as familiar as he was inert. By the war's waning months, he was like a creaky floorboard that was easier to walk around than to replace.

That such a situation had come to pass was shocking, given Halleck's credentials. He was born (along with a twin sister who died shortly after birth) the first of a large brood in Westernville, New York, to descendants of some of the state's oldest families. Though pressured to help run the family farm, Henry had dreams of going far afield—dreams that required an education to fulfill. The result was a very ugly impasse with his stubborn father, Joseph Halleck, a hard-bitten sort who had little use for the intellectual life and even less for a son who wanted it. With the sponsorship of his grandfather and a very understanding uncle, Henry managed to get the education he craved, but at the price of a relationship with Dad. Until well into adulthood, he had dropped "Halleck" from his official name, answering only to Wager (pronounced "Way-gur"), which was his mother's maiden name. As for Joseph—his eldest son never mentioned him again.

When Halleck entered West Point, he had an impressive amount of learning under his belt, including a stint at Union College. But he had also succumbed to the inflexibility that had made his father so easy to hate. Accordingly, much of his time at the academy was spent in judgment of his fellow cadets, most of whom showed a sincere disdain for sobriety that the uptight Halleck found repugnant. He soldiered on manfully, however, and showed a level of intellectual acumen that was truly striking, excelling in virtually every subject. So exemplary was his performance, in fact, that the faculty made him an assistant professor of chemistry six months before his graduation. He ranked third in the class of 1839, earning a coveted appointment in the engineers.

His first year after graduation was spent teaching under the esteemed and infamous Dennis Hart Mahan, West Point's demanding professor of military and civil engineering. A bona fide celebrity in military circles, Mahan was an ideal (if crabby) first mentor for Halleck, who would go on to do all the things he had once dreamt of as a young man, and much more. Halleck had a brilliant analytical mind that got stronger with all the exercise he gave it: designing and building fortifications in New York Harbor, speaking before Congress on the state of the nation's defenses, teaching at the Lowell Institute in Boston, traveling to France to learn about that country's renowned techniques in defensive architecture, and publishing a book that made him a military star, *Elements of Military Art and Science*. By the outbreak of war with Mexico, he had built himself into a one-man brain trust and one of the army's most admired engineering virtuosos. No wonder they called him "Old Brains."

He was sent to California in 1846 via a lengthy, storm-swept sea voyage around Cape Horn. Once there, he set about fortifying Monterey and even got to fight meager Mexican forces for control of the state. But Halleck made his biggest mark away from the shooting, serving as the military government's secretary of state in California and lieutenant governor of Mazatlan. For all these extraordinary services, he was awarded a brevet at the conclusion of the war and went on to play a leading role in California's early history. Having taken to the rough-hewn territory that had underwhelmed him at first sight, Halleck became indispensable to California—a scholarly entrepreneur whose training, education, and drive made him a founding father of the state that would one day be America's largest by population. In addition to maintaining his engineering duties as inspector of lighthouses and fortifications, he immersed himself in the study of law and even helped to write the California constitution before resigning his commission in 1854. He proved even more dynamic in civilian clothes, becoming a partner in the state's largest law firm, a very successful businessman, and the author of groundbreaking books on such scintillating topics as mining law. Even his choice in brides was meant to impress: In addition to being sixteen years his junior and an accomplished equestrienne, Elizabeth Hamilton was the granddaughter of Alexander Hamilton, founding father and Aaron Burr–nemesis. It seemed Old Brains could do no wrong.

All of which goes a long way toward explaining why he was considered such an asset by Union authorities at the beginning of the Civil War. After

Halleck's return to the army, Lincoln made him a major general and in autumn 1861 sent him to St. Louis. His first assignment—cleaning up the outrageous administrative mess into which his predecessor, John Frémont, had sunk the Department of the Missouri—was ideally suited to Halleck's managerial genius. After presiding as department commander over men like Ulysses Grant and John Pope, whose successful campaigns made the West a place of Union hope and victory, Halleck took the field himself for the advance on Corinth, Mississippi, in spring 1862. In truth, advance is probably the wrong word. It was more like a crawl. Nevertheless, a key rail junction had been captured; while his critics gasped at the fact that an enemy army was allowed to escape intact, Halleck was openly patting himself on the back for having taken a juicy target with such little loss of life.

If this was an indication of what Halleck was like in his first command over an army in the field, Lincoln didn't seem to notice. Unlike the eastern theater of operations, things in the West had been going the North's way, and Halleck was in ultimate command. Besides, he was Old Brains, the guy everybody looked up to as the egghead with the answers. For these reasons, the president called Halleck to Washington in July 1862 to assume the position of general in chief, previously held by the venerable Winfield Scott and, more recently, by George McClellan. The president, by his own admission no military man, needed an advisor who could span the gulf between civilian leadership and military expertise—a multifaceted director who would explain strategy, lead officers with firmness and charisma, and shape war policy in a time of momentous national crisis.

What Lincoln got was . . . well, something else. For years, Halleck had been convinced of his own superiority, a hubris supported by numerous impressive accomplishments. Now, imbued with supreme power, he dreaded suggesting that he wasn't all that. Fear of failure stalked him, nudging him into a strange sort of effort: He would use his authority to move responsibility onto the shoulders of others. A consummate intellectual, Halleck warmed to the role of advisor. It carried no burden of culpability. It allowed him to give full vent to the theories and cognitive efforts that had preoccupied him, and it put him into contact with the officers whose armies would smash their way to bloody victory. It conveniently left him out of the line of fire when it came time for heads to roll.

But Lincoln wanted a leader, not a poser. And, though Halleck's presence was like having a professor of military history around, Old Brains soon proved to be Old Bane. He buried himself in minutiae, a quality that had its merits when trying to whip the ungainly Northern armies into shape, but such pedantic pursuits were lost in the big picture, where Lincoln needed him most. Moreover, the tactics whose elucidation had made Halleck famous were quickly becoming obsolete in the face of a civil war increasingly decided by modern wonders like the telegraph, railroad, and the rifled musket. Halleck, the stern disciplinarian with a faith in dogma, began to look like a relic and a martinet, and worse, the ones who were making him look that way were the sort of fellows he once derided as boors, slackers, or amateurs. Chief among them were Grant, whom Halleck once thought a poor excuse for an officer, and Sherman, who had crossed tempers with Halleck back in California and would learn to loathe Old Brains with volcanic intensity. Men like these fought from the hip, making things up as they went along and sometimes ignoring the rules that had made Halleck a legend. But more important, they led within killing distance of the firing line—another fact that separated them from "Old Woodenhead." And, as indicated by his relentless refusal to travel to front lines only a few miles away, it was a contrast that clearly didn't bother him.

All of this provided more than enough reason to question why on earth Halleck was maintained as the highest-ranking officer in the land. But the worst thing about him was his complete lack of firm supervision. Halleck's deference to his subordinates was simply weird. McClellan, a fellow engineer who was much younger but far more charismatic, held Halleck's awe like a magician before a mystified onlooker, absolutely undermining the older officer's capacity to assume command over him. Other generals were just as unlikely to get cut-and-dried orders. "You must judge for yourself," he was fond of wiring to them. "In regard to the operations of your own army," he once told Joseph Hooker, "you can best judge when and where it can move to the greatest advantage." And so it went, month after month. "Make the particular dispositions that you deem proper." "Your army is free to act as you deem proper." "Do not be influenced by any dispatch here against your own judgment. Regard them as suggestions only." Here's a winner: "You have the same discretion in executing orders communicated through me that I have in sending them." But the quote that really says it all: "I don't like to subject myself to the charge of impertinent meddling."

What he lacked in assertiveness he made up for in animus. Having once been wealthy from his California ventures, he began to find it hard to support his family and his lifestyle on a military salary. This and the burdens of his office began to wear on his patience, making him notoriously irritable— to everyone, high and low, congressmen and corporals alike. Even foreigners caught his wrath: Once, on the steps of the Capitol, Halleck got into an argument with a Brit over the identity of the enormous new building. When the fellow attempted to defuse the situation by proffering his card, Halleck took it, threw it to the ground, and walked away.

At any rate, Lincoln eventually had a solution for the Halleck predicament. He demoted him to chief of staff under Ulysses Grant, who had been made commander in chief of all the Union armies in March 1864. That way, Halleck could still be squeezed for his excellent clerking abilities while lessening the impact of his damnable lassitude. It wasn't a perfect solution; indeed, the public continued to heap derision upon Old Woodenhead, dismissing him as less than useless. But it served the administration until peace could be secured.

Halleck proved difficult after the war as well, when he was put in charge of the Military Division of the James. From his headquarters in Richmond, Halleck acted as inflexibly as ever, making enemies among the freedmen and causing much gnashing of teeth up in Washington. He was eventually reassigned to his beloved California and then to the Division of the South. He died in Louisville, Kentucky, in 1872, and remains the highest-ranking Northern general of the Civil War to have been all but forgotten.

HALE AND HARDY HALLECK

The Confederate invasion of Maryland that culminated in the climactic Battle of Antietam was a troubled time for the Union. Northern armies had been routed at Second Bull Run, the North seemed doomed to a perpetual defensive stance, and George McClellan was back in charge of the Army of the Potomac, despite the fact that Lincoln and his cabinet were suspicious of his ability. To make matters worse, the new general in chief, Henry Halleck, was already making enemies—McClellan chief among them. But there was another, lesser-known factor at work: Halleck was laid up with a debilitating case of hemorrhoids. Worse, he was treating the affliction with opium, which exacerbated his already weakened state, restricting him to a couch for most of the day and transforming his command anxieties into depression.

As John Marszalek explains in *Commander of All Lincoln's Armies*, the stress seems to have led to a self-perpetuating cycle. If the hemorrhoids let up, they were replaced by crippling bouts of diarrhea and constipation, further ruining the general's ability and self-confidence, and leading him to rely on more opium, alcohol, and tobacco. Tragically, it wasn't long before the poor guy had become a balding, pasty, bug-eyed bundle of nerves with a contentious demeanor and a habit of absently scratching his elbow. No wonder he was irritable.

PRIORITIES

Scholarship was Henry Halleck's first love, and not even war could change that. Saddled with responsibilities as general in chief that he usually found draining, and hoping to supplement his income, Halleck devoted time to a project he'd been working on for years: the translation of Henri Jomini's *Vie politique et militaire de Napoléon*. It was a monumental accomplishment—and its publication in 1864, needless to say, did nothing to quell the widespread belief that Lincoln's top general wasn't exactly putting his nose to the grindstone. As longtime critic Count Adam Gurowski snapped, "What an inimitable narrow-minded pedant. If Halleck had brains, he would have realized that, during war, he could not have an hour leisure for translation."

FRIENDS IN HIGH PLACES

What little exercise Halleck could get was taken in Washington's Lafayette Park, where he liked to stroll and ponder the issues and challenges that confronted him. Unfortunately, he once allowed his mind to wander until the city's 10:00 curfew came and went. By the time he realized what had happened, he was locked in the park with only two options: escape somehow, or sleep within the park's confines, no doubt to be awakened the following morning like some poor hobo—a story that was sure to make the papers. Given his puttylike physique, however, Old Brains would never have made it out were it not for the fact that he encountered a private who was similarly imprisoned. The soldier soon found himself standing on the shoulders of Honest Abe's general in chief to get over the fence and find some help. From that night on, the fellow had a high-ranking guardian angel named Henry Halleck.

DON'T HOLD BACK, FELLAS

So many great things to say about Henry Halleck, so little time.

"Lincoln's military clown."—*Count Adam Gurowski*

"Little more than a first-rate clerk."—*Abraham Lincoln*

"Put Halleck in the command of 20,000 men, and he will not scare three setting geese from their nests."—*Senator Benjamin Wade, on placing Halleck in charge of Washington's defenses*

"He, in short, is a moral coward, worth but little except as a critic and director of operations, though intelligent and educated. . . . [Halleck] originates nothing, anticipates nothing . . . takes no responsibility, plans nothing, suggests nothing, is good for nothing."—*Secretary of the Navy Gideon Welles*

"A great sinner against the mass of respectable mediocrities."
—*Admiral John Dahlgren*

"Probably the greatest scoundrel and most bare-faced villain in America."
—*Secretary of War Edwin Stanton*

4 GEORGE BRINTON McCLELLAN

December 3, 1826–
October 29, 1885

HIGHEST RANK:
Union General

ASTROLOGICAL SIGN:
Sagittarius

NICKNAMES:
Little Mac, Young Napoleon

WORDS TO REMEMBER:

"The climate of Spitzbergen and Arabia are not more different than the characteristics of a Civil and a Military man, and as well might we expect those climates to change in an hour, as to see a citizen become a good officer without years of training."

What the hell was this guy's problem? It's a question that occurs to virtually everyone who reads about the career of George McClellan. Rarely has one so brilliant failed so spectacularly to deliver on prospects so glorious. He was the natural choice to lead the nation's military machine—and he was largely responsible for the army's inability to end the war in 1862. It's enough to give you a headache.

The young McClellan showed so much promise that West Point chucked its age requirement just to let him in. In 1842, at fifteen and change, he entered the academy amongst cadets who had to be sixteen to get through the door. Moreover, he came with more than the usual learning under his belt, having already attended the University of Pennsylvania for two years (!). The son of a prominent Philadelphia doctor, he was young but big on smarts, and he graduated second in his class.

The year 1846 was a wonderful one to graduate if you wanted to kill people as soon as possible. The war with Mexico was just getting underway, and great things beckoned for young lieutenants with the grit to squeeze the present situation for all it was worth. As one of his class's greatest stars, McClellan went right into the prestigious engineers, earning two brevets during the Mexican War. Afterward he developed into a man of protean

ability—a sort of wunderkind in uniform. Having acquired an impressive facility with languages, he translated French training manuals while teaching at West Point. He explored the source of the Red River and surveyed possible routes for a transcontinental railroad. He was an inventor, builder, instructor, and explorer. He was also an observer: In 1855, his superiors sent him and several (much older) colleagues to witness the Crimean War and report on military developments that might prove of use. McClellan, still a young man, had become a big shot.

The unlimited prospects of civilian business beckoned, and he resigned his commission in 1857 to become a railroad engineer. When civil war came in 1861, McClellan was sitting behind a desk in Cincinnati, having become president of the Ohio and Mississippi Railroad. Governor William Dennison pounced on him to whip Ohio's volunteers into shape, though President Abraham Lincoln—who had been an attorney for the Illinois Central Railroad when McClellan worked there after leaving the army—was keeping his eye on the impressive young West Pointer. McClellan was soon elevated from the head of Ohio's militia to a major general in the United States Army in charge of a crucial department that included Ohio as well as parts of Kentucky and Virginia.

Talk about a missed opportunity: Union general George McClellan once stumbled across the battle plans of the Army of Northern Virginia—then spent so much time second-guessing himself, the opportunity was squandered.

A juggernaut of efficiency, McClellan shaped his command into a force to be reckoned with, and he used it to secure two crucial areas for the Union: Kentucky, a vital border state that had hoped to remain neutral, and western Virginia, a largely pro-Union region whose citizens were hoping for deliverance from the state's Confederate authorities. They got it when bluecoats under McClellan's authority cleared the area of Southern forces during a series of battles in the second half of 1861, thereby laying the foundation for what would become West Virginia. McClellan found reasons to whine about his subordinates throughout the campaign ("In heaven's name give me some general officers who understand their profession," he once wrote his superiors), but his greater numbers prevailed. The victory would elevate McClellan to national importance with the help of a certain Union humiliation at Bull Run. Suddenly, the young buck from Philadelphia was the North's only real war hero. Lincoln, quick to seize on anything that might conceivably offer some hope of success in what was turning out to be an awful debacle, made George McClellan the solution to everything.

In August, the general assumed command of the enormous fighting force that would soon be dubbed the Army of the Potomac. By November, he had replaced the retired Winfield Scott as general in chief. He was thirty-four friggin' years old.

With incredible energy, the "Young Napoleon" set about turning the mass of recruits under his leadership into an army. This was a Herculean feat, and perhaps no one in the country was more qualified to pull it off. Tireless, pedantic, and self-assured, McClellan drilled his men endlessly, saw to every conceivable need, demanded perfection and absolute professionalism, and held reviews—lots of reviews. The result was the most powerful martial host the western hemisphere had ever seen, by a long shot. Though well fed, heavily armed, and thoroughly disciplined, the Army of the Potomac's most conspicuous characteristic was loyalty—to the spitfire called "Little Mac." This is understandable, in light of what McClellan had given them: structure and pride, two indispensable qualities in every victorious army. But McClellan's popularity with the troops would in time produce frightening problems for the Lincoln administration—as would McClellan's inability to use armies with anything approaching the brilliance he displayed in creating them.

The general set a pattern that would end up driving those in power crazy. More afraid of failure than anything else, McClellan obsessed over preparation. The army had to be at a state of perfect preparedness before engaging in operations. There were never enough stockpiles of food and munitions, never enough spare shoes, and there was never enough time—to drill, drill, and drill some more. It had the effect of making McClellan look like a man in a hurry to avoid clashing with the enemy. The president would end up calling it "the slows."

By the time McClellan was ready to move, the cabinet was ready to snap. The general had even suffered a bout of typhoid fever in December, further delaying any action. When he finally did take the field, the Confederates had withdrawn from the positions with which they had been threatening Washington. Nevertheless, McClellan had been devising the perfect plan for his perfect army. Leaving troops behind to protect Washington (barely enough, as an uneasy Lincoln saw it), McClellan proposed sending the Army of the Potomac, with the navy's help, down to the Peninsula, the district between the York and James rivers, from which it would march on Richmond. A giant flanking maneuver that utilized the North's strengths in numbers and sea power, the plan offered real hope of ending the war with one fell swoop.

While in Europe, McClellan had witnessed firsthand the siege of Sevastopol, an epic tableau of entrenchments and elephantine siege guns. Now, faced with Rebel works at Yorktown, he settled down for an American version of the same. Once he got the men situated on the Peninsula, McClellan wasn't planning a lightning thrust toward the Confederate capital: He intended to wage war at a snail's pace. This was an exact science, after all, and one that he—the great West Point–educated engineer—knew better than anyone, especially that rogue's gallery of civilians in Washington who wouldn't shut up about moving things along.

Like a hungry, sluggish leviathan in the habit of sleeping off its meal after every engagement, the Army of the Potomac crept inexorably toward Richmond, its Confederate opponents frantically stabbing at the oncoming mass to no avail. By the end of May 1862, things looked truly dire for Richmond.

Then Robert E. Lee assumed command of the Rebel defenders, when Joseph E. Johnston fell wounded at Seven Pines, fundamentally altering the spirit of the struggle around Richmond. Though Johnston was one of the most revered military leaders on either side of the struggle, Lee possessed something that McClellan seemed absolutely incapable of handling: reck-lessness. By going over to the offensive on his left and leaving Richmond protected on his right by a skeleton force, Lee was gambling that his oppo-nent wouldn't spot the weakness and exploit it. He was right. McClellan, ever the cautious and prudent plodder, could not conceive of an army com-mander doing something so insane.

Worse, McClellan met his enemy's aggressiveness with panicked timidity, withdrawing like a turtle into its shell. During the Seven Days' Battles in June, the Young Napoleon retreated steadily before Lee's poorly coordinated attacks, checking him nearly every time but pulling further back neverthe-less. McClellan was lashing Lee but losing the campaign. Too unnerved to risk taking the initiative, he found it safer to respond to his enemy's actions, convinced that he and his army were fortunate to escape. Indeed, he exuded no small amount of pride in "saving" the Army of the Potomac from certain destruction.

For such an exceptionally bright fellow, McClellan had shown himself to be a little out of touch—indeed, delusional. Everyone was to blame for the failure of the Peninsula campaign except the man in charge of it. He railed against the men in Washington, particularly Lincoln (whom he dis-missed as a backwoods monkey-man) and Secretary of War Edwin Stanton (whom he loathed viscerally), for not giving him everything he requested. In fact, his demands were becoming so unrealistic that one wonders if McClellan had heard a reliable rumor that the President was hiding a genie in the Executive Mansion.

He also blamed the enemy, and in this he had a little help. Allan Pinkerton had helped to establish the federal government's secret service in 1861, then joined McClellan to become chief detective of the Department of the Ohio. The two had been inseparable since. McClellan, a man whose self-importance could not allow him to explain the failure of his own genius without conjuring insurmountable obstacles, had an unwitting accomplice in his spymaster—who, it can safely be said, needed to go back to intelligence-gathering school. In overlong, officious-looking reports based on interrogations of people with extraordinary imaginations, McClellan built a case that the Confederacy was fielding a veritable horde. From the moment he landed on the Peninsula to the day he realized that the Army of the Potomac would have to be evacuated, McClellan never doubted that he was outnumbered. In fact, the reverse was always true: the real Confederate numbers were less than half of those that mocked McClellan in his nightmares.

The general's superiors were beginning to catch on to the McClellan treatment: lots of boasting and secrecy followed by glacial maneuvering, hand-wringing, excuses, derision, accusations, and bitching. While McClellan waited on the banks of the James to be the last one to leave the Peninsula, his units on their way to Washington were being reassigned to the Army of Virginia under John Pope, a bombastic fool who would lose badly at the Second Battle of Bull Run in August. McClellan, stuck in Washington with little to do but watch Pope misuse the Army of the Potomac that had once been his, inwardly cheered at the Bull Run disaster. With the capital threatened, a desperate Lincoln once again turned to the damnable Young Napoleon, who seemed at once the solution and the doom of the Northern cause. Having lost his title as general in chief during the Peninsula campaign (an administration tactic to help McClellan focus on the Army of the Potomac and its march on Richmond), Little Mac was once again put in charge of all the forces in the eastern theater.

Though it tasted like a bitter pill to guys like Lincoln and Stanton, bringing McClellan back electrified the men in the ranks. Upon hearing the news during the retreat from Bull Run, the men raised a cacophony of ecstatic cheers that could be heard for miles. It was perhaps the greatest moment of McClellan's career. How could he possibly top it?

The answer to that arrived soon enough. On September 13, a copy of Lee's "Special Order No. 191" fell into the hands of a Union soldier, who found it lying on the ground wrapped around three cigars. In it Lee spelled out, in great detail, the entirety of his plan to capture Harpers Ferry, Virginia, in preparation for his invasion of Maryland—a plan that involved the splintering of his army into several columns. McClellan now had the means to run down and defeat the Army of Northern Virginia. It was, quite simply, the greatest intelligence coup of the American Civil War.

But it fell into the hands of the man least prepared to exploit it properly. McClellan was elated at first and convinced that he had the means to destroy his wily opponent at last. But with a giant break comes the pressure not to blow it. What if he acted on this invaluable information rashly and failed? Unforgivable. Better make sure and do it right. See to the details. Prepare the men for what will surely be the showdown of the war. Yeah, that's it. Slow and easy.

By the time McClellan got his ass in gear, the window of opportunity had vanished. Lee, eventually alerted to his predicament, did his frantic best to gather the disparate elements of his army for the blow that was about to fall. Had McClellan acted with anything approaching the alacrity that defined the best Confederate operations, he could have easily destroyed a large chunk of the Army of Northern Virginia and hastened the end of the war. Indeed, Lee's best efforts to gather his strength behind the Antietam Creek near Sharpsburg, Maryland, still wasn't enough: He faced a two-to-one disadvantage against McClellan. But when the armies met on September 16, McClellan—incredibly—believed once again that he faced a larger foe. The battle that he initiated on September 17 brought on the bloodiest day in American history, producing some 23,000 casualties.

Antietam was emblematic of all that was wrong with George McClellan. Interestingly, it was the first time that he'd been present for a major engagement from beginning to end. Like Xerxes at Thermopylae, he directed it like a player moves his chess pieces—aloof, intellectual. He even slept through the first bloody clashes in the morning, as if the gears he had set in motion no longer required his full attention. Obsessed with the notion that the South was able to put more men in the field than he was, he fought the battle with the mind-set of a demigod doing his minions a favor: If the Army of the Potomac was ruined by this nonsense, it wasn't his fault. After all, he was fighting against the odds, so any gains at all should be considered virtually incredible and a testament to his infinitely sound judgment. In fact, Lee's army was fighting for its life at Antietam, and would have been in very grave shape had the Federals pressed it hard at all points with everything they had. As it happened, McClellan never committed more than three-quarters of his army throughout the day, and that only in piecemeal thrusts.

It is not too much to say that Antietam should have been the end of the Army of Northern Virginia. Instead, the Union had to settle for a check on Lee's tepid invasion of the North—enough of an accomplishment for Lincoln to release his preliminary Emancipation Proclamation. But it was a lost opportunity of the first order, which McClellan never seemed to fully grasp. "Those in whose judgment I rely," swelled the general, "tell me that I fought the battle splendidly and that it was a masterpiece of art." Unfortunately for him, he followed his masterpiece of art with a masterpiece of procrastination, letting Lee's mauled army flee unmolested to the refuge of Virginia.

This was the last straw. Since the beginning of the war, the headstrong generalissimo from Philadelphia had been testing the patience of everyone who stood for the Union. He had been known since his West Point days to have professed affinity for Southerners and disdain for his fellow Northeasterners. And no one could forget the pamphlets he had printed in 1861, during his advance into western Virginia, assuring citizens he would protect their right to hold slaves and even forcibly crush any Negroes bold enough to look at his campaign as an excuse to rebel. McClellan was a conservative Democrat, a feverish foe of abolitionists, and a man who—it seemed—had dithered a bit too conspicuously in his military duties. The final nail in his coffin came in October, when Jeb Stuart's ubiquitous cavalry once again rode around McClellan's army. The Young Napoleon was relieved of his command.

So intense and universal was Little Mac's popularity with the troops that Lincoln and his cabinet actually feared a military coup. But his perceived popularity went to the heart of the misunderstanding between McClellan and the men who directed him. That he hated them was less an indication of his disdain for civilian rule than it was proof of a petulant man's hatred of interference from nonprofessionals. Moreover, few men in uniform despised secessionists more than McClellan, whose genuine fondness for Southern manners and society stood totally separate from his ruthless insistence on union. With these dubious credentials, Democrats nominated him to take on Lincoln in the 1864 presidential election. He was the unlikely candidate of a divided party—a professional soldier committed to total victory representing men who pushed for peace. With such an insecure platform and a troubled party, McClellan's candidacy made it easier for those on the fence to vote for his opponent, whose reelection ensured that the war would be prosecuted to its end. In other words, McClellan—quite unintentionally—helped defeat the South in a way he never could have on the battlefield.

Not that he never won political office. In 1877, he won election as governor of New Jersey, where he displayed an admirable degree of effectiveness with very little effort. But it was, to say the least, anticlimactic. He had become a huckster cashing in on previous exploits. In the end, his greatest tribute came from the unlikeliest of sources. Five years after Appomattox, Robert E. Lee was asked to name the ablest opponent he faced throughout the War Between the States. "McClellan, by all odds," he replied without hesitation.

Go figure.

BACK IN THE SADDLE

When George McClellan returned from his European tour in 1855, he had acquired numerous ideas that would influence the American military establishment. But none of them acquired the longevity of his ideas on cavalry equipment. Armed with designs from Hungary and Prussia, the young McClellan set about overhauling the standard-issue saddle for American cavalry units. The result was the "McClellan saddle," an easily maintained design that became the standard for all units on horse until the mounted arm was abolished by the United States Army, well into the twentieth century.

ALTERED STATES

A native of Philadelphia, McClellan wanted to fight for Pennsylvania when war broke out. Though impressed by Ohio governor William Dennison's eagerness to sign him up, he earnestly lobbied the authorities of his native state to give him a commission. As it happened, they ended up doing just that. But the telegram informing McClellan of his new rank in the Pennsylvania volunteers was accidentally sent to Chicago, rather than Cincinnati. By that time he had accepted the offer from Dennison. As a result, McClellan was attached at the beginning of the war to Ohio, where he made a name for himself against inferior Confederate forces, rather than Pennsylvania, whose attachment to the eastern theater would have associated him with the defeat at Bull Run. The result—stemming from an errant telegram—was the abrupt rise of a hero.

Spanking the Monkey

"The original gorilla" is how a piqued McClellan loved to refer to Abraham Lincoln. It's a term he first heard from Secretary of War Edwin Stanton, another man for whom the general—after an initial friendship—ended up embracing a long and sincere distaste. McClellan hated deeply and for keeps, like a testy little prince whose vulnerability brooked no slights. When combined with his gift for the drawing room snub, it produced legendary results. In November 1861, the president and Secretary of State William Seward called on McClellan and were told that he was attending a wedding. The executive party decided to wait. An hour later the general returned—and went right up the stairs to bed without so much as acknowledging his esteemed visitors or, for that matter, his orderly's announcement that the president of the United States was paying him a call.

ULYSSES S. GRANT

April 27, 1822–July 23, 1885

HIGHEST RANK:

Union General

ASTROLOGICAL SIGN:

Taurus

NICKNAMES:

Useless, Sam, Unconditional Surrender

WORDS TO REMEMBER:

"The truth is I am more of a farmer than a soldier. I take no interest in military affairs, and, although I entered the army thirty-five years ago and have been in two wars, in Mexico as a young lieutenant, and later, I never went into the army without regret and never retired without pleasure" (to German Chancellor Otto von Bismarck).

On April 6, 1862, the history of warfare in North America took an abrupt turn for the terrible. On the west bank of the Tennessee River near a place called Pittsburg Landing, Tennessee, five Federal divisions began their morning with a bang—or, more accurately, thousands of bangs. Alerted by pickets just after sunup that an army of Rebels was on its way from the southwest along the Corinth road, the bluecoats exchanged their coffee cups for cartridges and began frantically deploying to meet the great mass of butternut that was even then bearing down on them. The vast Union encampment, however, had

Ulysses Grant loved horses and refused to tolerate any sort of animal cruelty. After witnessing a teamster beating his horses, Grant ordered the man to be tied to a tree for six hours "as a punishment for his brutality."

not been laid out with defense in mind—everyone was convinced that Albert Sydney Johnston and his Confederates were all the way down in Corinth,

huddled behind elaborate defenses. But Johnston had brought his army up, determined to strike a blow at his enemies before they could do the same to him. His appearance was a complete and unnerving surprise.

At just over one hundred yards, the serried Rebel ranks halted and unleashed a devastating salvo, punching great holes through General Benjamin Prentiss's hapless division. Before long, perhaps two hours, that division would all but cease to exist as a fighting unit. The others would fare little better by the end of the day. Shiloh—the costliest, most savage battle yet seen in America, named incongruously for a nearby church—had begun.

Ulysses S. Grant had heard the rumble of guns from his base across the river, at Savannah. Pittsburg Landing was the forward encampment of his army—those were his men getting shot at. By the time he boarded a riverboat and raced to the battlefield, the onslaught was more than an hour old and just heating up. For the next nine hours and more, in fighting of thunderous, unprecedented ferocity, the oncoming Confederates pushed their confused enemies inexorably back, taking one Union camp after another—each of which offered up Yankee goodies that barefoot Johnny Rebs were not in the habit of passing by. Their plundering, along with pockets of fierce and desperate Union resistance, served to slow the rout to a fighting retreat. Grant, cool and alert amidst the crashing violence, used the time he had to organize a last line of defense—a bristling cordon of cannon to prevent his army from being pushed like a crumbling levee into the waters of the Tennessee. With the sun dropping fast, 8,000 exhausted Rebels made a final attempt to break Grant's line, only to wade into a flood of shot and shell from field pieces, siege guns, and the arching ordnance of Union gunboats. The attack disintegrated.

The Southerners recoiled, satisfied with their tremendous victory. Albert Sidney Johnston, Jefferson Davis's favorite general, lay dead on the battlefield. But his army was truly victorious. It had caught five Yankee divisions almost literally with their pants down, and proceeded to shove them, as if by a giant push broom, out of their tent cities into a precarious bridgehead on the banks of the Tennessee. The Federal losses were appalling, including 7,000 men killed or wounded and 3,000 captured. Some forty pieces of artillery had been wrecked or captured. Strung out along the river like refugees, thousands of unnerved farm boys in blue cowered and milled about, a veritable army of broken deserters. Little wonder so many of Grant's subordinates were thinking about retreat across the Tennessee. Indeed, not a few of them had been thinking about it for hours, since before the cacophonous roar of battle had faded.

One of them was William Tecumseh Sherman, who had handled his division remarkably well that long day under the circumstances. A sensitive cynic and recovering depressive who was only just learning how terribly talented he was at war, Sherman had begun to take a shine to Grant. That night, as rain soaked the two armies and the acres of dead and dying that lay between them, Sherman went looking for his superior to pick his mind. He found Grant standing beneath a tree, his slouch hat and overcoat drawn tight against the weather, a cigar clenched in his teeth. The commanding general, who had recently suffered a riding accident, had been resting his lame leg at a field hospital. But the screaming, and the sawing, and the effusion of blood and viscera had been too much for him, driving him away to find peace in this dark, wet sanctuary. "Well Grant," said Sherman through the downpour, "we've had the devil's own day, haven't we?"

Grant sucked the glow back into his cigar. "Yes. Lick 'em tomorrow though."

Such an attitude was a little crazy, at least to officers who thought they knew better than Grant. (And there was no shortage of those.) Grant had been receiving reinforcements since late afternoon, to be sure. And the Rebels had shot their wad in the long battle that day. But so had Grant's men—thousands killed and captured, thousands more shattered in spirit. As everybody at the top knew, these were volunteers and raw recruits. They had been surprised, whipped, and deprived of their kit and baggage. They had LOST. You couldn't just order them to take it all back in the morning. Better to skedaddle across the river to safety and fight another day.

But Grant was different. Relying on his reinforcements, and the strength of his veteran commanders, he endeavored to resuscitate his battered army with his own indomitable spirit. Very early the next morning, he offered simple, straightforward commands to his subordinates that got them off in the right direction and left the details of battle to them as circumstances required. His contribution to their effort was his sublime, self-assured calm and infectious enthusiasm. The thought of retreating had literally never occurred to him—nor had it occurred to him the previous February at Fort Donelson, another occasion in which his troops had rallied decisively after being thrown back in a grueling match. As had been the case at Fort Donelson, Shiloh was a test of wills: both sides had reached the breaking point. Whichever side attacked next, won.

Believing they would make short work of the broken Federals the following day, the late Johnston's Confederates—now under the command of P. G. T. Beauregard—slept the sleep of the confident, satisfied from a day that, despite its consuming destruction, had seemed like Christmas in April with its Yankee largesse. At first light, Grant's men went forward into Rebel ground that had lately been theirs, driving enemy pickets before them in a haunting reverse of the previous day's events. The armies grappled again, loosing storms of lead into each other in a series of awful, concussive melees. By mid-afternoon, the Southerners had had it, forcing Beauregard to organize a fighting retreat back to Corinth. He left behind him more than 10,500 killed, wounded, or missing. Shiloh was a holocaust: More casualties were inflicted in two days of fighting than in all of America's previous wars combined.

But Grant was left standing on the field. His forces had been surprised and thrown back, but that didn't count for much in his world. He had gotten up off the ground and kicked his assailant in the teeth with a dirty boot. That counted for much in his world. "The art of war is simple enough," said Grant. "Find out where your enemy is. Get at him as soon as you can. Strike him as hard as you can and as often as you can and keep on going." Phil Sheridan, who ultimately became Grant's cavalry tsar, said that Grant "was the steadfast center about and on which everything else turned." President Lincoln would one day praise Grant for "his perfect coolness and persistency of purpose." But how does one describe or encapsulate the genius that allowed this gentle, soft-spoken little man to become the conqueror of the South? William Sherman, who knew the sphinx-like fighter from Point Pleasant, Ohio, better than most, said it best: "He is a mystery to me and I believe also to himself."

He was a mystery to his father, too, who nicknamed him "Useless" as a boy. Virtually everything about Ulysses was paradoxical or misleading, including his name. He was christened Hiram Ulysses Grant, only to be accidentally renamed Ulysses Simpson Grant in the paperwork that got him into West Point (Simpson was his mother's maiden name). The academy, which gave him the only skills he ever really used and that allowed him to become one of the most important figures of the century, was his father's idea—Hiram "Useless" had no desire to go whatsoever, and would never take to regimentation, studying, uniforms, or killing. Short and slightly built, he did not care for athletics. He was a lousy student. Though an extraordinarily gifted artist, he would proclaim a lack of interest in painting later in life and abandon it altogether. His other talent, riding, made him famous at the Point; nobody—nobody—could handle horses like Grant. Where did he end up upon graduation? The infantry. There were no spots available in his first and natural choice, the cavalry. (Sigh.)

The story just gets stranger. During the War with Mexico, he served with both of America's preeminent military leaders—Zachary Taylor in the north, and Winfield Scott on the coast, receiving two brevets for bravery in a conflict he considered morally repugnant. After being assigned to the remote Pacific northwest, he pined for his beloved wife, the daughter of a man who not only had eagerly supported the Mexican War but who also owned slaves, something else that Grant found unethical. His solution to loneliness was to drink, which he didn't do very well at all. It never required much whiskey to get Grant stumbling, bullet-proof drunk. Compelled to resign his commission in 1854 on account of his bibulous behavior, he embarked upon a series of professional failures the likes of which American history has rarely witnessed in a future president. He borrowed money and even slaves to help his doomed farm; got work as a real estate agent, but could neither sell houses nor collect rent with anything approaching com-petence; hit up his hostile father for loans; looked for work along the streets of St. Louis; pawned his possessions to buy Christmas presents for the kids; and peddled firewood he had cut himself. His younger brothers finally took him in as a clerk in their Galena, Illinois, leather goods shop—a cruel irony, considering the fact that the stench and gore of his father's tannery had always made Grant sick as a child.

Then war came.

Within a few years he would be the closest thing to a generalissimo that America had ever produced, holding a rank, lieutenant general, that Congress had resurrected especially for him—an almost incredible reversal of fortune. But he had a hard time convincing folks in 1861 that he wasn't the incompetent, sulking lush that everyone seemed to believe he had become. He managed to get a colonelcy and a regiment of miscreants to drill, but his most important acquisition was a patron in Elihu Washburne, congressman from Galena, Illinois. A friend of the president's, Washburne helped Grant get a brigadier general's star in the volunteers. After whipping his men into shape, he saw action at Belmont in November, a battle that did little more than offer newbies on both sides an opportunity to fire their rifles at a moving target. But bigger things were waiting just around the corner.

In February 1862, Grant managed to get permission from his overly pru-dent superior Henry Halleck to lead an expedition into Tennessee with the support of ironclads under the command of Flag Officer Andrew Foote. The resulting campaign changed the entire complexion of the war in the West. Foote's floating monsters managed to pummel Fort Henry on the Tennessee River into surrender, but not before most of its garrison escaped to Fort Donelson, ten miles away on the Cumberland. Without hesitating, Grant decided to send his force overland to take the second fort, wiring Halleck of his intentions almost as an afterthought. Donelson proved a tougher nut to crack: Foote's ironclads got much worse than they gave and were forced to retire for repairs, and the Rebel garrison, reinforced before Grant's army showed up, was as large as the Union force, making a successful siege all but impossible. Recovering from Confederate attacks that nearly achieved a breakout, Grant launched a final furious assault, completing the encirclement and rendering the fort's defenses untenable. "No terms except an unconditional and immediate surrender can be accepted," he famously and quite brashly informed his enemy. "I propose to move immediately upon your works." It proved effective. Fort Donelson fell, yielding a slew of prisoners, control of western Tennessee, and use of the Cumberland and Tennessee Rivers.

Soon hailed throughout the North as "Unconditional Surrender" Grant, he had become a hero, giving his president and his country the first major success of the Union war effort. But then came the April bloodbath at Shiloh, horrifying a public that had just recently been singing Grant's praises. Body counts on such a hitherto unknown scale were too ghastly, even in exchange for a Confederate reversal and Albert Sidney Johnston's corpse. The incident gave Henry Halleck the excuse he was looking for to treat his famous underling like excess baggage. As he crept toward Corinth in what may have been the slowest advance of the Civil War, the sluggardly Halleck kept Grant in tow as a sort of glorified page. Convinced that he had shot his bolt, Grant prepared to pack for home and what would doubtless have been another slide into undignified financial disaster. Then Sherman paid him a visit, and asked him what the hell he thought he was doing. In the frenetic speaking style that had become one of his dubious hallmarks, Sherman jabbered on and on about how things can turn around if you just stick it out, and somehow it worked.

Good thing, too, because Grant's next triumph would make military history and save the Union. Vicksburg, Mississippi, was the key to unlocking the South's undoing. A fortified stronghold perched on heights that overlooked a bend in the Mississippi, it was akin to the perfect river sentinel, frowning down on the "Father of Waters" with more than enough large-caliber artillery to rain hell upon anything stupid enough to float on by without permission. Unassailable from the river, surrounded by swamps and lakes, it seemed impervious. Grant went at the problem in the fall of 1862, doing everything short of sending a squadron of balloons over the city to bomb it into submission. He sent columns of troops overland from north of the bastion, landed divisions by boat, had canals dug to redirect the river, but nothing worked. Wallowing about in the mud, his supply lines harassed by Rebel cavalry maestro Nathan Bedford Forrest, Grant began worrying his superiors once again and giving the newspapermen something to moan about. Then, the following year, he struck upon an idea so daring that many of his best subordinates, including Sherman, begged him not to try it. (Grant didn't listen.) As the ships of Admiral David Porter sailed south on the current, bravely running the gauntlet beneath Vicksburg in a nighttime dash, Grant marched his men alongside them on the west bank of the Mississippi. Once well south of Vicksburg, the army was ferried in safety across the river and left to its fate on the east bank, deep within enemy territory. The Federal army was now totally on its own—Vicksburg lay athwart its supply lines to the north, and supply from the river was wholly unrealistic. Moreover, Grant had not only to deal with the defenders of his fortified target, but also with another Confederate army under Joseph Johnston that had come to Vicksburg's aid. No wonder Grant's lieutenants thought him soft in the head.

But he was way ahead of them all. Let loose like a virus in the flesh of his enemy, he lived off the produce of local farms and villages, moving without having to worry about lines of supply. The previous winter, morose with failure, the general had hit the bottle again. Now there was no whiskey in sight—in fact, the only possessions Grant brought with him, besides the uniform on his back, were a comb and brush. He descended on Joseph Johnston's army at Jackson, Mississippi, and routed it. Then, when the defenders of Vicksburg sallied out to crush him, he turned on them and, in a pair of sharp fights, sent them hastening back into their defenses. It was all so brilliant and dazzling and ballsy that nobody seemed to notice when his attempts to storm the works of Vicksburg itself ended in bloody repulse (except, of course, the nearly four thousand dead and wounded incurred during the two all-out assaults—they definitely noticed). Things settled into a siege, and on July 4, 1863, the city finally surrendered. He rounded out the year by breaking the Confederate siege of Chattanooga in the dramatic assaults up Lookout Mountain and Missionary Ridge. Grant had become the North's trump card.

And the president himself had become his greatest fan. Outwardly, the two had nothing in common. Lincoln, eight inches taller than his favorite general, was an effusive storyteller and humorist who, among his other talents, excelled at admitting and delineating his own faults. Grant, by contrast, had so little to say about anything, at all times, that even those close to him were hard pressed not to wonder if anything at all was present in his head to be expressed. And when he did speak, it was almost never to admit a weakness—Grant's abiding strength lay in a self-confidence that was manifest, indestructible. But they were both Midwesterners who had gravitated to Illinois. Both men had opposed the War with Mexico, one in his heart and the other on the floor of Congress, a shared experience of moral protest. And both men found themselves in agreement that the South must now be crushed utterly if there was to be any hope of peace. Both were looking to bring that other arm out from behind the Northern behemoth and start slugging away with both fists. Anything to shorten the war.

The president made his man a lieutenant general and set him at the head of all the nation's armies. Putting his friend Sherman in charge of all the forces of the West, Grant took his place with George Meade, the victor of Gettysburg, and the Army of the Potomac. He did so not because the West was less important than the eastern theater, for it certainly wasn't. But Robert E. Lee was in the East. And Lee had become a strategic target in and of himself—a symbol of Southern success and defiance that did much to prop up a sagging cause. And there were many in the Army of the Potomac who didn't believe that Grant, who had cut his teeth on inferior foes on the Mississippi, understood what he was in for in Uncle Bobby, the great bugbear of Washington soldiers.

Perhaps they had a point. Grant went south and got ambushed in that primordial woodland known as the Wilderness—the perfect place for Lee to cancel Grant's outrageous superiority in numbers and artillery. In the midst of the incredibly intense fighting, Grant, informed of horrific casualty figures and the possibility of disaster on his right wing, did a singular thing: He went into his tent, fell on his cot, and sobbed openly.

It was perhaps the last gasp of doubt left in him, purged in a moment of weakness. Nobody had ever witnessed anything like it before. At any rate, he soon did another singular thing. As his men pulled out of their positions in the Wilderness, rather than direct them back north, as every previous Army of the Potomac commander would've done, he sent them east and south—a profound decision to maintain contact with the enemy that evinced roars of approval from the men, elated at having a fighter at the helm. Grant's plan was to move to the left, sliding his army around in an attempt to get at Lee's weak spots while never losing touch with him. He knew that he could use the proximity of Richmond as a weapon, forcing his opponent to position himself for the city's defense. But the Rebel capital was never Grant's object—the Army of Northern Virginia was. Lee obliged throughout the Overland Campaign, as it was called, clashing with Grant at Spotsylvania, North Anna, and Cold Harbor. The latter, in which Grant ordered a final all-out assault against entrenched positions, produced terrific slaughter—7,000 casualties in an hour. It was the only event that Grant regretted during his Civil War career. Undeterred, he kept sliding around Lee's right and got the drop on him at Petersburg. There, P. G. T. Beauregard put up a valiant defense until Lee and the Army of Northern Virginia could show up and prevent the Federals from sweeping in to Richmond. The siege of Petersburg had begun.

Grant had bottled up his enemy—someone had finally beaten Lee. Throughout the final winter and spring of the war, Grant gradually extended his encirclement, stretching Lee to the breaking point and launching assaults to probe for weakness. After the Battle of Five Forks, the Rebel line at last became untenable, forcing a mass evacuation of forces west toward a very uncertain future. The following April, Grant ran his opponent down and received his surrender. Lee, wearing his dress uniform with a sash and gilt sword, was obliged to wait at the assigned meeting place for Grant, who showed up in an unbuttoned, mud-spattered uniform, devoid of sword or even spurs. The scene was perfectly apt.

Grant had never been comfortable in the army, yet summoned and directed its awesome power better than almost anyone. Unlearned in war almost in spite of a West Point education, he relied on common sense, surreal clarity of thought, and dogged persistence to fashion victory from adversity. Rarely has such a lethal combination of qualities resided in such an innocuous package.

The great unlikely warlord never again did anything so well as he did in those tumultuous years between 1861 and 1865—except write about it all in his outstanding memoir, published by Mark Twain. By then, dying of throat cancer from a life wreathed in cigar smoke, he had served two terms as president of the United States and traveled the world. Though rife with corruption and cronyism, his presidency witnessed a tenacious and ultimately doomed struggle on behalf of the freedmen, whose fate, Grant sincerely believed, was emblematic of the nation's future. As a traveler, he was praised the world over—a symbol of America resurgent in all its rumpled, egalitarian glory. Once out of the limelight, he became a businessman and lost everything, bringing himself and his wife, Julia, perilously close to destitution. It was out of this that the memoir emerged—a pecuniary necessity that exposed its author as a literary prodigy. The thing saved Julia from a life of poverty, earning nearly half a million bucks after Grant's death—a fitting denouement to a life that had witnessed unparalleled extremes of failure and ruin, all against the backdrop of a nation's violent redemption and gilded comeback. Ulysses Grant may just be the quintessential American after all.

EASY RIDER

During much of the Vicksburg campaign, Ulysses Grant rode a horse named "Kangaroo." Left by the retreating Rebels on the field at Shiloh, the animal—ugly, unkempt, neglected—wasn't much to look at when Grant found him. But while most observers dismissed the horse as a lost cause, the general recognized what was, in fact, a thoroughbred. He took Kangaroo under his care and in time produced a mount that was the envy of his officers.

Grant loved horses, and horses loved him back. It was a gift that Ulysses had from the time he was a small boy, driving his father's team of horses with striking ease. As a teenager, people from all around brought difficult mounts to the Grant home for "Ulys" to pacify and train. His fellow West Point cadets were in awe of his riding abilities, watching him once jump the academy's most difficult mount over a bar set to a height that would've been virtually impossible for everyone else. The record stood for twenty-five years. After the conclusion of his second presidential term, during the Grants' world tour, a stop in Turkey produced an historic equine moment. Sultan Abdul Hamid II honored his esteemed guest with a visit to the royal stables, telling the former president to choose any two horses to keep as his own. Stunned, like a kid in the world's greatest candy store, Grant made his two choices, only to be told, "Any other two." An amused Grant chose two other magnificent beasts, and had them shipped home. Named Leopard and Linden Tree, they ultimately established the Arabian purebred strain in North America that exists to this day.

As for all those who didn't share his appreciation for horses, Grant could be uncharacteristically wrathful. Once, during the Overland Campaign in 1864, the general came across a teamster whose wagon was stuck in the mud beating his horses on the face. Grant, enraged, commanded the brute to stop. The man was defiant: "Who's driving this team anyhow, you or me?" Grant immediately had the man tied to a tree "for six hours as a punishment for his brutality." His staff had never seen him so undone.

GENERAL ORDER NO. 11

One of the most irritating parts of General Grant's job during the 1862 attempts on Vicksburg was dealing with the illicit cotton trade. Cut off from the world's markets, Southern planters sold their goods to throngs of Yankee traders and speculators who followed in the wake of the army's advance south. Plenty of soldiers and officers dallied in the traffic as well, producing a situation that the government thought had grown out of control—profits that made their way back to Southern authorities, after all, could prolong the war. To get a handle on this burgeoning black market, Federal authorities gave their generals conflicting directives that were often impossible to enforce, insisting that only those traders with legal permits could carry on trade in cotton. Grant in particular found the whole situation untenable along the Mississippi. As a result, he sought to simply prevent traders from doing business in his jurisdiction.

It was against this backdrop that Grant, on December 17, formally expelled all Jews from the Department of the Tennessee. Fixating on several prominent Jewish traders in the area and allowing his own ignorance to run amok, the general simply began assuming that the vast majority of illegal merchants were "Israelites." Officers on his staff did their best to prevent Grant from issuing "General Order No. 11," but to no avail. Aside from being a heinous act of anti-Semitism, the proclamation was impossible to enforce—what to do, for instance, with the thousands of Jews fighting in his own army? Fortunately, the order was short-lived. Rightly pilloried in the press, the act appalled President Lincoln, who ordered that it be immediately revoked. That Grant did so the following month only because he had been ordered to, further impugns his judgment. It remains a strange and ugly smudge on his record.

THAT TOTALLY BITES

As if it weren't bad enough watching all his attempts to take Vicksburg fail and having a hellraiser like Bedford Forrest cutting his supply lines to ribbons, Grant had a nasty shock one morning in February 1863. The night before, he had broken the usual habit of sleeping with his dentures in, and instead placed them in a bucket of water—which his servant, unaware of the dentition lying within, threw into the river early the next morning. Grant wouldn't have replacement choppers for almost a month. No wonder he fell off the wagon and started drinking again.

Quick! Take the Picture!

Of all the close brushes with death that General Grant faced during the stunningly bloody war he helped to end, one of the scariest occurred . . . in a photographer's studio. After being promoted to lieutenant general, Grant agreed to sit for the capital's image-capturer par excellence, Matthew Brady. Unfortunately, the general didn't show up until late in the day, when the sun was well on its way toward the horizon. To maximize what little sunlight remained, Brady sent an assistant up to the roof to open the shades on the skylight. Instead the fellow slipped and broke the skylight, sending huge shards of glass cascading down upon the illustrious subject, who had taken his seat as requested. Grant, who casually looked skyward to see the cause of all the commotion (the glass was two inches thick), gave "the most remarkable display of nerve" that the photographer had ever seen as the pieces crashed and shattered all around him. Now that's coolness under fire. (Not a single bit of glass managed to hit him.)

6 WILLIAM TECUMSEH SHERMAN

February 8, 1820–February 14, 1891

HIGHEST RANK:
Union General

ASTROLOGICAL SIGN:
Aquarius

NICKNAMES:
Cump, Uncle Billy

WORDS TO REMEMBER:
"Its glory is all moonshine; even success the most brilliant is over dead and mangled bodies, with the anguish and lamentation of distant families" (on war).

"War is all hell," said William Tecumseh Sherman. And he oughtta know. Sherman's Civil War truly was hell—for him, for those around him, and for the South he adored and crushed. His checkered career continues to inspire awe, respect, and hatred, virtually all at once, as if refracted through a prism into a spectrum of savageries. From his unbalancing intensity to his forward-looking strategy, from his searing eyes to the igneous hair atop his grizzled head, Sherman stands like a totem for the unprecedented destruction of America's defining tragedy.

Blood and connections ensured him a place on the national stage. His father, an Ohio supreme court justice named Charles Robert Sherman, died when "Cump" was nine, forcing Mrs. Sherman to disperse her children for want of financial means. Red-headed Cump was informally adopted by Thomas Ewing, a prominent politician who ultimately gave much to the boy—including his daughter Ellen, whom Cump married in May of 1850. Ewing's wealth and political clout (he would go on to become a senator and presidential cabinet member) did much for William in the chaotic years to come.

To begin with, Ewing was instrumental in getting him into West Point. There Cump proved especially adept at making his "midnight hash," a potato-based concoction that was eagerly devoured by fellow cadets in Sherman's

room after lights-out to compensate for the academy's dismal fare. And his talents didn't stop there: He was sharp, animated, and popular, and he graduated sixth in his class.

More culinary adventures followed in Florida, as Sherman spent much of his time catching turtles and spearing sharks during the Seminole "war." His artillery unit was later posted to California during the war with Mexico, where Cump earned a brevet and made a valuable friend in Henry Halleck. Wary of supporting his family with a military salary, he resigned his commission in 1853 and embarked on a series of abortive ventures, proving that his decision to quit the Army was a bad one. Like Grant, Sherman was luckless in many fields: banking, finance, law. From San Francisco to Leavenworth, Kansas, Cump left a trail of frustrated dreams. Then in 1859 came a posting that seemed ideally suited to him: superintendent of the Louisiana State Seminary of Learning and Military Academy. Since his posting in Alabama and Charleston as a young officer just after his stint in Florida, Sherman had warmly embraced the South and its cultural idiosyncrasies and come to look upon its people as his friends and neighbors. Now, ensconced in a position in Louisiana that took his learning and intellectual talents into account, he could make a home among the folks he had come to understand so well.

In the years before the Civil War, William Sherman once suffered the misfortune of surviving two shipwrecks on the same day.

Or so he thought. If he understood Southerners, he certainly didn't understand secession. In the wake of Lincoln's electoral victory, as friends and associates in Louisiana bound their fates to a nascent Confederacy, Sherman felt like he had suddenly stumbled into an insane asylum. Worse, his decision to leave and go north was going to put him right back into the impecunious situation he had hoped was long behind him. But leave he did—into a future that frightened him.

Cump worried most about getting another job—which seems pretty silly now, given the fact that he had a West Point education and a war was breaking out. Moreover, he had better connections than most of the fellows pestering Lincoln for a battlefield commission. Two of Cump's brothers were in a position to lobby on his behalf: Charles Taylor Sherman, who was organizing Ohio volunteers, and John Sherman, a prominent Ohio senator who would go on in later years to become a treasury secretary and secretary of state. They, in addition to brother-in-law Tom Ewing, a prominent lawyer and Washington insider, set the gears in motion (which included meeting personally with the president) to get their man a colonelcy in the infantry.

Voilà. If worrying over his profession seemed a little unwarranted, it was. But fretting had become one of his traits—and it would get much, much worse. Despite a lousy performance at First Bull Run, Cump was made a brigadier general of volunteers in the summer of 1861, bringing him up to the grade that many thought he should have had from the beginning. He was then sent west as part of the effort to keep Kentucky in the Union—a task so onerous that Robert Anderson, the hero of Fort Sumter and now his superior, felt compelled to resign, citing "the mental torture" of his command. Cump, who had intentionally asked Lincoln for a subordinate position, suddenly found himself in charge of the whole Department of the Cumberland. And if it had been hard on Anderson, it would be positively brutal on him.

Something had gone awry in Sherman since the beginning of the war, as if the natural sensitivity that had made him so famously gregarious and cerebral in his brash youth had been twisted by awful truths. Life was a mean struggle to survive; friends he had once esteemed (still esteemed) were now embarked on a mad scheme to ruin the country and destroy his command; and, most significantly, the war that everyone thought was going to be brief was certainly going to be anything but. Indeed, it promised to be an interminable, gory, and consuming conflagration. Why didn't anybody see that except him?

There were other things that only he saw in Kentucky: such as Confederate brigades beyond number. He felt all but abandoned to face a

Rebel host that—in his imagination—grew to prodigious proportions. Always suspicious of the quality of volunteer soldiers (an opinion that intensified in the rout of Bull Run), he saw the useless humanity paraded before him for training and despaired. That so many of them simply deserted every day hardly helped. And he knew all those Southerners who faced him—knew that so many of the army's finest had gone with Dixie and would be coming for him. They were good, and they were his enemy. It was a hopeless situation as he saw it, driving him to pace and chatter and smoke and fume like some caffeinated sociopath.

And then there were the newspapermen, scorned by Sherman as little better than swamp gas. When they were forbidden to enter his encampments, the feeling soon became mutual—and those few who did get in printed stories that he had gone insane, an opinion shared by some in the government who had read his frantic correspondence and heard the rumors. Sherman was finished.

Well, not quite. There seems no doubt that Cump suffered at least a nervous breakdown in the fall of 1861—hardly the sort of thing that draws encomiums from one's superiors in a time of war. Nevertheless, Sherman had allies. And one of them was Henry Halleck, into whose care he was now shunted in the wake of the Kentucky humiliation. Sherman remained anything but stable, however, a fact that would've ended his career were it not for his connections in high places and a thoughtful, laconic fighter named Ulysses Grant.

Sherman was senior in rank, a fact that disappeared when the two generals got to know each other while serving in Halleck's western command. Drawn to his fellow Ohioan, Cump offered to waive his higher grade and take a command under Grant, beginning one of the most extraordinary and fruitful relationships in military history. They were both outwardly flawed, a fact that seemed entirely at home with their mutual understanding that war had become—and must be—a hard business devoid of glory. Such realism brooked no illusions, and they could be nearly as hard on each other as they were on the Rebels. But respect flowed between them as if through a palpable connection—galvanized, perhaps, by a shared confusion over how on earth either of them had become lead players in one of history's grandest martial epics.

Sherman needed a new beginning, and he got it—sort of—at a bloodbath called Shiloh in April 1862. On the first day of the battle, his lack of caution allowed General Albert Sidney Johnston's Confederates to make a surprise assault that drove the bluecoats almost to destruction on the banks of the Tennessee River. Grant's decision to counterattack the next morning, however, turned the battle into a Union victory, partially erasing Sherman's carelessness. With this awkward Renaissance, and a promotion to major general of volunteers, Cump began his climb to military immortality.

It was to begin along the Mississippi River, in the drive to take the crucial stronghold of Vicksburg. Again, Sherman's tactical sense failed him in a tragic frontal assault at Chickasaw Bluffs, which doomed Grant's attempt to take Vicksburg by a direct approach. Placed under the command of Major General John McClernand, Sherman played a crucial role in taking the irritating Confederate strongpoint at Arkansas Post. And in Grant's successful capture of Vicksburg, Sherman led the Fifteenth Corps, wrapping up the campaign with the siege of Jackson. Promoted a brigadier general in the regular army, he took part in the relief of Rosecrans's forces at Chattanooga, and secured the relief of Knoxville. By then it was the winter of 1863, and Sherman—a capable commander at best with plenty of mistakes and mediocrities to ponder—made history mostly with his words, particularly those spoken to a lady who took issue with his soldiers for their pillaging in the Knoxville campaign. "War is cruelty," he responded to the red-faced woman. "There is no use trying to reform it; the crueler it is, the sooner it will be over."

Of all the year's casualties, the one that hit Sherman hardest was that of his son Willy, struck down by typhoid fever at the age of nine while campaigning with his father. His loss was the final layer of Sherman's waxing hardness; violence, destruction, and the necessity of Herculean duties had turned him into a machine of war. Like one who had stared down the abyss of psychosis (or something like it) and understood how terrible it was, he mustered the wrath and direction needed to bring an end to the great national craziness around him.

When Grant was appointed commander in chief, Sherman succeeded him to overall command in the West. Now at long last he would be afforded the stage and circumstances to which his peculiar talents were truly suited. Never a great tactician, Sherman's assets lay in the organization and sweep of armies across vast distances, a mission appropriate not only to the scale of his calculations but also to the scope of his harsh vision. From here on out, he would essentially *march* the South to death.

Atlanta was first, arrived at by using superior numbers to outmaneuver his Confederate opponents. Despite a bloody repulse in late June at Kennesaw Mountain, Sherman repeatedly flanked his opponent's positions, forcing them farther and farther back. Taking Atlanta in one of the most significant turning points of the war, he turned it into a pyre that burned for days. And then he made the most important decision of his life. Leaving enough men under George Thomas to deal with the remaining Rebel resistance to his rear, he divided his 62,000-man army into two columns and struck east, burrowing through Georgia's vitals like a pair of parasitic worms. Unlike every Civil War general up to that point, he sought no enemy army, anticipated no climactic battle. He meant to cut his supply lines and feed his troops off the fat of the foe, turning them loose in the great expanse of home front that was feeding and arming the Rebel armies. He would eat the enemy's chickens, tear up his railroads, steal his livestock, and burn his crops—and he would do it without butchering hordes of young men, which was more than his buddy Grant could say up in Virginia. Sherman would make the civilians of Georgia understand the privations that afflicted the soldiers that they were so eager to send to the front. And this, he was sure, would bring peace to a broken populace.

Like a prophet, Cump was unleashing the future—a horrifying future of total war. But in 1864, his decision seemed a rejection of the ritualized killing that was extending the nation's agony into a dark, perpetual Iliad. The men under his command, however, held no such notions. Called "bummers," his blue-coated foragers fanned out before the army like harbingers of hell, searching for provisions and securing them for the army that followed. And it doesn't take an extraordinary mind to imagine what 62,000 young veterans on a juggernaut through the Confederate candy store might have been capable of. Indignant Confederates retaliated brutally, leading to an ongoing and sometimes ugly guerrilla conflict, all along Sherman's "march to the sea."

Sherman's march through Georgia also marked a dramatic meeting of the races. It is ironic that Sherman, far from being an abolitionist, should become one of the great black saviors of the Civil War. Indeed, he maintained a callous opinion of slavery until late in the conflict, by which time it seems as if circumstances had wrought a change upon him (though he would later argue fervently against black suffrage). As Sherman's columns made their way east, whole communities of freed slaves gathered about the rear of the army, a situation Sherman tolerated and then welcomed. To his soldiers he had become "Uncle Billy." But to the ex-slaves whose lives seemed reborn, he was something much greater.

Not all of his officers, of course, approved. On December 9, General Jeff C. Davis, one of Sherman's principal lieutenants, ordered the pontoon bridge that had carried his men across Ebenezer Creek to be taken up before five hundred fleeing slaves on the opposite bank were allowed to cross. In full view of Northern witnesses, many were slaughtered by Confederate cavalry. It was a horrible reminder that many men in blue were still fighting for the Union exclusively, rather than for the freedom of others—and that Sherman had unleashed a maelstrom in Dixie that often raged beyond his control.

Cump wheeled his army north, gutting the Carolinas as he had Georgia, and ended up wrapping up the war with a series of controversies. In April 1865, roughly a week after Lee surrendered to Grant at Appomattox and just days after Lincoln's assassination, Sherman secured the surrender of Joseph Johnston's army. Or so he thought, anyway. The terms he ended up giving his Confederate archrival, however, were outrageous. In addition to allowing Johnston's troops to momentarily keep their arms (they were to be surrendered later at their state capitals), Sherman "waded into the turbulent waters of Reconstruction," as biographer Stanley P. Hirshson put it, and essentially agreed to allow the Confederate states to rejoin the Union with their present governments. Inherently preposterous, the surrender was flatly rejected by the Johnson administration. But to war secretary Edwin Stanton, the document was an excuse to heap infamy on Sherman, whom he and others in government considered dangerous—a Copperhead who was soft on slavery and sympathetic to Southerners and who meant to run for president in '68 if he hadn't already taken over the government by then with his army. Stuff like this, as well as the administration's acrimonious rejection of the Johnston surrender terms, hit the rumor circuit and the press, casting Cump in the role of a fool and a traitor.

The whole sordid affair abruptly and absolutely ended Sherman's friendship with Halleck, one of those who had suspected him of selling out to the enemy. But it was Stanton who earned the Ohioan's fiercest ire. His "revenge," however, was rather less than glorious: At the Grand Review of the Armies in May 1865, Sherman pointedly refused the hand of Stanton while greeting President Johnson and his cabinet, causing a scandal that made Sherman feel as if he'd smitten another foe.

Having twice received the Thanks of Congress during the war, Sherman had made it as a soldier, and a soldier he would stay. Promoted to lieutenant general in 1866 and full general in 1869, he assumed the role of commander in chief of the army when Grant became president. Throughout much of that time he would visit upon the Plains Indians the same ferocity and remorselessness that had characterized his war against the South, considering them little more than oddities whose resistance against the inevitability of white expansion was idiotic. As he once wrote to his wife, "My solution is that war is popular with them, and they only look at it from the stand point wherein it is easier to starve than work. Probably in the end it will be better to kill them all off." He built upon his legacy by founding the School of Application for Infantry and Cavalry at Fort Leavenworth, and by repeatedly and emphatically turning down requests that he run for president, a prospect he found nauseating. Retired in 1884, he later moved to New York City, where he died of pneumonia in 1891. Even in death the old warrior was lethal: Joseph Johnston, Cump's wiliest opponent, attended the funeral and refused to don his hat in the wet weather out of respect. He soon took ill and died a month later.

HOLY %&*@!

Sherman was named Tecumseh in honor of the admired Shawnee leader who proved so formidable until his death in the War of 1812. It was preempted by "William" only after the boy had moved in with the Ewing family, when he was baptized by a Catholic priest. William was his baptismal name, and it stuck.

What certainly did not stick was an appreciation for Catholicism—or, for that matter, any other religion you can think of. Sherman's wife, Ellen, pursued the possibility that he would make a sincere conversion to her Roman faith, and did so more imploringly as the Civil War's carnage—and Cump's role in it—stretched on and on. He never did, and he maintained a suspicion of religion that seemed only to increase with time.

And so, when his son Tom announced that he would use his expensive law school education to become a Catholic priest, Sherman called down a lit- tle fire and brimstone of his own: "Death—suicide on his part could have been borne, but deliberately to abandon us all, and shut himself up in a Catholic Cloister as the slave of Religion, his very existence instead of being a support will be an enduring nightmare. . ." (A chilling choice of words, con- sidering the fact that Tom would indeed attempt suicide in 1911.) The break virtually destroyed any closeness that remained between father and son.

WHO LET THE DOGS OUT?

Sherman's march from Atlanta to Savannah has gone down as one of the most controversial campaigns in American history. Though his intent was to curb any wanton destruction or thievery on the part of his foraging "bum- mers," he soon began to worry his lieutenants by turning a blind eye a little too often, allowing plunderers to rage out of control.

Interestingly, it was four-legged Confederates who had the most to fear. As Sherman's columns advanced through the countryside, word of their approach inspired slaves and Union prisoners of war alike to make escape attempts. Knowing that Rebel authorities were in the habit of using dogs to chase down fugitives, Sherman's troops acquired the habit of shooting every canine they came across, littering the army's line of march with their carcasses.

GOIN' TO CALIFORNIA—THE HARD WAY

In 1853, Sherman sailed for San Francisco to assume a new position in his friend's firm. But it soon appeared as if the fates had decided against the idea and were trying to thwart his journey. After taking a ship to Nicaragua and crossing over to the Pacific, he boarded a vessel for California that enjoyed a smooth journey until less than one day's sailing from San Francisco, when it caught up on a reef. He and the rest of the passengers and crew got safely ashore via lifeboats, whereupon he commenced looking for another ship. The crew of a schooner hauling lumber offered to give him a ride. But as the vessel approached San Francisco Bay it capsized, making it two marine disasters in one day. Sherman did in fact make it to his destination, though he was soaked when he got there.

Hard Bargain

"Indians are funny things to do business with," Sherman once said, and he was speaking from personal experience. On one occasion, he offered a box of cigars to a chieftain who had stopped in to visit while in Washington. The fellow kindly accepted the gift, then offered it back to Sherman in exchange for Minnie, Cump's fetching daughter. No deal.

7 AMBROSE EVERETT BURNSIDE

May 23, 1824–September 13, 1881

HIGHEST RANK:
Union General

ASTROLOGICAL SIGN:
Gemini

NICKNAME:
Old Burn

WORDS TO REMEMBER:
"Probably very few of the general officers in the army have seen more dark hours than I have."

In January 1862, an armada of nearly one hundred vessels—gunboats, transports, steamers, and various other shallow-draft types—wound its way out of Chesapeake Bay, heading south. It carried a precious cargo: Union soldiers, most of whom were none too pleased at the notion of braving the Atlantic in storm season. Their leader was Ambrose Burnside, known for a carbine that bore his name and for the fact that he could be identified at quite a distance by the flamboyant wings of facial hair that hugged his face. Concerned by the fear of weather spreading through his soldiers, the general transferred his headquarters from the sturdiest ship in the flotilla to the *Picket*, a dinky little thing that would surely be the first to disappear beneath a wrathful sea. The move was intended to inspire confidence by example, the sort of gesture that Burnside

General Burnside's magnificent facial hair was a legend in its own time. The style was known as burnsides for many years after; eventually the words were reversed, resulting in the sideburns we know today.

loved and that sprang from a sincere concern for the welfare of his men. Not quite a month later, in the wake of fighting on Roanoke Island, he would come across a wounded lieutenant and order him placed on the

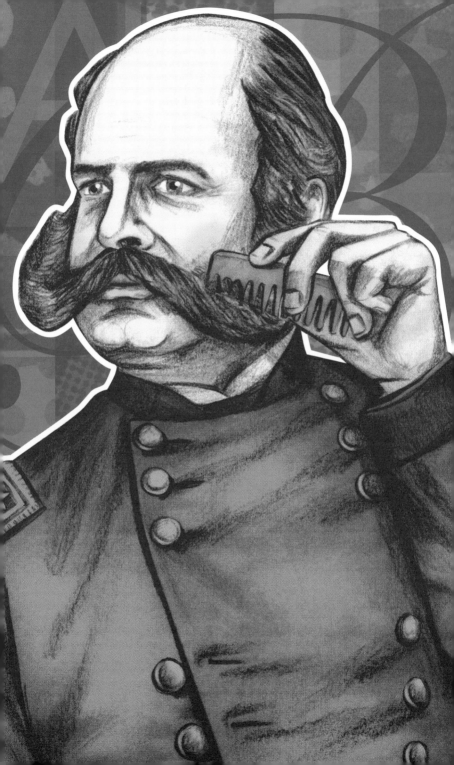

Picket to receive the services of his staff physician. The lieutenant, an ordinary officer of the ranks, never forgot that moment.

Generous, engaging, and intelligent, Burnside was a likable guy who had lots of friends and admirers. By the end of the war, however, he had acquired just as many, if not more, detractors. One of the most ill-starred of Union generals, "Old Burn" is an example of how bad things happen to good people—a man whose ability could not save him from lousy luck, bad decisions, and military debacles of historic dimensions.

But none of those things hampered the operation heading south from Chesapeake Bay that winter in 1862. Conceived with the help of his friend George McClellan, Burnside's mission was to take the war to the North Carolina coast in a daring amphibious campaign. The weather did indeed play havoc with his ships, but without loss of life, and by February 8, he had safely landed his division on Roanoke and taken 2,500 prisoners in a hot, quick fight. With the island secured and occupied, he took his special landing force to the mainland, capturing New Bern and Beaufort in March, and striking all along the North Carolina coast until he was recalled north in July. The whole campaign came off nearly without a hitch and was a smash hit with the folks back home. Burnside had removed the North Carolina coast as a haven for blockade runners and provided another base of operations for the Union. Unlike so many other Northern generals by this time, Ambrose Burnside was still considered hot stuff.

He had risen to such lofty heights from humble beginnings. Born the fourth of nine children to a court clerk in Indiana, he was apprenticed to a tailor and ended up practicing the trade for a while until his appointment to West Point. "Burn" racked up an astounding 198 demerits as an academy plebe, just two short of the limit, mostly because of his penchant for visiting friends at unauthorized times. Fortunately, he was almost as smart as he was convivial and managed to graduate eighteenth in a class of thirty-eight. He was sent to Mexico at the tail end of the war, arriving just in time for the soul-destroying boredom of garrison duty. Transfer to Rhode Island offered a pleasant change of pace, until he found himself out west again chasing hostiles. He got an arrow in his neck and lived to tell the tale.

Setting his sights—literally—on something at once more lucrative and less dangerous, Burnside resigned in 1853 and went back east to become an entrepreneur. He had designed a cavalry carbine that promised to be more efficient than anything presently in use, and after fleshing out the design, started turning it out at the Bristol Rifle Works in Rhode Island. There he became a man of some stature, getting an appointment as a major general in the state militia and even making an unsuccessful run for Congress. But he had staked his fortune on a promise from the secretary of war that Burn, in his agreeable naïveté, treated like a contract for his rifles. When the "deal" fell through, so did Burn's business, and he was forced to sell everything. Now a married man with little in the way of financial prospects, he headed west in search of opportunities, where his good friend George McClellan got him a job at the Illinois Central Railroad.

It was back in Rhode Island, however, where his destiny awaited him. When war broke out in 1861, William Sprague, the state's governor, hoped Burn would come back and organize the First Rhode Island Infantry. He accepted, and after marching the regiment to Washington, Burnside was put at the head of a brigade, which he led well enough at Bull Run to be commissioned a brigadier general of volunteers.

Already drawing the favorable attention of President Lincoln, Burnside was placed in charge of the North Carolina scheme. There, from the organization of the ships to the training of the troops to the relatively efficient actions on Roanoke and beyond, the general exhibited strong administrative skills and a gift for getting the most out of his subordinates. But it was also a campaign, from beginning to end, against inferior numbers and desultory organization. It had yet to be seen how he would handle Confederates who were at their best. Nevertheless, promoted to major general and given command of the Ninth Corps, Burnside's star was on the rise. Indeed, Lincoln—in the throes of his frustration with McClellan—offered the whole Army of the Potomac to him, though the ever-loyal Burn begged off, sincerely insisting that he wasn't up to it and that his friend was the better man for the job.

Whether or not that was true, neither he nor Little Mac performed brilliantly the following September at the epic clash along Antietam Creek. To Burnside was assigned the role of left hook: The Ninth Corps was to cross the creek at a stone bridge and nearby fords, massing on the opposite side to assault and crumple Lee's right wing. Unfortunately, Burnside's reconnaissance of the fords wasn't thorough enough, requiring part of his corps to march farther south in search of traversable crossing points. And his efforts to seize and secure the bridge (which has ever since borne his name) in the face of fire from the Confederates proved unimaginative, time-consuming, and costly. He was not able to get his corps organized on the far bank until midafternoon, by which time the Federal attacks farther north on the Rebel left had already been repulsed. Marching toward the town of Sharpsburg, it looked as if Burnside's attack, though late, might just crumple Lee's exhausted line—until A. P. Hill's Rebels appeared, having been force-marched all the way from Harpers Ferry, and waded into Burnside's flank. The Ninth Corps fell back, and the battle was over.

So was McClellan's career, though it would take another two months to become reality. By that time, he had finally gotten the Army of the Potomac moving in pursuit of Lee, only to have it snatched from his grasp and handed to his friend. Lincoln and War Secretary Stanton had had quite enough of the Young Napoleon, and as far as they were concerned, Burnside was going to take command if it had to be stuffed down his reluctant throat. Burnside accepted out of a sense of duty.

Such a development was hard on a man like Burnside, who put much stock in the ties that bind. Though his relationship with McClellan had been strained for months, another casualty of the waspish Philadelphian's descent into paranoid delusion, Burn was not a man to test friendships quite so openly as he felt himself doing now. Nevertheless, duty was duty, and after an emotional farewell to his old West Point chum, the new commander of the Army of the Potomac set about doing his job.

He had quite a chore ahead of him, not least because he was a virtual unknown outside the Ninth Corps, replacing a figure thoroughly beloved in the ranks. He would never truly win over the officers of the Army of the Potomac, many of whom squirmed under his command, missed their precious Little Mac, and anticipated an excuse to disgrace Burnside.

They soon got one, and it was a doozy. Charged by the Lincoln administration with keeping the pursuit of Lee in motion, Burnside had to find a safe place to cross the Rappahannock and get at the Army of Northern Virginia. He settled on a place called Fredericksburg, developing a plan which seemed sound enough: By quickly deploying his army there and crossing the river with the help of the Union army's train of pontoon bridges, he could be in a position to threaten Richmond and bring a fight with Lee's army before it was able to concentrate. But it didn't work out that way. To begin with, Burnside failed to get his troops at the point across from Fredericksburg quickly and all at once. As units began to mass, they tipped Lee off to the idea and inspired him to occupy the high ground behind Fredericksburg in anticipation of a crossing. But the worst misfortune may not have been Burnside's fault. Owing to bureaucratic incompetence that went all the way up to General in Chief Henry Halleck, the pontoon bridges—seminal to the whole operation—did not arrive until November 25, by which time the Army of Northern Virginia had been able to concentrate its strength. Pressed to make a move before the end of the year, Burnside decided to go ahead in December with a plan whose crucial element of timeliness had expired and to force a crossing in cold weather at a location that clearly seemed well defended.

After laying the pontoons under fire on December 11 and clearing the town of enemy resistance on the 12th, the battle descended into a bloodbath on the 13th. Though some progress was initially made on the Confederate right, the focus of the clash ultimately shifted to Lee's left, where Rebels under James Longstreet crouched behind a stone wall at the foot of Marye's Heights, a crest that overlooked Fredericksburg proper. Into their furious fire marched wave after wave of Union manhood, blown into oblivion by an unrelenting tempest of lead. As superheated Confederate gun barrels fouled from the furious pace, blue-clad bodies began to carpet the ground in great writhing heaps, producing a vision of mortality that left onlookers agape in horrified disbelief. Burnside, aghast, offered to personally lead another attempt the following day, as if joining the panoply of dead and dying across the river was the only way to redeem his honor. He was talked out of it.

In a day of fruitless assaults, the Army of the Potomac had reaped nearly 13,000 casualties. Fredericksburg became a byword for Union death and failure.

Burnside, still feeling pressured to pull off an offensive as soon as possible, planned to make another attempt at the Rappahannock farther downstream before year's end. But the horror show at Fredericksburg had rendered his position all but untenable. Convinced that his plan was dangerous, officers in his command took the idea directly to Lincoln, who canceled it. Obviously, morale in the Army of the Potomac was approaching nil. Outraged by the virtual mutiny in his own ranks, Burnside nevertheless pressed ahead with yet another plan to cross the river, this time upstream from Lee's position. This one needed no human intervention to veto it, for the weather did just fine on its own. January rains turned the Virginia roads into every teamster's worst nightmare, and the army soon found itself utterly immobilized. Referred to even in official reports as the "Mud March," it was the final nail in Burnside's coffin, and he knew it. Buffeted by the weather into a perfect rage over the disloyal sentiment that was now widespread, Burnside prepared for the president's consideration a document that authorized the firing of five prominent officers in the Army of the Potomac and the outright dismissal of four others from the service altogether. Lincoln instead accepted the transfer of just one: Burnside.

Sadly, command of the army would go to one whose name had been mentioned in Burnside's message of dismissal: Joseph Hooker, an inveterate enemy. But such were the politics of war. Lincoln hadn't given up on Old Burn, and soon sent him west to command the Department of the Ohio, where he ran into some other thorny wartime politics. Faced in Ohio, Indiana, and Kentucky with what appeared to be pervasive anti-Lincoln sentiment, Burnside issued General Order Number 38, which threatened

execution for all those found guilty of benefiting "the enemies of our country."
Even the expression of pro-Confederate sentiments warranted banishment to
enemy lines, or worse. Of all those who found the dictum acutely intolerable, one stood out: Clement L. Vallandigham, a staunch Peace Democrat and
former Congressman from Ohio whose purpose in life had become the public excoriating of Lincoln and his unconstitutional policies. After speaking
out against Order 38, the vituperative Vallandigham was promptly arrested
by agents working for Burnside, jailed, and tried before a military court—
enough, by itself, to send the protestor's system into a rage-induced infarc-
tion. Though Vallandigham was convicted and sentenced to imprisonment
until the end of the war, the president thought it better to banish him to the
Confederacy. Vallandigham eventually made his way to Canada and ran for
the Ohio governorship in absentia. He lost.

The Department of the Ohio was full of military responsibilities as well.
Burnside oversaw the capture and incarceration of John Hunt Morgan, the
celebrated Rebel raider, only to see him escape the following November. And
Burn advanced to Knoxville, enduring a siege by Longstreet's Rebels until
relieved by William T. Sherman, a campaign for which he received the
Thanks of Congress. But despite these laurels, the war would end back east
for Burn, where it began.

By the spring of 1864, his old Ninth Corps had been recruited back up to
strength, and he was placed at the head of it. In Grant's relentless and gory
Overland campaign, a lackluster Burnside—gripped by vivid memories of
Fredericksburg—led his men with reluctance and a lack of bold imagination
(which, to be fair, had never been his strong suit anyway). That uneasiness
still remained when the war in the east settled into the siege of Petersburg,
partly accounting for the final—and most bizarre—catastrophe of Burnside's
military career. In June, the commander of a Pennsylvania regiment in the
Ninth Corps approached him with an intriguing idea. Using his men's coal
mining expertise, the officer proposed digging a tunnel under the enemy
salient opposite his unit, filling it with explosives, and detonating it. A tactic as old as siege warfare itself, the plan was intended to create a gap in the

enemy's defenses that infantry could quickly exploit and, so it was hoped, break the trench-enforced stalemate.

Burnside approved and took the idea to Grant, who reluctantly gave the OK. The Pennsylvania men did indeed know their stuff: In about a month of hard work in the heat of July, they excavated a five-hundred-foot shaft culminating in two lateral tunnels that formed a giant "T" running beneath the Confederate works. Very early on the morning of July 30, they detonated eight thousand pounds of gunpowder in their makeshift subterranean gallery, instantly obliterating some three hundred hapless Confederates and hurling enough earth into the sky to leave a thirty-foot-deep crater that stretched over 150 feet along the shattered Rebel line. The Southerners were quick and efficient in their recovery, however, and the Union infantry who were intended to exploit the enormous gap were poorly led and disorganized. The crater became a mass grave for many of them. A court of inquiry laid the majority of blame on Burnside as corps commander, who—though badly served at the crater by both his subordinates and his superior George Meade—patiently accepted the verdict and all that it meant. After returning from leave and awaiting orders that never materialized, he offered his resignation in April 1865.

And so ended the convulsive Civil War career of Ambrose Burnside. Disgraced in military circles, he remained an iconic figure to many in the North, particularly in Rhode Island. He served three consecutive and fairly popular terms as governor of his adopted state and was later elected to the United States Senate. He had one final wartime adventure, however, and one that spoke to his trustworthy, genuine nature and his belief in the essential goodness of men. Having traveled to London on business in 1870, Burnside took the opportunity to cross the channel and witness the climactic final act of the Franco-Prussian War being played out in the siege of Paris. It wasn't long before Old Burn had ingratiated himself to the Prussians and secured a pass into the embattled city, where he endeared himself to the French as well. Soon he became an envoy, shuttling messages between the two camps in an earnest effort to secure peace. But like so many of his good intentions, the effort came to naught. He died a decade later from heart failure, and has ever since remained a symbol of controversy and human limitations.

CASH FLAW

Like most newly minted young officers during the final months of the war with Mexico, Ambrose Burnside found garrison duty a royal bore. He dealt with it by gambling often, a habit that apparently got the better of him. By the time he was transferred to Fort Adams back east, the guy had accrued six months' salary worth of gambling debts. Reassignment to Rhode Island spared him the trouble of doing something about it.

Financial troubles seemed to follow Old Burn wherever he went. During his tour of duty in New Mexico around 1850, he took over the quartermastering responsibilities of his little post for want of officers and eventually became associated with $5,700 in army funds that were unaccounted for. Though the bookkeeping error (or embezzlement) may have been somebody else's, Burnside was held responsible for it, a debt that dogged him even after he resigned from the army. But his most intriguing money mishap must be the one that involved A. P. Hill, who made a loan to his friend Burn before the outbreak of war that was never repaid. In the eleventh hour of the Battle of Antietam, after elements of Hill's Light Division had made their dramatic entrance on the battlefield and thwarted the Federal Ninth Corps in its flanking attack, one of the Confederate general's men pointed out to him that it was Old Burnside they had foiled. "Don't you know him?" asked the fellow. "I ought to," quipped Hill. "He owes me $8,000!"

GUNS AND BUTTER

Inspired by his experience fighting Indians on the western frontier, Burnside's carbine design was an excellent one. After a few modifications, he acquired a patent for the firearm in 1856, and established his Bristol Rifle Works. It was an impressive accomplishment and testament to Burn's ingenuity and resourcefulness. But his damnable luck reared its ugly head once again, ruining what seemed a foolproof enterprise. Given the impression by Secretary of War John Floyd in 1857 that the war department intended to buy thousands of his carbines, Burnside shot himself in the foot by failing to secure a real contract, borrowing capital to churn out guns that had nowhere to go. When Floyd went with someone else, the bottom fell out of poor Burn's venture. To his investors and creditors went everything, from the weapon's patent to the rifle factory to his old uniform. Burnside had to start all over again from scratch, as if his industrial adventure never happened.

The worst part, ironically, is that the rifle was such a good one. The army ended up buying more than 55,000 Burnside carbines during the Civil War, making it the third most commonly used weapon of its type by Federal cavalry. And the man whose name it bore saw not a penny of that tremendous profit.

GETTING CHEEKY

Those magnificent swatches of whiskery goodness that cradled General Burnside's face were a legend in their own time. In postwar America it became customary to refer to the style as burnsides, a word that evolved over time to describe only those patches of hair that grew along the side of the face to the jawline. Not long after that, the word was reversed, and *sideburns* was born—a curious legacy indeed for a man who patented a rifle design and presided over the ignominious slaughter of thousands of young men.

8 JOSEPH HOOKER

November 13, 1814–
October 31, 1879

HIGHEST RANK:
Union General

ASTROLOGICAL SIGN:
Scorpio

NICKNAME:
Fighting Joe

WORDS TO REMEMBER:
"I was at the Battle of Bull Run the other day, and it is neither vanity or boasting in me to declare that I am a damned sight better general than you, sir, had on that field" (to Abraham Lincoln).

It is said that the word *hooker*, as a synonym for prostitute, came into common usage with all the women of ill repute who followed Joe Hooker's camps during the Civil War. The assertion may well be true, though some would argue that hooker was already slang for a streetwalker (a lady, if you will, who "hooks" a john) in parts of the English-speaking world before Fort Sumter was ever fired upon. In any event, even one who is skeptical of the story is confronted with the question of why the connection was made at all—the answer being, of course, that *so many women of ill repute followed Joe Hooker's camps.*

Hooker was more than just a libertine. He was also a braggart and an intriguer. But it was in spite of these exemplary qualities that he rose for a brief moment to become commander of Lincoln's precious instrument of force, the Army of the Potomac. For Hooker was also a pretty decent general.

His Mexican War experience was representative of his life in general. Awarded three brevets for his gallant and meritorious service (a rare achievement indeed for any lieutenant in that conflict), Hooker managed to jeopardize all he had fought for by backing into a contentious personal battle between two higher-ups: Winfield Scott and Gideon Pillow. In the

hearings that resulted, Hooker testified on the latter's behalf, carving a place for himself in Scott's memory that he would one day come to regret.

But that lay in a distant future. Born in Massachusetts, the grandson of a Revolutionary War hero, Hooker's accomplishments in Mexico seemed to confirm that martial blood ran in his veins. Hell, with his steel blue eyes and the way his broad frame filled out a uniform, he even looked like a conqueror. But California's charms weaned him off the army. Stationed there in the wake of the Mexican War, he settled in Sonoma and began spending his meager officer's salary at the card table. In 1851, he acquired a two-year leave of absence and an old rancho to settle on, where he gave farming a try (unsuccessfully) and ended up selling the timber off his land for a modest profit. Formally resigning his commission in 1853, he dabbled in local politics, acquired an appointment as superintendent of military roads up in Oregon, and became a colonel of California militia. Money remained an issue, however; by 1861 he was broke.

> Joe Hooker's headquarters had the reputation of being like a government-sponsored saloon, full of alcohol and gambling and women of ill repute.

Naturally, he hoped to fix that back east by offering his services to the North as a general. But Winfield Scott, now general in chief, made that a difficult proposition, and Hooker observed the first months of the war as a civilian. It wasn't until after Bull Run, when he secured a personal interview with the president and informed him of the army's dreadful mismanagement, that he was able to get his foot in the door. Lincoln was impressed by the boastful fellow, and a commission as brigadier general of volunteers soon followed.

It is significant that Hooker acquired his post and began his Civil War career with a meeting in which he berated other officers. Such slandering, in addition to gulping whiskey and leading troops with relative efficiency, essentially became his modus operandi. He went with McClellan to the Peninsula, where he led a division in the van of the march on Richmond and fought effectively in the Seven Days' Battles. He was with his division in the defeat at Second Bull Run and was then given a corps to command. By now known popularly as "Fighting Joe" Hooker, he lived up to the moniker at Antietam when he rode with his First Corps against the Confederate left, the flanking assault that initiated the day's furious bloodletting and that climaxed in a cornfield that became one of the most notorious killing grounds in American history. While astride his horse during the struggle, Hooker took a bullet through the foot, putting him out of action for the day. His mauled corps soon followed, falling back with 2,500 casualties. The attack on that part of the battlefield petered out an hour later, leaving the second and third acts to be decided farther south.

Convinced after Antietam that the army's leadership was lackluster at best and that he was one of the very few who knew his business, Hooker began complaining to anyone who would listen. That he was fond of drink didn't do anything to help keep his mouth shut, and it was soon common knowledge that Hooker had a low opinion of his superiors. The tragedy that unfolded next only poured fuel on the fire. Watching his troops get shot to pieces on the fields beyond Fredericksburg was more than many could handle. For Hooker, it was the last straw. He had hated Burnside's Fredericksburg plan to begin with; now, having seen it fail in biblical fashion, he openly inveighed against Burnside and virtually everyone else in authority—including the administration. Indeed, it was widely known that Hooker advocated a military dictatorship to successfully prosecute the war.

To the hotheads in the U.S. Congress Joint Committee on the Conduct of the War, before whom he testified against Burnside, Hooker looked like the sort of man who could fix the carnival of errors that the Union war effort had become. Fighting Joe was just as good at impressing newspapermen and politicians as he was at holding his hooch, and his hard line—on fumbling Union generals and Confederate enemies both—had endeared him to the radicals, in and out of Congress, who fretted over Lincoln's foundering leadership. Having done well enough on the battlefield to attract favorable attention, spoken out against all the right demons, and escaped the scandalous failures that had doomed the likes of McClellan and Burnside, Hooker became that most peculiar of Civil War generals: the politically inescapable appointee. Lincoln, though aware of Fighting Joe's ability, was personally disgusted by his insubordinate behavior, particularly toward Burnside. But with so much pressure to promote him from influential folks who needed to be satisfied, the president had little choice but to bow to popular opinion. "Hooker talks badly," remarked a world-weary Lincoln, "but the trouble is, he is stronger with the country today than any other man." And so it went. After Burnside's removal, the bourbon-slugging mudslinger from Massachusetts would lead the Army of the Potomac.

Rarely has a head of state voiced so much reluctance in the commissioning of a commander. "I have placed you at the head of the Army of the Potomac," began Lincoln's famous letter to Hooker. "Of course I have done this upon what appear to me to be sufficient reasons. And yet I think it best for you to know that there are some things in regard to which, I am not quite satisfied with you." The document is a delicious window on the moment, the men involved, and the perils faced by those in civilian government forced to crawl into bed with military men from whom they must have victory for survival. "I much fear that the spirit which you have aided to infuse into the Army, of criticizing their Commander, and withholding confidence from him, will now turn upon you," chided the chief executive. And yet, the new commander was to "go forward, and give us victories." Not exactly a pep rally.

Lincoln needed his general to understand him, and it seems as if he succeeded. But in this awkward relationship, both parties had what they wanted: Fighting Joe had an outlet for his vision of victory, and Lincoln had a warlord who sincerely believed in the marrow of his bones that Robert E. Lee was about to meet his match. Not for Fighting Joe the quavering doubtfulness of Burnside. Hooker did not lack confidence. "May God have mercy on General Lee," he puffed, "for I will have none." And though many critics North and South thought Hooker's appointment a bad idea, he set about proving them dead wrong. With his reorganization of the Army of the Potomac, his attention to the needs of the rank and file, and his injection of professionalism, Fighting Joe acquired the nickname "Administrative Joe." The army bounced back from the nightmares of Fredericksburg and the Mud March, acquiring a level of efficiency and élan that it had thought impossible since Little Mac had first sharpened its resolve. Great things were possible again.

And not for lack of indulgence. Hooker had long been a drinker and a carouser, and his headquarters became a sanctuary for officers who couldn't see the point in moderate behavior or abstinence. But amidst the saturnalia emerged a plan of unimpeachable brilliance—a strategy worthy of the reluctant confidence placed in him. Fighting Joe meant to wheel his great army around Lee's left like the sweeping arm of a hurricane, maneuvering counterclockwise behind the Army of Northern Virginia's flank and scooping it up like so much storm debris. Using stealth and aggressiveness, the Army of the Potomac would cross the Rappahannock well west of Lee's positions, then swing eastward to destroy him while he was busy with a diversionary effort made around Fredericksburg.

It was great stuff. And it even caught the wily Lee by surprise, at least at first, partly because of the impenetrable forest known as the Wilderness that would prove as much a bane to Hooker as a shield. As the Army of the Potomac moved south toward its quarry, it ran into the dark expanse of the Wilderness, negating much of the superiority in numbers that Hooker enjoyed over his opponent. Alerted to the move by Jeb Stuart's cavalry, Lee shifted west to meet the challenge and used the confusion of the Wilderness to his advantage. Once the two armies met near the crossroads of Chancellorsville, everything that defined Joe Hooker—his chutzpah, confidence, domination over events—simply vanished. It was as if Robert E. Lee possessed a pin that Hooker's balloon hadn't counted on. Sensing his enemy's hesitation, Lee sent Stonewall Jackson to crash into the Union right, collapsing what little remained of Hooker's confidence. A cannonball did much to finish Joe off, smashing through a pillar that he was leaning on at his mansion-headquarters and knocking him senseless for a time.

Chancellorsville could easily have been the end of the Army of Northern Virginia and a vindication of Joe Hooker's otherwise insufferable self-promotion. Instead, it was Robert E. Lee's finest hour. And the Army of the Potomac was bundled back beyond the Rappahannock once again.

It is hard not to compare our subject to the playground bully whose delusions of tyranny are dashed by the one clever kid bold enough to challenge him and defuse his inflated self-image. Nevertheless, Joe Hooker still had a few cards left to play. Replaced by George Meade just days before the climactic Battle of Gettysburg, Hooker ended up leading two corps west to help deal with the crisis there in the wake of Chickamauga. In the western theater, he led like the hero he used to fancy himself as, particularly at the charge up Lookout Mountain outside Chattanooga. But at Atlanta, Sherman promoted a subordinate of Hooker's to command the Army of Tennessee in the wake of James McPherson's death. Fighting Joe, insulted beyond hope of repair, insisted on being relieved and was promptly satisfied. He was reassigned to the Midwest and finished the war as far as possible from the action he hoped to shape decisively. Spending much of his remaining life disagreeing with the history being written about himself and his fellow officers, he died in 1879 a symbol of Union controversy.

FRESH START

In January 1853, Joe Hooker ran into trouble while gambling over a game of cards. Failing to pay his losses, Hooker was taken to court. But because gambling debts were not honored by the state, he was let off the hook and left with only a smudge on his honor.

Such behavior was apparently routine for Hooker during his California days before the war. He was constantly wanting for funds. William Sherman and Henry Halleck both claimed later that they had loaned him money out west that was not repaid. The outbreak of war found him destitute just at the time he needed money to get back east. In fact, he would never have gone on to greater glory at all were it not for an extraordinary act of charity. While in San Francisco, he happened into the popular tavern owned by Billy Chapman, whom he knew. Taking note of his patron's pathetic demeanor, Chapman approached and asked if anything was wrong. After hearing Hooker's plight, the tavernkeep asked him how much he thought he needed to get back east. His reply was $700. Chapman disappeared and returned with $1,000 in bills. He even made sure that Hooker's cabin in the upcoming sea voyage was liberally stocked with cigars, free of charge. With friends like that, who needs guardian angels?

Please Don't Feed the Animals

With an abortive effort at farming, a constant lack of profit, and no shortage of gambling debts, Hooker's attempt at playing the country squire out in California didn't fool anyone. Even the wildlife was uncooperative. Once, while hunting near his Sonoma property, he happened upon a bear. Hooker discharged his rifle, missed, and the great beast charged. In the tussle that followed, the two disappeared over the precipice of a canyon, very nearly killing them both. A search party later found the future commander of the Army of the Potomac hanging like somebody's bloody laundry in the limbs of a redwood tree.

COURAGE IN A BOTTLE

Joe Hooker most likely didn't drink when he graduated from West Point in 1837. But things change, and for him they changed in California. While still in the army, Hooker started hanging out at an infamous Sonoma haunt called the Blue Wing Inn, where whiskey brought the frontier's disparate elements together under one riotous roof. He soon acquired a reputation for enthusiastic imbibing that endured his entire life. During the Civil War, his habits were put to song. Early in the war, William B. Bradbury wrote a patriotic tune called "Marching Along," which became quite popular throughout the North. Its chorus went:

Marching along, we are marching along,

Gird on the armor and be marching along;

McClellan's our leader, he's gallant and strong;

For God and for country we are marching along.

Soldiers in Hooker's command sang a slightly different version—they switched out the third line with, "Joe Hooker's our leader, he takes his whiskey strong."

The subject of alcohol even came up after the defining failure in Hooker's life, the Battle of Chancellorsville. Though some in Congress were concerned with finding out whether the general had been soused during the battle, others of a more cynical bent turned the question on its head: It was well known that Hooker had given up drink as soon as the Chancellorsville campaign commenced, and plenty of officers wondered if there would have been a victory in the Wilderness had Fighting Joe's nerve been buttressed by its usual medicinal aid. Oh well. Damned if you do, damned if you don't.

IF THE SHOE FITS

"Fighting Joe" was a pretty flattering nickname as far as such things go for a general. But Hooker hated it, believing that it made him sound like some quarrelsome malcontent. Besides, he acquired the sobriquet under the silliest of circumstances. Reporting in 1862 on the furious combat near Williamsburg in which Hooker's division was playing a leading role, a New York newspaper flashed the following terse headline: "Fighting—Joe Hooker." Within weeks the line had become a name, and the rest is history.

9 PHILIP HENRY
SHERIDAN

March 6, 1831–August 5, 1888

HIGHEST RANK:

Union Officer

ASTROLOGICAL SIGN:

Pisces

NICKNAME:

Little Phil

WORDS TO REMEMBER:

"If I owned hell and Texas, I'd rent out Texas and live in hell!"

In May 1865, virtually everyone who was anyone in the victorious Union army was preparing to march through Washington in the Grand Review of the Armies. And Phil Sheridan was certainly someone. Of the three Federal generals to emerge from the conflict with the most laurels, the plucky little Irishman had done more at the eleventh hour than either William Sherman or Ulysses Grant to checkmate Robert E. Lee. But Sheridan, much to his dismay, was not slated to participate in what was surely going to be one of the most memorable parades in American history. Instead, he'd been ordered west of the Mississippi by Grant to secure the

---

Philip Sheridan was notorious for his violent temper. In one of his more famous outbursts, he literally threw a rude conductor off a train before calmly resuming his conversation with a friend.

---

surrender of Edmund Kirby Smith and the only Confederate force of any size still fighting. Sheridan was the man for the job if Smith was really a serious threat—which he wasn't. As many people have since speculated, it seems more likely that Grant was less concerned with running Rebels to the ground in the West than he was with facing the prospect of inviting Sheridan to the Washington fete. Doing so would have meant putting him in the same reviewing stand with Army of the Potomac commander George

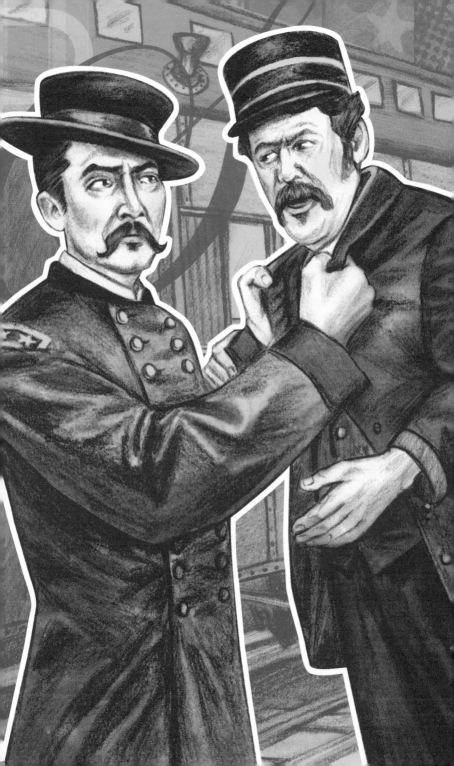

Meade—and Meade, like a few other Northern officers, was as likely to chew coal slag as sit next to Phil Sheridan.

Another one of those officers was Gouverneur Warren, a hero of Gettysburg whose corps at the 1865 Battle of Five Forks failed to move quickly enough for Sheridan, who promptly destroyed Warren's career by sacking him on the spot. Warren had to wait fourteen years to clear his name: An 1879 inquiry exonerated him of any culpability at Five Forks and impugned the decision to relieve him, a verdict that couldn't reverse years of undeserved infamy. Then there's William Woods Averell, a previously wounded Indian fighter and respected cavalryman who attracted the unwanted attention of Sheridan in the wake of the Battle of Fisher's Hill in 1864. While Averell was regrouping his troopers after the stunning Union victory, Sheridan was wondering why he wasn't off bagging Rebels on the run, famously giving him the order to engage in "actual fighting, with necessary casualties." Averell, whose victory at Kelly's Ford the previous year was widely credited with having turned the tide against Southern cavalry, found himself exiled to West Virginia for his alleged lethargy. He also strove to undo the damage done his good name by "Little Phil," to no avail.

Fortunately for Sheridan's reputation, he was harder on the enemy than he was on his fellow officers. The diminutive, short-tempered son of an immigrant Irish laborer, Philip Henry Sheridan seemed innately confrontational—a quality that, when properly harnessed, would take him from painfully humble origins to the dizzying heights of power. He was born in Albany. Or Boston. Or was it County Cavan, Ireland? The fact is, we may never know. He grew up believing he'd been born in Ohio, but his mother later told him that it was Albany. Still later she is known to have told others that Phil had been born at sea on the trip from Ireland. In any event, he grew up in Somerset, Ohio. After an obstreperous, demerit-filled stint at West Point, he graduated in 1853 and was stationed at Fort Duncan, Texas, where he was quickly instructed in the morally ambiguous, casually violent chaos of the frontier. Once, after watching a young herder get massacred by Lipan Indians on a cattle raid, he and a company of troopers gave chase, only to see the murderers slip to safety over the nearby Mexican border. That night, Sheridan ran into the raiders during a dance at a local rancher's house, very nearly ending the evening with an explosion of violence. Living so close to the natives of America's trackless West was the source of two very different reactions from Sheridan. On the one hand, he sincerely mourned the passing of the ancient way of life, but on the other, he dismissed the native people as "red savages" in need of civilizing. After moving on to Fort Reading in the Pacific Northwest, Sheridan turned heads even in Washington, D.C., for his expansive attitude toward local Indian nations as well as for his coolness under fire when tracking down hostiles. It was during such a campaign that Sheridan received his first and only battle wound: a nick across the bridge of his nose from a bullet that killed the enlisted man next to him.

Like many officers stuck on the perimeter of the country when the Civil War broke out, Sheridan was desperate to get posted back east and get into the action. The only wound he was likely to receive during his first real assignment, however, was a paper cut. In St. Louis, Major General Henry Halleck lassoed Sheridan to sort through the Byzantine accounting mess left by his predecessor, John Frémont. Even in an army rife with systemic embezzlement, the labyrinth of misappropriations bequeathed by Frémont to his successor ranked as "a system of reckless expenditure and fraud perhaps unheard of before in the history of the world." Relying on skills he had acquired as a store clerk during his adolescence, Sheridan managed to audit the Department of the Missouri out of its bookkeeping nightmare, making a valuable and lasting ally out of Halleck.

By May 1862, having labored manfully through a series of quartermastering jobs, Sheridan was convinced he would never see duty at the front. His break came when the governor of Michigan went looking for an officer in the regular army to lead his state's Second Cavalry Regiment. Sheridan's name floated upward, probably by way of Gordon Granger, the unit's previous commander, and the eager Irishman was chosen. Phil Sheridan had his foot in the door.

He soon knocked the door right off its hinges. After borrowing the eagle-inscribed shoulder boards of a colonel from Gordon Granger's uniform, Sheridan hit the ground running (galloping?) and, after playing a major role in a raid south of Corinth, Mississippi, was appointed to command the whole brigade. A promotion to brigadier general followed after a decisive skirmish with Rebel cavalry at Booneville. And the following October, he traded in his cavalryman's spurs for command of a division in the Army of the Ohio.

What could account for such a meteoric rise? Sheridan had leadership ability, to be sure. But despite his churlishness, he also had a few friends (namely Halleck, whose recent promotion to commander in chief made him a functionary in Lincoln's tight circle). And he had married that old instinct for confrontation to his thirst for advancement, birthing a potent gift for intraservice politics. Plus he was able to exhort the men under his command to great things with his combustive severity (in time he would become notorious for having laggard officers publicly "drummed out" of camp before the assembled ranks of their units). The combination of these qualities allowed him to pummel his way into greatness.

Sheridan and his division did well enough at the confused and indecisive Battle of Perryville; the following December, however, they made history at the Battle of Murfreesboro. The former quartermaster was as assiduous in preparation as he was aggressive in battle, preparing his men the night of December 30 for a Confederate assault he assumed, via reliable intelligence, was coming early the next morning. When the storm broke as he'd predicted, Sheridan's division was the only one targeted by Braxton Bragg's oncoming Rebels to keep its cohesion and offer a stiff resistance. Confronted by a furious onslaught and surrounded by fleeing bluecoats, Sheridan, steadfast, directed his men through one of the most exquisite fighting retreats of the entire war. A difficult maneuver to perform under the kindest of conditions, it prevented the disintegration of the Union position, which staved off further attacks the next day and convinced Bragg to give up and pull out.

If Sheridan's performance at Murfreesboro was heroic, his showing at Chickamauga was awful—a failure somewhat tempered by the fact that nearly everyone in the Union Army of the Cumberland performed miserably that day except George Thomas, the "Rock of Chickamauga." Forced back to Chattanooga by Bragg, the Federals waited for William Sherman to arrive with reinforcements while their Confederate pursuers besieged the city from the heights of Missionary Ridge. Then, commanded by the newly arrived Grant, they struck. On November 25, 1863, streams of Federal soldiers spontaneously went beyond their objectives at the foot of Missionary Ridge and assaulted the slopes themselves, carrying the fortified Rebel position and routing its defenders in one of the most sensational and unexpected victories of the war. Sheridan's division was as prominent as any that day— a fact not lost on Grant, who watched the whole thing in befuddled amazement. From that moment, Phil Sheridan's future was assured.

His reward was as surprising as it was considerable: command of the Army of the Potomac's cavalry corps. Grant may have thought him more than adequate for the job, but many had their doubts—including Army of the Potomac commander George Meade, who kept a tight leash on Sheridan and used his horsemen for everything except the sort of lightning-quick strikes they were trained for. The mounting tension between the two soon came to a head during the Wilderness campaign in May, when Meade quite rightly gave Sheridan a lashing for using his cavalry clumsily and holding up the advance of the infantry. In the heated argument that followed, Sheridan openly accused his superior of interfering with the proper use of the army's troopers. All he wanted, he insisted, was to be given an opportunity to prove what he knew he was capable of: whipping Jeb Stuart, the dashing bane of Federal cavalry. After the tête-à-tête, an enraged Meade went to Grant in the hopes of having the commander of his cavalry arm slammed with insubordination. But Grant, intrigued by Sheridan's claim that he could defeat Stuart if given the chance, merely dismissed Meade and told him to allow Sheridan an opportunity to make good on his boast. And so Sheridan, by turning a legitimate gripe about his own incompetence into a convenient change in tactics, had laid the groundwork for one of the most memorable events of the war: the raid at Yellow Tavern. Riding south toward Richmond with a concentration of cavalry unusual for the Army of the Potomac, he drew the audacious Stuart out, roundly defeated his force, and killed him for good measure.

Sheridan was later checked in a clash at Trevilian Station, but was soon given an independent command of enormous significance: the Shenandoah Valley, verdant birthplace of legends. His orders from Grant were twofold: clear the valley of anything even remotely useful to the enemy, and get south of Confederate general Jubal Early to "follow him to the death." Early would live to a ripe old age, but everything else about Sheridan's campaign went splendidly—once he got moving. After what seemed to many in Washington an interminable delay, Sheridan acquired accurate intelligence about Early's weakened force with the help of an industrious pro-Union local named Rebecca Wright. Having readied his army and confirmed his superiority in numbers, Sheridan finally struck south, winning a costly victory at Winchester and blowing through the Rebels at Fisher's Hill. The following October, Sheridan was summoned to Washington for a conference with Lincoln and Secretary of War Stanton. On his return journey, he spent the night of October 18 in Winchester, a few miles north of his army, and awoke the following morning to the distant thunder of battle. What he and his retinue saw as they rode closer to the noise was every commander's worst nightmare: fleeing soldiers in blue, some wounded but most merely demoralized, all walking and limping in the opposite direction. Early had struck that morning in a surprise attack that sent most of Sheridan's army, in his absence, flying north from the field.

Had anyone there predicted that the day would end in a stunning Union victory, they'd have been dismissed as a raving lunatic. But that is precisely what happened, giving Sheridan his finest hour. He was aided, ironically, by Jubal Early himself, who dithered incomprehensibly in the hours following his men's extraordinary breakthrough. (Though Early himself denied it to his dying day, others claimed they heard him say something about having earned "enough glory for one day.") As hungry Rebels fell to plundering the captured Union camp, Sheridan began to encourage his scattered forces for a counterstroke, at one point riding his horse, Rienzi, along the length of the reassembling line of infantry, hat in hand, to let them all see him. The troops, electrified by their general's return, stole their last bit of strength for another fight. Within weeks, "Sheridan's Ride" would be immortalized in a poem recited throughout the North. And within hours, Sheridan's counterattack was sending Early's routed Confederates back up the Valley Turnpike, their earlier triumph a distant memory.

The Battle of Cedar Creek sealed the fate of Jubal Early's army and left the Shenandoah mostly in Northern hands, freeing Sheridan to complete the destruction he'd been wreaking since making his appearance. The year 1864 was a bad one to live in the valley. Though preceded by despoilers like David Hunter, Sheridan went about his beastly business with an especially dreadful thoroughness. No one's property was safe, whether Rebel, Unionist, or even Quaker pacifist. If you grew, built, or owned anything in the Shenandoah that could possibly aid Confederate troops, you were going to lose it. Buildings were razed, crops were burned, animals were slaughtered. "The Burning," as it came to be known, made a fitting backdrop to the merciless brand of warfare that both sides began waging. Southern guerrillas, particularly those under the ubiquitous John Singleton Mosby, made life hell for Union columns, which had no compunction retaliating without consideration for the Articles of War. Impromptu executions and lynchings (and worse), by both sides, became all too common. And Sheridan used it all as further proof of the need for more plunder.

Leaving a smoldering moonscape in his wake, he headed southeast for the endgame. After sending George Custer's hardened cavalry to sweep Early's remaining skeletons aside at Waynesboro, Sheridan arrived in the Petersburg theater and was given most of the Army of the Potomac's cavalry, as well as Gouverneur Warren's Fifth Corps. With this considerable host, Grant intended that Sheridan take Five Forks, a road junction west of the Confederate fortifications that, if seized, would put Lee's Army of Northern

Virginia in an untenable position. Sheridan did just that, defeating a Rebel force under George Pickett. Right on cue, Lee and his army fled west, the hope of hooking up with Joseph Johnston's army quickly dissolving. Sheridan followed closely, destroying much of Richard Ewell's corps at Sayler's Creek and getting ahead of the quarry near Appomattox Court House until it seemed pointless for Lee to continue. The end had come.

Sheridan, thirty-four years old at Lee's surrender, had already lived a lifetime. But the end of the war was merely the beginning for him. In the years that remained before his relatively young death, he would carve out a rather sensational career that was, in many ways, emblematic of nineteenth-century America itself—for good and ill. For twenty-six months, he reigned (and that is definitely the appropriate word) as military governor of Texas and Louisiana, during which time he intimidated Maximilian, French-backed puppet of Mexico, by secretly (and illegally) supplying his enemies with arms; made an ardent enemy out of President Andrew Johnson for routinely ignoring his policies; and frequently intervened scandalously in state politics, from dismissing legitimate court cases against occupying soldiers to removing freely elected governors. Years later, after Sheridan had moved on to a different and more agreeable post, President Grant would ask him to return to New Orleans as an unofficial observer of a contentious election season. While there, Sheridan would famously dismiss the opposition Democrats as "banditti" for whom the "what-do-you-call-it" (writ of habeas corpus) should be suspended.

If unreconstructed secessionists had a serious beef with Sheridan, many Native Americans would soon learn to speak his name with fear and loathing. In 1868, he assumed command over the Department of the Missouri, commencing a long stint as scourge of the Plains Indians. Adopting the strategy he had followed in the Shenandoah Valley, Sheridan sent his scant forces out to surprise and destroy Indian settlements in winter, when forage for their mounts was scarce. The death of women and children was considered regrettable, but acceptable—the belligerent native warriors had brought violence upon their people, not the soldiers under Sheridan's command who were compelled to act. He also supported a policy that punished hostile action with death or imprisonment, rather than negotiation or treaty, insisting that Indians who went on the warpath were more like murderers than enemy combatants. His immediate superior for most of these years, William Sherman, was even more sanguinary; but Sheridan caught most of the heat from millions of Americans who looked at the whole bloody business as essentially genocidal. Whatever Sheridan's merits or failings, the fact remains that few had as large a role as he in the "winning of the West."

For a man who had craved and secured the thrill of absolute control in so many theaters, the ultimate reward from Sheridan's country—promotion to commanding general of the United States Army in 1883—was conspicuous for its lack of real power. An appropriate fate, perhaps, for a man who had to be reminded on occasion of the Constitution's insistence on civilian authority over the military. His final act was strangely incongruous. After a heart attack in 1888, Sheridan—his once lithe frame having ballooned from years of rich living—retreated to a small Massachusetts resort community named Nonquitt with Irene Rucker, his wife since June 1875. He eventually died on August 5 in an environment of peaceful quiet that couldn't have been less like the long angry melee that had been his life.

AT ARM'S LENGTH

Phil Sheridan was short, with a bullet-shaped head that made it difficult for him to wear a hat. As for the rest of him, perhaps it's best to rely on a description by Abraham Lincoln. Little Phil was "a brown, chunky little chap," said the president, "with a long body, short legs, not enough neck to hang him, and such long arms that if his ankles itch he can scratch them without stooping."

FIGHTIN' PHIL

Sheridan graduated from West Point in 1853—five years after he had entered. Why the extra year? During his third year, the bilious young Sheridan ran into the sort of trouble that usually cuts careers short. Insulted somehow by the tone of an order given by Cadet Sergeant William Terrill during an exercise, Sheridan shouted, "Goddamn you, sir, I'll run you through!" and charged the stunned Terrill with his fixed bayonet. The attacker was brought under control and no harm was done. When Sheridan came across Terrill sitting alone the next day, he shouted, "Goddamn you!" and laid a haymaker on the cadet's head that sent him sprawling. The two then fell into a scuffle that finally exhausted the patience of the academy's authorities, who decided to suspend the hotheaded Sheridan for nine months. Sheridan's hiatus did nothing to cool his jets: He earned more demerits in his final year than he had in the previous three combined.

Needless to say, Sheridan didn't mellow with age. In the summer of 1863, Little Phil was conducting an inspection tour by train with General George Thomas when an unusually long delay held up the schedule. When Sheridan got up to question the civilian conductor, he was dismissed without an adequate explanation. The general then ordered the fellow to get the train moving and was met with another snide retort that, it is safe to say, the fellow should have seriously reconsidered. Sheridan promptly unleashed a storm of flying fists upon the conductor, then physically threw him off the train before returning to his conversation with Thomas as if nothing had happened.

California Girl

In 1869, Phil Sheridan arrived in Washington, D.C., to confer with his friend, newly elected president Ulysses Grant. With the possibility of his reassignment hanging in the air, Sheridan insisted that he not be sent to the Pacific Northwest. His reason was Sidnayoh, daughter of Klikitat Indian chief Quately. Sheridan had lived with her during his years at Fort Reading in northern California. "Frances," as her white friends called her, had visited Sheridan in Washington at the conclusion of the Civil War, but had since married a Canadian fur trapper. Citing "personal reasons" that he knew Grant would understand, Sheridan wanted to avoid any chance of opening that wound, and he stayed in the Division of the Missouri.

WINDY CITY BLUES

In October 1871, Chicago nearly burned to the ground in one of the greatest conflagrations in American history. With his division headquarters stationed there, Phil Sheridan found himself smack dab in the middle of what has come to be known as the Great Chicago Fire. Predictably, he helped fight the inferno with impressive gusto, particularly during demolition efforts to stem the spreading flames. But it was during the fire's aftermath that Sheridan truly came into his own, assuming martial law by order of the city's mayor and organizing whatever troops and volunteers he could lay his hands on to restore order in the city. Unfortunately, having droves of armed toughs roaming the streets coiled for action can lead to trouble—as it did the night city prosecutor Thomas Grosvenor was shot dead by a young buck in the "Sheridan Guards," an ad hoc volunteer regiment. John McAuley Palmer, governor of Illinois, had never authorized the decision for martial law in the first place; upon hearing of Grosvenor's death, he started firing some shots of his own. Palmer sought to have Sheridan and Mayor Roswell B. Mason indicted for murder, but failed to get a grand jury to charge anyone in the case.

ROYAL PAIN IN THE ASS

Considering all the violent moments Phil Sheridan passed through, it is perhaps a miracle that his worst wound was a scratch on the nose from a Yakima Indian's bullet. Even stranger is the fact that one of his closest brushes with death came years after the lethal maelstroms of Murfreesboro and Chickamauga. In 1872, Grand Duke Alexis, heir to the Russian throne, was paying a visit to America and had voiced interest in taking part in a real buffalo hunt. Phil Sheridan was more than happy to oblige, and he arranged the whole affair. Several days out of Omaha, the hunting party—which, in addition to Sheridan and his Romanov guest, included such notables as George Custer and "Buffalo Bill" Cody—arrived at a herd and began dropping the great beasts with their giant-caliber hunting rifles. After being thrown from his new mount a couple of times, a bruised Sheridan decided to set off on foot with a friend to go after some wounded buffalo he had spotted. Then, seemingly out of nowhere, Custer and the duke came charging over the hill from the opposite direction, blasting away at the same buffalo Sheridan had eyed. After hitting the deck and waiting for the bullets to stop flying, Sheridan stood up and, flushed with fury, began giving Custer and the eager young Romanov a profoundly vulgar piece of his mind. It may not have been the manner in which the grand duke was accustomed to being addressed, but one can hardly fault Sheridan under the circumstances.

DEAD INDIANS AND SUCH

"The only good Indian is a dead Indian." Though Phil Sheridan never said that, he almost certainly did say, "The only good Indians I ever saw were dead." It was addressed to a Comanche chief named Tosawi, who, during a meeting with Sheridan, described himself as a "good Indian," inspiring the general's infamous retort. Though Sheridan did express a degree of heartfelt respect for the Plains Indians and their right to fight for the preservation of their culture, particularly later in his life, his actions as the country's principal general of the West bespeak a brutal severity that is hard to dismiss merely as nineteenth-century racism. One example is particularly telling. Conscious of the Indians' reliance on buffalo hunts, the Texas legislature once considered passing a law that would outlaw poaching on native lands. Sheridan, convinced that killing off the herds was a valuable tactic in the war to break native spirit, felt strongly enough about the subject to make a personal appearance before the legislators. Instead of punishing poachers, he argued, the state should give them a medal featuring a dead buffalo on the front and a despondent Indian on the reverse.

10 DANIEL EDGAR
SICKLES

October 20, 1819–May 3, 1914

HIGHEST RANK:

Union General

ASTROLOGICAL SIGN:

Libra

NICKNAME:

Devil Dan

WORDS TO REMEMBER:

"Satisfied as I was of his guilt, we could not live together on the same planet" (regarding Philip Barton Key).

On July 5, 1863, Dan Sickles lay feverish in a Washington, D.C., boardinghouse, contemplating the loss of his right leg while chatting amiably with Abraham Lincoln. Sickles was no stranger to the president's company, having long since become familiar enough at the White House to tease the Lincoln children and join the first lady's séances. But the painful stump that challenged his legendary composure that hot Sunday afternoon bore testament to the grim turn events had taken since his last occasion to speak with the president. And as he fought off delirium by sucking on a cigar, Sickles took this opportunity to do more than exchange pleasantries with his friend and commander in chief.

In fact, General Sickles had damage control on the mind: a keen desire that his cherished reputation should not share the fate of his leg. Two days earlier, on the second day of the epic struggle at Gettysburg, he had performed a maneuver with his infantry corps that was either courageous or disastrous. Sickles was determined that the world, and President Lincoln in particular, should know it as the former. And as the wincing, sweat-soaked general calmly pleaded his case, Lincoln no doubt showed one of his knowing and world-weary smirks. For as everybody in the country knew, Dan Sickles was a man of many talents. But avoiding controversy, on or off the battlefield, was definitely not one of them.

A native son of New York City, Sickles was emblematic of the churning, opportunistic, multicultural stew that produced him. His old Dutch ancestry

went back six generations, making him a "Knickerbocker" with inroads to the city's most privileged circles. But besides his father, George, Sickles's closest associates were Americans whose pedigree in the New World didn't run nearly as deep. The Da Pontes, worldly Italian immigrants who had befriended Sickles's parents, educated young Dan in the requisites of sophisticated bachelordom: opera, theater, poetry, the moral relativism of dissolute gentry, etc. And the Irish at Tammany Hall provided Sickles with his calling: the Democratic Party, which began grooming him for politics at a very young age. (At sixteen he was delivering rousing speeches on behalf of presidential candidate Martin Van Buren.) Men of dash, wit, and character were required for the organization's demanding schedule, packed with graft, intimidation, pamphlet-burning, ballot-stuffing, and street brawling. Though Sickles attended New York University, his education and law study were nearly superfluous compared to his close Tammany ties. Party connections allowed him to pass the bar, set up a practice, and get elected to the New York State Assembly. In late 1853, he secured the post of corporation lawyer of New York City, but he decided soon afterward to risk it all on a posting abroad.

Daniel Sickles lost his leg in the Battle of Gettysburg, but the limb was preserved in a glass case in the District of Columbia's Army Medical Museum. In later years, Sickles would visit his old appendage on the anniversary of the battle that took it from him.

Sickles's name had reached the ear of senior Democrat James Buchanan, the newly appointed minister to Great Britain. "Old Buck" needed someone to be his first secretary, and Sickles, though hesitant at first to give up his cash cow as New York's corporation counsel, realized the opportunity he was being offered and took it. He would never regret the decision, for it commenced a long relationship with Buchanan that would serve him well in times to come. In the meantime, Sickles set about doing what he did best: stirring up trouble.

Sickles was already a controversial figure before he hit London in 1853. The purest creature of Tammany Hall's clannish chicanery, he had narrowly sidestepped an 1846 charge of grand larceny—an imbroglio over a misplaced property deed that came to nothing with the help of political friends. He was also very publicly connected with one of New York's most successful prostitutes, Fanny White. And it was she, rather than Sickles's wife of barely a year, who accompanied him to the Court of St. James, resulting in a scandal that confirmed Sickles's uncanny gift for flouting public censure. Sickles's wife, Teresa, eventually came over to join him with their young daughter in the summer of 1854—in time to be present at a July 4 celebration in which Dan made headlines on both sides of the Atlantic by refusing to stand for a toast to Queen Victoria.

But this stuff would look like amateur theatrics compared with what was coming. After returning to America, Sickles got elected to the New York State Senate and then, in 1856, to the United States Congress. He had come a long way; the Sickles family was soon dividing its time between a country home in northern Manhattan and a plush mansion along Washington's Lafayette Square. Though Sickles continued to carry on extramarital affairs, it was Teresa's infidelity that would lead to sensational catastrophe. Sickles was virtually the last person in both New York and the nation's capital to learn that his wife was regularly sleeping with Philip Barton Key, the Washington, D.C., district attorney and son of Francis Scott Key, composer of "The Star-Spangled Banner." His sacred honor thrashed beyond hope of repair, a raving Sickles shot his wife's paramour to death in Lafayette Square on February 27, 1859, before numerous witnesses.

It was a spectacle, to be sure. And the murder trial was just as memorable. Drawn by tight political ties, his legal team featured some of the toughest lawyers on the East Coast, including future secretary of war Edwin Stanton. In a bravura performance of legal gymnastics, they argued that their client could not be held responsible for the blood rage that had consumed him, originating as it had in response to a heinous betrayal that undermined everything Christian society stood for. They buttressed their case by pointing out that Key had done more than just indulge in adultery: He had polluted another man's property. Because the body of Sickles's wife belonged to Sickles, his violent act was not unlike self-defense. The jury agreed. It was the first successful temporary insanity plea in American history.

Interestingly, pumping Philip Barton Key full of holes in broad daylight and getting away with it did little to tarnish Sickles's public standing. Indeed, quite the opposite. Free to resume his congressional career, he found himself more than just vindicated: He was now feted by many of his countrymen as an avenging hero who'd boldly taken a matter of honor into his own hands, damn the consequences. He was a killer, to be sure, a fact that sickened many, but his reputation seemed mostly to benefit from this spectacular tragedy.

No, what really ticked everyone off is what he did next: forgive his wife. Dan's public pronouncement that he was reconciling with Teresa was received with scorn and even outrage. Once a cuckold, Sickles had rectified the situation, only to go crawling, it seemed, after the wanton woman who'd shamed his good name. He had the welfare of his daughter, Laura, in mind when he did it, but that was lost on his countrymen. His political career was all but ruined.

Sickles needed something to resurrect his prospects, and he would get it soon enough. Like so many at Tammany Hall, he was a devout Democrat with plenty of friends in the South and no use whatsoever for Republicans and their abolitionist caterwauling. The very thought of taking up arms against another state—even a state that seceded from the Union—was anathema to Sickles. But when the Southern states began occupying Federal installations and forts, he changed his tune. After all, secession was one thing; aggression against the nation's property was quite another. The shelling of Fort Sumter decided the issue for him: He was now a "war Democrat."

After raising, equipping, and drilling a brigade of troops (which he named the Excelsior Brigade), it looked as if Sickles had found his true calling. Military culture and leadership came naturally to him, and the company of men in a dread cause appealed to his sense of honor. In 1862, as part of McClellan's Army of the Potomac, Sickles fought up the Peninsula toward Richmond and back down it again in the retreat of the Seven Days, displaying a remarkable coolness under fire that would distinguish him as a fighting general. He was rewarded by his superior, "Fighting Joe" Hooker, with command of a division, which was spared the butchery of Fredericksburg by being assigned a supporting role in the battle. Then, when Hooker was elevated to command the whole Army of the Potomac, he gave Sickles his old corps. Dan was truly going places.

And not because he was a military genius. Though brave and clearly popular with his men, Sickles was relying on his connections, as much as anything else, to get ahead in the army. Rumor had it that James Buchanan, who was president during Sickles's murder trial, had worked behind the scenes to take some of the punch out of the prosecution's case. Now Sickles was getting close to another president. His relationship with Lincoln began in 1861, when Sickles, who risked losing much of his brigade to the governor of New York over a militia jurisdiction dispute, went directly to the president to plead his case. The two hit it off, and Sickles had been getting closer to the Lincolns ever since. First Lady Mary Todd Lincoln was particularly taken with Sickles's dangerous reputation and aura of rakish urbanity and began inviting him to swing by the White House whenever his duties allowed.

Sickles's most important patron, however, was Fighting Joe Hooker, a hard-drinking West Pointer who shared Sickles's enthusiastic moral turpitude. The two scoundrels got on swimmingly, turning the Army of the Potomac's headquarters into what one indignant officer dubbed "a combination of bar-room and brothel." The party came to an abrupt end at the Battle of Chancellorsville in 1863, when Hooker allowed himself to be hoodwinked and mauled by the one-two punch of Bobby Lee and Stonewall Jackson. Chastened, Hooker backed up to defend Washington and then gave the Army of the Potomac over to George Meade.

The reversal at Chancellorsville meant more to Sickles than the sacking of his sponsor and drinking buddy. It had also imparted a lesson that would have tremendous consequences. During the battle, he'd been ordered to retire from a strategic bit of high ground called Hazel Grove, and after grudgingly doing so, he watched the Confederates occupy it with batteries that proceeded to pour shot and shell into Union ranks with deadly effectiveness. It left in him an obsession with high ground that came back to haunt him two months later near a Pennsylvania town called Gettysburg.

It was there, upon the ridges that overlooked the town in a broad arc, that the Army of the Potomac was afforded an opportunity to turn back Lee's invasion of the North. It would do so, of course, during three of the most important days of the Civil War—but not before "Devil Dan" Sickles had his controversial day in the sun. Arrayed along a ridgeline that dominated the local terrain, Meade's forces were in an ideal situation to receive an attack—which, given Lee's relentlessly aggressive style, they were sure to get. But there was one stretch of the Federal line, all the way down on the left wing, that dipped below the rest, looking very much like a break in the high ground.

And guess whose corps occupied it.

The ignominy of Chancellorsville fresh in his mind, Sickles wasn't happy with his situation, not at all. But a solution presented itself three quarters of a mile to his front, where higher ground beckoned. All he had to do was get permission from his superior to go seize it. Granted, that would mean breaking the integrity of the Union line, exposing his flanks on an exposed crest almost completely devoid of cover, but it was high ground, and he wasn't going to stand idly by while the Rebels took it and used it against him.

Though instructed to maintain his position on the left flank in line with the corps to his right, Sickles thought the matter important enough to see Meade in person. After asking whether he could dispose of his troops according to his own discretion, Sickles was testily told by Meade (the two didn't particularly like each other) that, of course he could, "within the limits of the general instructions I have given you."

Sickles rode back to his position with a member of Meade's staff, who concurred with Sickles's opinion and then rode back to Meade's headquarters for further consultation. An hour then passed without hearing anything more from Meade. So Sickles acted.

Moving forward in splendid formation, Sickles marched his corps toward the Emmitsburg Road and established a line short of it that went through a peach orchard. But with more ground to cover, the corps was spread thin, jutting out from the rest of the army like a bubble just waiting to be burst. He had taken the high ground. But at what cost?

The answer to that question came soon enough. Sickles's corps had barely completed its redeployment when the Rebels unleashed an assault on both wings of the Union line, giving his exposed troops a dreadful punishment. The orchard and a neighboring wheat field became a frenzied killing ground, forcing the Third Corps back—to its original position, the line it had held before moving forward. But in the time it took to beat back Sickles and his troops, the Federals had brought up reinforcements to secure the far left wing. The Union flank had not been turned. And the Confederate attack, despite harvesting a slew of Yankee lives and tearing Sickles's right leg to bits, had failed.

Historians continue to debate whether that failure was due in part to Sickles's rash move. Many good men in the Army of the Potomac believed that, had Sickles remained where he was, the Confederates would still have been repulsed, without the bloodbath in the orchard and wheat field. The battle was barely over before acrimonious debate began in earnest. Meade lost no time dismissing the old Tammany lawyer as reckless and insubordinate, and Sickles gave as good as he got, taking every opportunity to blast his commander as dilatory and confused. Though unconvinced of his tactical ability, the nation never doubted Sickles's bravery: thirty-four years later, he was awarded the Medal of Honor for "conspicuous gallantry."

Whatever the truth, the cannonball that slammed into Sickles's right leg that afternoon ended his wartime career. Perhaps sensing this, he maintained the presence of mind to light a cigar for his departure from the battlefield, affecting a dispassionate demeanor in his stretcher that no one present would ever forget.

His days in uniform may have been over, but he was far from done. After pestering the president for something to do, Sickles was charged with touring occupied sections of the South in preparation for postwar reconstruction plans. Then he took on the jungles and highlands of Central

America, sent there by Lincoln to negotiate passage across the Isthmus of Panama for American troops and to inquire about the possibility of settling freed slaves in Colombia. After the war, he served as military governor of the Carolinas, only to be dismissed in 1867—the same year his wife, Teresa, died. Two years later, President Grant appointed him minister to Spain, where he married again, to a woman named Caroline de Creagh, and proceeded to alienate her with sensational extramarital affairs that galvanized his reputation as an incurable reprobate.

Even in old age, Sickles was incapable of avoiding controversy. After returning to New York City, he was made chairman of the New York State Monuments Commission, charged with overseeing the memorials at Gettysburg that pertained to soldiers from the Empire State. It seemed, at long last, that somebody had found a job for Dan Sickles that he couldn't turn into a front-page headline. But no. In 1912 more than $28,000 of the commission's budget went missing. Though Sickles had clearly purloined a hefty sum for his own use, public opinion was overwhelmingly forgiving. State officials began a subscription to raise the money, and he never served a day in jail. He died two years later, a rapscallion to the end.

THE TURN OF THE KEY

It was on the evening of Thursday, February 24, 1859, that Dan Sickles received an anonymous letter informing him of Philip Barton Key's ongoing affair with his wife. Key would lie dead in Lafayette Square the following Sunday afternoon.

Sickles had heard of the affair before that fateful Thursday, but dismissed the rumor out of hand. His angelic Teresa had never shown anything but ardent devotion to him. And Key was a friend; indeed, Sickles had used his political connections to reconfirm him as district attorney. That the two could betray Dan in such a fashion was inconceivable to him.

Inconceivable or not, they'd been doing just that—and for nine months. Teresa was quite taken by "Barton," as he was commonly known, whose family legacy and easygoing aristocratic manner made him a popular fixture in the capital's social scene. As for Teresa, she was a legendary beauty, a lively socialite who was fluent in numerous languages, and very young—less than half her husband's age, in fact. She had never lacked male admirers. For the older Barton, capturing this ingenue's heart was something of a coup.

Smitten, Barton went so far as to rent a house on Fifteenth Street, not far from the Sickles home on Lafayette Square, for their assignations. It was reckless behavior like this that set tongues to wagging and ultimately got Barton killed.

Since receiving the anonymous letter, Sickles had had some close friends look into its veracity and discovered the monstrous truth. Life in the Sickles household had since become, to put it mildly, tense. Dan loudly confronted his distraught wife, then forced her to write out and sign a confession (which, in the weeks to come, would ingloriously find its way into the pages of *Harper's Weekly*). He then fell into a depressive funk punctuated by crying jags.

It was in this state of mind that an incredulous Sickles saw the agent of his destruction brashly waving a little hanky out in Lafayette Square to signal his beloved. Wild-eyed, Sickles donned an overcoat and stuffed several firearms into it. He then stormed into the square yelling, "You must die!" and fired a shot at Barton, grazing him in the hand. Barton, pathetically, hurled a pair of opera glasses at his attacker. The two then grappled before Sickles produced another revolver and perhaps a derringer and shot Barton twice, mortally wounding him. He died soon afterward.

Though Sickles forgave Teresa not long after his acquittal, he maintained an uneasy emotional distance from her for the rest of their marriage.

FRIENDS IN HIGH PLACES

Though President James Buchanan was in the White House when his friend Dan Sickles slew Philip Barton Key, he did not witness the altercation. A White House page, however, did. Electrified by the drama in Lafayette Square, J. H. W. Bonitz ran into Buchanan's office and began recounting what he'd seen. Buchanan, unaware that **Bonitz** wasn't the only witness to the murder, was worried that his excited employee might be called to court as an eyewitness. His reaction was to give the fellow some money and tell him to get out of town on indefinite leave, back to his home in South Carolina—by any standard, a suspicious act for a practiced lawyer and president of the United States.

OBJECTION!

Based as it was on moral outrage, the defense of Dan Sickles during his murder trial stood the very real chance of derailing if the prosecution brought up the defendant's own unrestrained behavior. Whether because of gross incompetence, pressure from politicians (such as President Buchanan himself), or the inequity of nineteenth-century mores, Sickles's sexual shenanigans were never at issue in the courtroom.

Which is rather astonishing, because they were spectacular. Throughout most of the time in which his wife was carrying on with Barton, Sickles was carrying on with an anonymous married woman in a Baltimore hotel they'd established as the location for their regular trysts. And during the war he quite possibly produced a child with another woman. This was hardly unusual for Sickles, who, despite his undeniable attachment to Teresa, seemed woefully unsuited to monogamy.

His long relationship with high-profile New York prostitute Fanny White is a prime example. Sickles never held himself to the restrictive Christian standards of behavior that shaped so much of his era's social structure. Hence his decision to embark upon his new assignment as first secretary to the American minister in London with Fanny on his arm instead of his wife, home with a new daughter too young to travel. This was bold, to be sure. But when Sickles went to a royal reception and formally presented Fanny, under an alias, to Queen Victoria, folks on both sides of the Atlantic blanched. The papers back home were neither fooled nor amused, and responded accordingly—partly because it had all happened before. While a member of the New

York State Assembly, Sickles had taken Fanny to Albany (before his marriage to Teresa) and given her a tour of the assembly chamber. Disgusted, the speaker of the assembly issued a censure.

Another of Sickles's more scandalous relationships occurred years later, after he'd been appointed minister to Spain. On a trip to Paris, he met Spain's deposed monarch, Isabella II, who reputedly maintained an insatiable sexual appetite into her twilight years. Sickles obligingly accommodated her whenever the wooing of his future second wife, Caroline de Creagh, allowed. Such a precarious state of affairs was bound to backfire, especially when Isabella was the most famous of his numerous liaisons. In time, despite producing two children, his marriage to de Creagh fell apart.

Sickles would play his hand out in the company of aged widow Eleanor Wilmerding, his housekeeper in New York during his final years. While Sickles's somewhat estranged wife, Caroline, and the kids lived just blocks away, he carried on with Eleanor as if it were the most normal thing in the world. And for Dan Sickles, it was.

Getting a Leg Up

Sickles was astride his horse on the Gettysburg battlefield when, on July 2, 1863, a twelve-pound cannonball crashed into his right leg, destroying the tibia. Delivered to the Third Corps field hospital behind the battlefield, the doctor sedated Sickles with chloroform and amputated his leg a little above the knee. But instead of being thrown aside to join all the other bloody limbs that were removed that day, Sickles's leg was quickly wrapped for shipment to the Army Medical Museum in Washington, which was looking for displays. And there it remained for years, behind glass, a curious gift to posterity. Sickles himself was known to visit his old appendage on the anniversary of the battle that took it from him.

11 FREDERICK DOUGLASS

February 1818–February 20, 1895

HIGHEST RANK:

Abolitionist Leader

ASTROLOGICAL SIGN:

Aquarius or Pisces

NICKNAME:

The Lion of Anacostia

WORDS TO REMEMBER:

"We must . . . reach the slave-holder's conscience through his fear of personal danger. We must make him feel that there is death in the air around him, that there is death in the pot before him, that there is death all around him."

A wet Frederick Douglass fumed. It was a rainy evening in Rochester, New York, and the Congress Hall Hotel had no rooms to let. So he marched around the corner to the Waverly House, only to be told, once again, that there were no vacancies. That did it. Trembling as much from rage as from the damp, he impolitely reminded the clerk who he was and insisted he be given a room. Douglass had just arrived back in the city after receiving a telegram the day before that his house had burned down, and he was in no mood for the usual bigotry that greeted black patrons in hotel lobbies. The clerk, no doubt aware of the famous Rochesterian's identity (and probably having read in the newspaper that his house was now a hissing ruin), apologetically explained that, no kidding, there really were no rooms available. Douglass backed off, concealing his embarrassment with a tempestuous exit. He ended up locating his family members at a neighbor's house and spending the night there.

The Waverly House was indeed full of guests—including, interestingly enough, a few who happened to be black. The following day, Douglass would see the charred husk that had been his beloved home for twenty-five years, lost—along with piles and piles of invaluable letters and documents—to a fire that was almost certainly caused deliberately. It was a pathetic moment

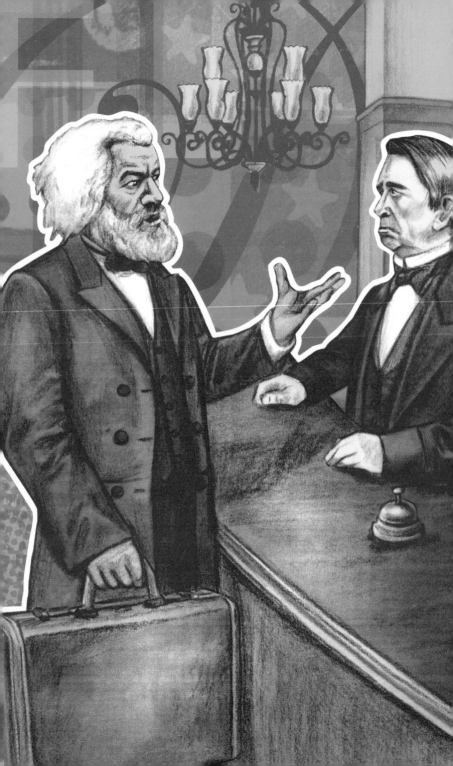

for a great man who, not eight years earlier, had been welcome in the White House in the midst of the worst war the nation had ever known. But Frederick Douglass couldn't remember a time when arson didn't immediately spring to mind when a prominent black person's house burned to the ground; or, for that matter, when it was possible to take a hotel clerk at his word when he told a black man that no rooms were available.

Douglass could remember vividly, however, when the possibility of owning a house that anybody would want to torch was as laughably inconceivable as rudely challenging a white clerk's judgment and getting away with it. Once upon a time, such things were as remote from Douglass's experience as the rings of Saturn. Back then, in the hard world that had made and scarred him, he was known by another name: Frederick Augustus Washington Bailey. He was born a slave to a slave woman, though he never knew her well. She was dead by the time he was eight. As for Frederick's father, he was not a slave but a white man whose identity would never be decided beyond doubt. On Maryland's eastern shore, where Frederick grew up, slaves lived a life of extreme anticipation on bondage's frontier: with Pennsylvania and freedom beckoning to the north, masters kept their property on a tight leash or, worse, "sold them south" to Mississippi or Alabama, as far away from the Underground Railroad as one could get. Frederick would see some fifteen of his close relatives disappear to such a fate before he seized his own freedom.

> **In a time when few blacks dared to raise their voices in anger, Frederick Douglass wasn't afraid to berate a white hotel clerk who refused to give him a room.**

The seeds of escape were sown in his mind when he was still young. Sent to work in Baltimore for the Auld family, he became the recipient of an astonishing breach of the master's code: On her own initiative, Sophia Auld, intrigued by the boy's sharp mind, began teaching him how to spell and read. He was a quick and hungry student, and made good progress. To Frederick, this remarkable experience made Baltimore a sanctuary where new things were possible. One day it would be the springboard for his flight.

But that lay beyond a wide chasm of suffering and indignation. In 1833 his master of six years, Thomas Auld (who inherited Frederick from Aaron Anthony upon the latter's death), brought the teenager back from Baltimore to St. Michaels on the eastern shore. Frederick was soon hired out to neighboring farms, one of which was owned by Edward Covey. Popularly known as a "slave-breaker," a title bestowed on those who prided themselves on the persuasive power of their unyielding brutality, Covey was unsparing with the lash. From him, Frederick—now a large, muscular man—would learn to fight back: Daring to physically take on the "slave-breaker" in front of other slaves on the farm (the match went on for quite some time), Frederick humiliated the tyrant before his victims—a triumph destined to become one of the most celebrated moments in Douglass's autobiography. Remarkably, he was no longer whipped on the Covey property. In 1835, Auld sent Frederick to work on the farm of William Freeland. There, having continued his self-educating and taken on a few clandestine pupils as well, Frederick would at last plan an escape attempt with several fellow laborers.

It ended disastrously. Betrayed, probably by a fellow slave, the party of conspirators were bound and hauled behind horses into St. Michaels. In the face of cries to lynch the men, Thomas Auld interceded, arguing that Frederick and the others be jailed for future trial (they hadn't killed anyone, after all). It was a dramatic act by Auld on Frederick's behalf, and not the last time that he would do such a thing. After lying to people that he was going to sell Frederick south to Alabama, Auld made a decision that would mark the turning point in his extraordinary slave's life: He sent him back up to Baltimore to become a skilled laborer.

The intention was to turn Frederick into a profitable worker who could be hired out at a decent profit. But what happened was rather different. Taken on by Hugh Auld, Thomas's brother, Frederick did indeed become a caulker in the shipbuilding trade. But he did some other things, too—like meet a free Negro woman named Anna Murray. By 1838, they had decided to marry and make a home for themselves in Baltimore. Hugh Auld, unusually liberal with the strictures he placed on his brother's slave, had gradually allowed Frederick to become as close to free as a man in bondage could be. Such liberties went to Frederick's head one day when he decided, on his own authority, to stay at an African Methodist Episcopal camp meeting outside Baltimore a little longer than Auld had anticipated. When Frederick came back, a furious Auld began stripping Frederick of the privileges he had begun to take for granted—including living apart from his master's household. With his dream of marriage and a home of his own with Anna suddenly threatened, Frederick decided on escape.

The fruit of three tense weeks of planning and preparation, his flight from slavery was made possible by a remarkable acquisition: the papers of a free seaman, identifying him as a sailor. Whether sold or given as a gift has never been divulged. But they identified their carrier as a member of a very respected class of men in the ports of the eastern seaboard, a fact that more than compensated for the fact that the description of the bearer did not resemble Frederick Bailey at all. Armed with a false identity and a lot of very real courage, the runaway soon found himself—via train, then ferry across the Susquehanna, and train again—in New York City. Anna followed as soon as he could write to her, and they were married in September 1838. By the end of the month, with help from agents on the Underground Railroad (for slave catchers lurked everywhere), the happy couple was in New Bedford, Massachusetts.

Making his break with the past complete, Frederick Bailey became Frederick Douglass. Now his labor would be putting money in his own pocket instead of someone else's. (It would not be caulking, however, as white men in his new home would not build ships with him.) And, soon enough, so would his speaking. Eloquent, passionate, charismatic, and extremely intelligent, this self-taught, self-made intellectual—who, were he unlucky enough to bump into the wrong men, would instantly be whisked off to a life sentence of soul-destroying labor under some scouring, deep Southern sun—began acting on a natural gift for stirring captivated audiences. Douglass turned the curse of his birth into an account of struggle to enlighten and shock abolitionists keen on acquiring firsthand knowledge of the netherworld they were fighting to destroy. And it worked. By 1842, having attracted the admiration of William Lloyd Garrison and other abolitionist leaders for his enrapturing speeches, he was making a living as an anti-slavery orator, logging thousands of miles to make uniquely powerful contributions to the debate that was increasingly tearing the nation apart—and, in light of the angry crowds, threatened to tear him apart as well. His autobiography— *Narrative of the Life of Frederick Douglass, an American Slave*—appeared in 1845, dropping him into the peculiar predicament of becoming an even bigger target for slave catchers who looked at his book as a giant "bring it on" sign. Because of this, as well as the opportunity to take his message to foreign audiences who wanted to hear him, he was off to the British Isles.

Threatened and cheered by turns across the Atlantic, Douglass had become an international celebrity, standing like a lightning rod for the age's cause célèbre. Once back in America, his personal life and public views became inextricably intertwined in an ideological maelstrom that was as captivating to the public as it was representative of slavery's capacity to confuse and enrage. In 1846, Hugh Auld, having already acquired "ownership" of the guy formerly known as Frederick Bailey from his brother Thomas Auld, manumitted his slave when British admirers of Douglass's raised enough money—a little over seven hundred dollars—to purchase his freedom. Now a free man in both the North and the South, Douglass became shackled to the contentiousness that defined his life's work. William Lloyd Garrison, the radical whose early sponsorship had been instrumental in Douglass's rise, broke with the former slave in what became the defining philosophical clash of antebellum abolitionism. Garrison, uncompromising but extremely critical of violence, saw the struggle to end America's peculiar institution as a sweeping revolution, denouncing political parties, religious institutions, and the Constitution itself as complicit—they were part of the problem, not a means of solving it. Douglass, by contrast, was willing to fight within the system, relying on political compromise if absolutely necessary. The break remained bitter and vituperative. Ultimately, John Brown attempted to woo the great orator to the side of violent force; he was staying at Douglass's Rochester home when he hashed out the final details of his Harpers Ferry plan. In the wake of its sensational failure, Douglass once again hit the sea road a fugitive, fleeing the authorities that fingered him as part of the plot.

He returned from England in 1860 to a country on the verge of implosion. Lincoln's election and its climactic aftermath settled much, bringing former ideological enemies together again. By the end of the following year the breech between Douglass and Garrison had all but disappeared, replaced in wartime by an urgent need to get Lincoln on board the abolitionist train. For Douglass, the defining issue became the administration's refusal to put black men in uniform—a policy of unutterable stupidity as far as he was concerned, given the scale of the war, the stakes involved, and the eagerness of so many black men to sign up. "Why does the government reject the negro?" he asked rhetorically in one of his monthly publications. "Can he not wield a sword, fire a gun, march and countermarch, and obey orders like any other?"

When the government came around, largely due to partisans like Douglass, it inspired a bold career change. Since the 1840s, Douglass had been regularly publishing the *North Star* (renamed *Frederick Douglass's Papers* and then *Douglass's Monthly*), one of the leading abolitionist papers in the country. Though a celebrated speaker, he had defined himself primarily as an editor. Now he was to be a recruiter, throwing his efforts directly into the destruction of slavery—an endeavor made possible by the administration's shift in policy. Douglass had two sons enlist in the famed 54th Massachusetts Regiment, traveled throughout the North to inspire enthusiasm for the war effort, and managed to secure a pass to recruit in occupied Southern territory. It was as if all the struggling, arguing, punching, and shouting of his prewar career had been leading up to this: a desperate and very lethal effort to change things once and forever. There was promise in the air.

Lincoln, once pilloried by Douglass as too soft on slavery, had become an ally. The relationship exemplified Douglass's willingness to keep pounding away at solutions within the system, rather than destroying the system itself. Indeed, his initial meetings with the president were to protest the government's awful treatment of black troops. Impressed by Lincoln's candor and willingness to try new courses of action, Douglass decided to trust the Illinois "rail-splitter" and back his reelection. Lincoln himself greeted the great abolitionist at his second inaugural ball in March of 1865.

It was obvious to Douglass that Lincoln was a man he and his fellow freemen could work with. But they didn't get Lincoln's version of Reconstruction. Martyred for a cause he came to embrace only in the cauldron of war, Father Abraham left his flock in the lurch. Andrew Johnson was no replacement. Horrified by the new president's sickly Reconstruction policy, Douglass devoted the rest of his life to two things: black freedom and the Republican Party (Johnson was a Democrat). Both would give him as much pain and trouble as they would satisfaction. The Fifteenth Amendment, for instance, forced him to make a difficult choice. Supporting a law that ensured the right to vote for every male American, regardless of race, meant ticking off many of his dear friends in the women's movement who wanted to wait for an amendment that also included gender. To realize his dream of black enfranchisement, he broke with supporters of a cause—women's rights—that he had warmly embraced for years. As for the Republicans, they were a political party. And like all parties, they were more than capable of misgovernment, corruption (lots of that), underhanded chicanery, and entrenched cronyism. Douglass seized on Grant as he had on Lincoln, believing him to be the man that prudence dictated should be the anointed champion of freemen. There was little Grant could do, however, that wouldn't later be undone, especially in a two-term presidency that was saddled with scandal.

But for better or worse, politics had become Douglass's main gig. In the ensuing years, he would rack up some impressive titles: U.S. marshal for Washington, D.C.; recorder of deeds for the District of Columbia; chargé d'affaires for Santo Domingo; minister resident and consul general to Haiti. But all of it was done against the background of Reconstruction's grand failure—a gradual reemergence of the racialist order in the old Confederacy.

Now ensconced in Anacostia, in the District of Columbia, he embarked on his twilight years. In 1894 he delivered his last major speech, "Lessons of the Hour," against the evils of lynching then sweeping the South—a sad and telling indication of how things had come full circle for him and the causes he had fought for.

The following February 20, he attended a feminist rally in which he was greeted warmly by Susan B. Anthony. Later that night he collapsed and died. Douglass had been many, many things, from activist and politician to businessman, editor, and one of the towering voices of his century. Yet the identity that continued to define him for so many of his countrymen was the one he desired most to leave behind: the former slave who had become so much more than was expected of him. Not even Frederick Douglass could escape the realities of his age.

AULD LANG SYNE

Slave-master relationships were often strange, and those shared by Frederick Bailey with the Auld family were no exception. Thomas Auld and his wife, Lucretia, were observant enough to see something special in young Frederick and to send him up to Baltimore. Sophia Auld, Hugh's wife, saw the same extraordinary sensitivity and took it upon herself to forever change his world by introducing him to the incredible power of words. And perhaps most importantly, Thomas Auld made the brave decision, after Frederick's abortive escape attempt, to spare him from a life of hard labor in a Deep South that might well have broken him. Sent instead up to Baltimore without disciplinary action for an act that most of the white South considered deserving of a hellish punishment, Frederick was apprenticed to Hugh and taught a trade.

Nevertheless, the Aulds were still masters. Good, kind masters, but masters all the same, who could not summon the conscience, humanity, or imagination to understand why a young black man should have his freedom. Douglass justifiably hated them for this—and yet knew, at the very same time, that he owed much to them. As William S. McFeely writes in his biography of Douglass, "For his freedom—for his life—he would for the rest of that life be beholden to a white man whom he had loved and whom he now had to remember to loathe."

The resulting storm of feelings would shape much of Douglass's writing and thinking on the evils of slavery. It would also lead to one of his strangest compositions. Featured in the *North Star* in 1848, the tenth anniversary of his successful escape, Douglass's letter "To My Old Master, Thomas Auld" sought to reconcile the author's conflicting emotions on servitude, cruelty, forgiveness, and his own troubled past. Publicly and politely taking issue with Auld, it accused him of being the sort of abusive, tyrannical slave-driver that Douglass knew he wasn't, perhaps in an attempt to create a focus for the rage that remained for having spent his first twenty years in bondage. Strangest of all, however, is the letter's assertion that Auld had abandoned Frederick's grandmother, Betsy Bailey, in her old age without having seen to her welfare. The accusation was false on two counts: first, Betsy had not been inherited by Thomas Auld, but by his brother-in-law; and second, she had in fact been brought back to St. Michaels to be cared for before she died.

Douglass would not know this for sure until 1877 when he found himself, for the first time in forty years, face-to-face with his former master once again. Thomas, very old and infirm, was able to correct Frederick on the point of his grandmother, and Douglass apologized. Despite this—and the fact that Douglass had excoriated Thomas Auld and his family in countless public speeches—the two men, choked with emotion, spoke like old friends and parted warmly.

JOB "SECURITY"

Frederick Douglass was a large, powerful man. And he needed to be. Taking on Edward Covey in his youth was just the first of innumerable physical confrontations that simply came with being one of those "uppity blacks." In 1841, Douglass had the gall to choose his own seat on a train ride up to an abolitionist meeting in New Hampshire, and was promptly thrown off for refusing to sit in the "negro car." Not long after this incident, he once again found himself confronted on a train by a conductor who had no intention of allowing Douglass's black skin to ruin everyone else's ride. Calling for help, the conductor and several buddies attempted to wrestle the recalcitrant passenger out of his seat, only to find that the iron grip he maintained on his bench made such an effort hopeless. Douglass arrived at his destination in that very seat.

Trains were a piece of cake compared to anti-slavery meetings. In 1843, Douglass and two white companions were in Indiana for an abolitionist meeting slated to be held in a local Baptist church. Unfortunately, the congregation was denied use of the building because of threats from local rowdies determined to break up the proceedings. The town did manage to provide an alternative meeting place in the woods, in which the anti-slavery group congregated the following morning. The toughs showed up once again and drew the meeting's leaders into a debate that grew into a shouting match and then quickly degenerated into a brawl. Douglass grabbed a piece of wrecked podium to use as a club, but someone managed to break his hand before he got a chance to use it. One of his white companions, William White, was luckier: all he got was a deep gash across his head before they all ran for their lives.

Not that anti-slavery meetings were the only occasion for getting beat up. Consider the balmy spring evening in 1850 when Douglass, in his monstrous temerity, dared to stroll along the Battery in New York City with two British women friends of his. Imagine! To many New Yorkers at the time, this was the equivalent of . . . well, there really is no modern equivalent. They simply considered a black man bold enough to keep the company of white ladies really bad. Faced with such naked injustice, a group of onlookers dragged Douglass away from his screaming companions and kicked the crap out of him.

Then there are those anniversary meetings, which can be very dangerous indeed—when the anniversary being celebrated is that of John Brown's execution. It was December 1860 in Boston, Massachusetts. Gathered in the

Tremont Temple to observe the "martyrdom" of Brown were quite a number of anti-slavery folk. But they soon found that they were not numerous enough— for, as was bound to happen at these affairs, a horde of uninvited guests showed up. They were staunch pro-Union men who objected to abolitionism's focus on a cause that was pouring fuel on sectional tensions and threatening the very cohesion of the nation itself. They soon took over the meeting and the podium through the Temple's rules of order and elected their own representative to the chair. When Frederick Douglass rose to speak, he was grudgingly recognized, thrust himself head-first through a gang of antagonists on his way to the podium, and began what amounted to a shouting match with bigoted hecklers. One thing led to another until the podium erupted with violence, with spectators, speakers, and police all trying to sort the others out with whatever means necessary. At one point Douglass found himself wrestling for possession of a chair with more than a few opponents who finally resorted to yanking his hair and having the police throw him out of the hall.

That night, at an abolitionist meeting that would not be interrupted, Douglass spoke of war against the powers that allow slavery. He didn't have long to wait.

12 SARAH EMMA EDMONDS

December 1841–
September 5, 1898

HIGHEST RANK:
Union Soldier, Spy, and Nurse

ASTROLOGICAL SIGN:
Sagittarius or Capricorn

NICKNAMES:
Frank Thompson, Our Woman

WORDS TO REMEMBER:
"I think I was born into this world with some dormant antagonism toward man. I hope I have outgrown it measurably, but my infant soul was impressed with a sense of my mother's wrongs before I ever saw the light, and I probably drew from her breast with my daily food my love of independence and hatred of male tyranny."

It is easy to forget through all the enormous casualty figures, savagery, and hateful noise of sectional rivalry that the American Civil War occurred during the Victorian Age—that its participants, in addition to being trapped in a mortal struggle that seemed interminable, were also imprisoned by a cage of stifling moral attitudes. One of those attitudes stipulated that those who marched "Into the jaws of Death,/Into the mouth of Hell," as Tennyson wrote about another war, could only be men. Indeed, war was strictly the province of men, like voting or cigars or functional clothing. It was a man's life in the army.

Not quite. According to DeAnne Blanton and Lauren M. Cook in *They Fought Like Demons: Women Soldiers in the Civil War*, at least 250 women were "in the ranks" of Civil War armies, and probably many more. Many of them, confronted with the societal limits placed on their gender, conjured imaginative ways of realizing their martial ambitions. Simply put, they went to war incognito.

One of the most famous was Sarah Emma Edmonds. She was born Sarah Emma Edmondson into a remote New Brunswick community called Magaguadavic (say that ten times fast). Her mother was an earnest,

hard-laboring carrier of numerous children—all of whom, save one, were girls, a disaster to family patriarch Isaac Edmondson. Stuck with five girls and an epileptic son, Isaac assumed a permanently surly aspect, getting as much labor as he could out of his daughters on the family farm and generally treating everyone churlishly. Little wonder Emma grew up critical of men. When she was seventeen, Isaac arranged a marriage for her with an older widower without so much as consulting her. It was the last straw.

Desperate to get out of town before she lost her freedom, Emma cooked up an escape plan. It seems likely that her mother, Betsy, was a conspirator, having decided that arranging her daughter's exile was preferable to watching her suffer in a lousy marriage as she herself had. According to one story, Emma was a stowaway on a wagon belonging to Betsy's friend, who casually and inconspicuously delivered her young cargo beyond the reach of Isaac Edmondson's grasp. The rest of Emma's life had begun.

> Sarah Emma Edmonds was one of the many women who disguised themselves as men to fight in the Civil War. Her fellow soldiers hardly suspected a thing.

What followed was very odd indeed and offers a window on the resolution of this remarkable young woman. Determined to secure her newfound freedom by earning a living, Emma answered an advertisement for traveling booksellers from a subscription publisher in Hartford, Connecticut. Naturally, only men could be itinerant booksellers (duh!), so Emma . . . well, became a man. She responded to the publisher as "Franklin Thompson," a suitably manly name, and set about perfecting her alter ego with a new suit of clothes, a new haircut, and a new walk (it was always the walk that gave a male impersonator away). It worked. Frank never got so much as a snicker out of his customers.

Ms. Edmondson wasn't just good at transgender theater—she was also good at selling books. The spirited young woman from rural Canada had hit upon her dreams: She was as free as any bachelor, beholden to no one, and with plenty of money in her purse. Independence, which she was not raised to anticipate as a girl, had become her reality. It was intoxicating.

After some unidentified mishap in which she lost all her money and belongings (perhaps a robbery?), Emma journeyed to Hartford itself and secured another business relationship to sell books door-to-door. She soon made her territory in Michigan, where she found the same success that she had had in eastern Canada and New England. It was here that she cemented her relationship to her adopted country, acquiring a fondness for America that would soon be put to the ultimate test.

That being civil war, of course. Emma had become quite attached to the United States, whose sundering caused her no small amount of concern. Moreover, she was a very pious Christian who was brought up to view slavery as a dreadful sin. How could she stand by and let everyone else shed their blood for the cause?

It wasn't enough to love her adopted country and to feel compelled by moral necessity. There was something else in her decision to go to war—a sense of adventure that had always been there, deep inside, and that had inspired her to defy convention once before with spectacular success. Much of the world already knew her as Frank Thompson. Why shouldn't Frank volunteer with all the other wild-eyed young men?

Practiced as she was at passing herself off as a "him," the only real obstacle to Emma's—er, Frank's—goal was the physical exam. "Physical exam," indeed. The extent of Frank's examination was the hands, whose small size should've been a clue. Instead, the doctor took the prospective soldier's hands in his own and gruffly asked, "Well, what sort of a living have these hands earned?" Frank explained that he had been a student, which, rather mystifyingly, was enough for the examiner. Passed.

In fact, Mr. Thompson had been lucky. Depending on the location and circumstances, many physicals were much more thorough. And demands from officers in the field for closer scrutiny of volunteers would eventually produce standardized examinations that really got down to business. But in

May 1861, Frank Thompson managed to squeeze through the system and become a private in the Second Michigan.

She made a peculiar soldier: she grew no facial hair and her feet were unusually small (especially for a "man" five feet nine inches tall), something that her comrades loved to razz her about. In time they called her "our woman," having no idea how close to the truth they really were. To them she was a small, overly youthful man. But she earned their respect by taking their jibes in stride and by never shirking a task, no matter how onerous. She soon was assigned nurse's duty, a job many hated because of its constant proximity to the maimed and dying. There she confronted her worst fears, but also became renowned for her bedside manner: brave, soulful, comforting. From First Bull Run to March 1862, Private Thompson was a highly esteemed, valuable nurse at the hospitals of the Second Michigan Infantry Regiment. When Colonel Orlando Poe assumed command of the unit, he made Thompson a mail carrier, citing his "effeminate" qualities (the new commander didn't want to take a valuable soldier from the ranks). The freedom was like a breath of fresh air, and Private Thompson once again threw herself into her duties with impressive dedication, both in the east and when her unit was reassigned to Kentucky toward the end of 1862.

All of this is fact. What is open to speculation is Thompson's activities as a spy. In her very successful memoirs, Emma Edmonds (she ended up dropping the last syllable from her family name) claimed to partake in many clandestine missions on behalf of the Union forces that, for the most part, are impossible to verify. If true, Emma went behind the lines during the Peninsula campaign as an ersatz black man made possible by silver nitrate, which she rubbed onto her face to great effect, and a wig. She reported directly to McClellan, offering valuable information on Rebel fortifications. In later campaigns she assumed the identities of an Irish woman hauling goods on an old wagon and an older black woman. On both occasions, she found herself well behind enemy lines.

Whatever the truth about her spying activities, they were all conducted while maintaining the Frank Thompson falsehood—meaning that, on at least two occasions, Emma Thompson fooled everyone, North and South, by pretending to be a man who was pretending to be a woman. Quite a feat. But if anyone could have pulled it off, Emma Edmonds could.

Then, in April 1863, Frank Thompson disappeared as quickly as he'd been fabricated. Emma later said that she had contracted malaria, which, in addition to placing her life in danger, put her in another sort of jeopardy: that of being discovered in a hospital. On the rolls of the Second Michigan, Thompson's name appeared in the "deserter" column. Faced with court martial, Emma allowed Frank Thompson to die for good. She spent the rest of her war years as an outwardly female nurse.

She also began writing her memoirs, which went on to be published to great acclaim. More important, Emma found love, perhaps for the first time in her life. His name was Linus Seelye, a carpenter and fellow New Brunswick native whom Emma became reacquainted with after making a reluctant return to her Canadian home. The two married in 1867 and, through a series of homes that ran from the South to the Midwest to Texas, ended up raising a family. It was an astonishing saga for a woman who once believed she would never marry.

Though her years in a man's uniform (and, it seems likely, in other guises behind enemy lines) comprised an impressive accomplishment, her greatest triumph—the thing that ended up setting Emma apart from everyone else—was yet to come. Aided by former comrades (who were shocked to learn of Frank Thompson's true identity), Edmonds/Thompson initiated a campaign to validate her bold masquerade. To begin with, she worked to have the smirch of "desertion" removed from her record, which it was. But more significantly, she lobbied Congress to give her a pension, just like her fellow males. In 1884, a special act of Congress voted to give her a veteran's pension of twelve dollars a month. Now out in the open, the deception had been made complete by those it was meant to dupe. When she died in 1898, probably from a stroke, she had the satisfaction of knowing that she was the only woman to have been made a member of the Union Army's veteran organization, the Grand Army of the Republic. It would be impossible to conceive of a more fitting capstone to such an extraordinary life.

By the Book

Emma Edmondson didn't come to the idea of dressing like a man to realize her destiny entirely on her own. In fact, a traveling salesman had a lot to do with it. After being offered a place to stay one night at the Edmondson homestead, the peddler thanked his hosts by giving them a rare gift indeed—a book. It was a novel entitled *Fanny Campbell, the Female Pirate Captain*, in which a woman rescues her beloved by going to sea and disguising herself as a pirate captain. When Emma decided to flee her home and join the other gender, she no doubt had Fanny Campbell's adventures in mind.

THE SHOOTIST

When Emma Edmonds began her campaign to repeal her deserter status and get a pension, she needed to secure the testimony of old comrades-in-arms, many of whom had no idea that Frank Thompson had in fact been a woman. First on her list was an old tentmate, Damon Stewart, who was stunned by the revelation but more than happy to help. Though his account of the war years was flattering with respect to Frank's military service, it did mention in passing that Thompson hadn't been very handy at all with firearms—a point that Emma hotly disputed, as she had always considered herself quite a shot.

Though we may never know for sure how good her marksmanship was, a story from Emma's years before the Civil War certainly merits consideration. Feeling lonesome for home while out selling books, she once returned to Magaguadavic to see her beloved brother Thomas, who suffered from epilepsy. Concealing her visit from her despotic father, Emma savored her time with loved ones and prepared to leave. Before going, however, she went hunting and managed to drop six partridges with little effort—certainly not the work of an amateur.

As for the birds themselves, Emma gave them to Thomas to take back home after she departed. He then had to explain how he shot six partridges to his cynical father, who didn't think his son was capable of such a feat.

LEARNING TO REID

Emma may have grown to womanhood with resentment toward men. But she seems to have gradually gotten over it and long before she married Linus Seelye. While on the road as a subscription bookseller, she admitted to having actually courted women to make her character all the more convincing. During the war, she formed a close friendship with Jerome Robbins, a fellow recruit from Michigan who shared Emma's pious disdain for swearing, drinking, and gambling. In fact, their bond grew to the point that Emma felt secure enough to divulge her true identity to Robbins, who kept her secret safe. Despite this, and a likely attraction on the part of Emma for her friend, there was no romance between the two (Robbins was infatuated with a sweetheart back home).

James Reid, however, was another matter. A handsome Scottish lieutenant in the Seventy-Ninth New York Highlanders, Reid became the object of Emma's affections—and it seems that the feeling was mutual. They were careful to keep their romantic liaisons a secret, and not just because Emma was supposed to be a fella: Lieutenant Reid happened to be married. In any event, their efforts at remaining discreet failed. Stories that Reid was sleeping with the mail carrier, who was in fact a mail carrierette, hit the rumor circuit just as Reid was discharged to return to his ailing wife in Scotland. Very shortly afterward, an ailing Frank Thompson went AWOL. Hmmm.

13 HARRIET TUBMAN

ca. 1822–March 10, 1913

HIGHEST RANK:
Union Nurse, Spy, and Guerrilla

ASTROLOGICAL SIGN:
Unknown

NICKNAME:
Moses

WORDS TO REMEMBER:
"I had reasoned this out in my mind; there was one of two things I had a right to, liberty or death; if I could not have one, I would have the other."

Though known by name to virtually every American from grade school onward, Harriet Tubman has faded into the shadows of Civil War history and lore, obscured by the feats of generals, politicians, and writers. But she deserves a place of prominence in the American narrative as a woman of incredible courage and resourcefulness—and as a person whose triumphs and tragedies are emblematic of her tortured times.

Born to Ben Ross and Harriet "Rit" Green, two slaves living on Maryland's eastern shore, Araminta, as Tubman was originally christened, grew up in a world in which illiteracy was fiercely enforced by white masters. She would never learn to read or write, though she ultimately dictated much of her life for posterity. From a very young age, she was hired out to other whites in the area for temporary periods—a way for Tubman's master, Edward Brodess, to squeeze as much profit as possible out of his growing slave stock. The effect was terrifying, not only because the girl was separated from her parents and siblings for long stretches of time, but also because she had no idea how kind or sadistic each new master might be. On one notorious occasion, Tubman—repeatedly scourged by an impatient mistress until her neck and shoulders were permanently scarred—fled, hiding in a pigpen for days until fighting the sow for food scraps proved too exhausting. She then slunk back to receive her beating. With mistresses like these,

Tubman learned to hate household duties; she requested work as a laborer. The outdoors suited her, and in time she developed physicality and stamina that would serve her well in freer times to come.

But she would have to seize that freedom herself. After marrying a free black man named John Tubman in 1844, Araminta managed to save enough money to hire a lawyer. Many slaves were manumitted, or freed, by contracts that were drawn up as rewards for years of loyal service, and Tubman was interested in discovering whether such an arrangement had been made at any time in her family's past. The lawyer's findings were somewhat shocking: Apparently, Edward Brodess had concealed the fact that Tubman's mother was to be granted her freedom at age forty-five, which she had reached years prior. Moreover, all the children born to her after that date—i.e., the last of Araminta's siblings—were to be considered free. Brodess was ignoring the contractual obligations that had been handed down to him from his mother's side of the family.

A childhood injury left Harriet Tubman prone to vivid dreams and hallucinations for the rest of her life. Among the most common was a recurring dream in which she flew above the countryside.

This was awful news for a young slave woman whose legal options were essentially nil. But it was the death of Edward Brodess that inspired Tubman to act. Saddled with debt, the widow Brodess was forced to sell some of her slaves, a fate dreaded by people in bondage who relied on family ties to sustain them—and Tubman feared she might be included (a similar fate had already befallen her sisters). With nothing more to lose, an emboldened Tubman fled north to Philadelphia, leaving her captivity, family, and husband behind.

It was no easy task. Eastern Maryland was well known to those who operated the Underground Railroad, the clandestine network that strove to get black fugitives to safety in the North and in Canada. Accordingly, it was also patrolled by those keen on shutting down the flow of runaway slaves up to Philadelphia and beyond. Finding her way through such dangerous country required remarkable stealth, determination, intelligence, and luck—she had made contact with the Railroad shortly after making her escape. But her most outstanding trait was an intrepid willingness to go back—again and again, on missions of liberation that were extremely perilous and that would make her a legend in her own time. Adopting her mother's name after reaching freedom, she was now calling herself Harriet. But many others would soon be calling her "Moses," for delivering them to the promised land.

The risks being what they were, Tubman had no desire to bolt recklessly into slave country, advertise for willing fugitives, and bolt back again. The fact is that these were missions of patience, intricacy, and subterfuge, employing Underground Railroad tactics that remain shrouded in mystery to this day. Local terrain needed to be scouted, word had to be spread (without alerting the wrong folks), and contacts had to be made—a tricky business indeed when virtually every message had to be carried by word of mouth through an illiterate community. Tubman acted as part of the Underground Railroad, whose leaders and "stationmasters" she grew to know well. It was a world of closely guarded codes and late-night rendezvous, of duplicity, daring, stamina, and tension. And Tubman was its greatest "conductor." By 1860, she had made thirteen trips south and rescued perhaps as many as three hundred fugitives from slavery, including her parents and four brothers.

Secrecy was the key. Tubman carried a pistol, and not just for self-defense: Should one of her "passengers" get cold feet, killing them would prevent exposure of the network. Such confidentiality, combined with Tubman's feverish spirituality and self-image as a humble instrument of God, contributed to her anonymity. Aside from the rumors of a "woman called Moses," Harriet's precise identity remained elusive, both to those who hoped for her succor and those who put a price on her head. (Bounties from various incensed parties amounted at one time to an estimated $40,000.)

In abolitionist circles, by contrast, she was a celebrity. When John Brown arrived at her home in St. Catharines, Ontario, in 1858, it was like paying homage to a heroine. "General Tubman," as he insisted on calling her, agreed to drum up money for Brown's planned invasion of the South. The two made quite an impression on each other: Tubman believed in the fiery partisan wholeheartedly and was deeply crushed by his abject failure and execution the following year. Her next extraordinary effort on behalf of freedom, however, was both more successful and more direct—in fact, it would mark the first time that Tubman intervened openly on behalf of a fugitive without concern for her identity.

Since the passage of the Fugitive Slave Act of 1850, slaves caught on the lam in free states were no longer safe. Indeed, authorities in the North were required by law to hold them until the "owning" parties—or agents working on their behalf—arrived to reclaim the absconded property. This resulted in open clashes throughout the North between police bound to take runaways into custody and abolitionists willing to go to extraordinary lengths to thwart the effort. One clash happened in Troy, New York, on April 27, 1860—the day Harriet happened to be passing through on a visit to her cousin John Hooper.

Charles Nalle, a former slave who had been on the run for a year and a half, was arrested that day by a hireling sent from Virginia. A crowd, mostly black, gathered outside the United States commissioner's office in Troy, where Nalle was being held. After disguising herself to look, as one local paper reported, like a "somewhat antiquated colored woman" (she was around thirty-eight at the time), Tubman surreptitiously gained access to the building. The authorities soon decided to move the prisoner across town to the judge's office, producing an opportunity that Tubman wasn't going to pass up. As Nalle and his escorts descended the stairs to the street, a certain "antiquated colored woman" sprang into action and attacked the sheriff and his deputies in an attempt to free their charge. Her attacks were savage—punching, choking—and the officers gave as good as they got, producing a frenzied melee that eventually spilled into the street, where it evolved into a general engagement. Spurred and inspired by this wiry powerhouse of a woman (who must be, it quickly began to circulate, Harriet Tubman), the crowd got seriously physical with the officers. A running gun-and-knife fight ensued, rolling like a storm toward the Hudson River and beyond to West Troy, where rescuers hoped Nalle would be safe.

He wasn't—not yet. Seized by authorities there, he was spirited to the chambers of Judge Stewart, then released when the enraged mob of abolitionists essentially bashed their way into the room through a fierce hackfest at close quarters. Tubman, her clothes in scarlet tatters, allegedly carried Nalle—himself a bloody mess—over her shoulder "like a bag o' meal" amidst the snap of angry bullets. He was whisked into the countryside, where he lived like a fugitive until local antislavery elements bought his freedom.

Violent and sensational, the Charles Nalle incident marked Tubman's transformation, in the wake of the John Brown fiasco, to a more candid relationship with the struggle against slavery. The outbreak of civil war would change it further. She didn't approve of Lincoln, whose tepid stance on slavery infuriated her. But by 1862, she had joined the Federal forces as a nurse and cook, finding herself in the wealthy, rebellious lowlands of the South Carolina coast. Her skills as a scout and spy, however, were not lost on her superiors—particularly Colonel James Montgomery, a fellow ardent abolitionist who had been with John Brown in Kansas during the bad old days. In time she was infiltrating the area, acquiring intelligence on terrain, troops, slave populations, and more. This led directly to the Combahee River raid of June 1863, Harriet's greatest wartime achievement—and one of the very first examples in American history of a woman leading a military operation. Like a scalpel cutting into the heart of Carolina plantation country, Tubman's band of freed black soldiers made their way up the Combahee River, avoiding the "torpedoes" (floating mines) that Moses herself had assiduously reconnoitered prior to the mission. They landed with impunity wherever they wished, burning property, causing mayhem, and gathering eager slaves. Brushing aside desultory Confederate resistance, the mission played on the deepest of Deep South fears as surely as a maestro plays his violin: black soldiers led by a black woman burning white property in the heart of secession. It was an extraordinary triumph.

At war's end she was tending to wounded soldiers in Virginia. In New Jersey, on her way home to Auburn, New York, she was rewarded for her wartime services by being forced to give up her seat on the train by a bigoted conductor who couldn't imagine a black woman with a soldier's pass. True to form, she did her best to kick his ignorant ass before he and a few other half-wits overpowered her. She was compelled to spend the rest of her "homecoming" journey in the baggage car.

Nevertheless, the final half-century of Tubman's life seemed more like an attempt to make peace. John Tubman, her first husband who wished to remain behind when she fled slavery in Maryland, had long since moved on. In 1869, Harriet took a new husband, Nelson Davis. For more than ten years she had been living in Auburn on land purchased from William Seward, a good friend and secretary of state during the Lincoln administration. In addition to becoming a famous suffragist, she purchased a large piece of land next to her own in 1896 for the construction of a hospital for aged and indigent African Americans—a proud achievement whose operation eventually passed to a local church. By the time of her death in 1913, she had become a rare bird indeed: an African American who had won her own freedom, secured the adoration of abolitionists, become indispensable to the military, and helped pave the way for women in a new century. How many people could say that?

VISIONARY

Araminta was twelve or thirteen when she was thumped with the defining tragedy of her life. While attempting to help a fellow slave escape, she was struck in the head by an errant metal weight that had been hurled by an irate overseer with a wild arm. The result was disastrous. She nearly died and was hampered with noticeable cognitive issues for the rest of her life. In the years to come, many who knew her reported witnessing Tubman's habit of nodding off to sleep in the middle of an exchange, only to wake minutes later and resume the thread of conversation as if nothing had happened. She also experienced vivid fantasies, even while awake, that evoked images of religious renewal and liberation. Her dreams of flight above the countryside were graphic and indelible; she even felt warned of her association with John Brown through a dream involving a snake that turned into a man with an especially long beard. Much has since been diagnosed to offer a scientific explanation of her behavior, from narcolepsy and cataplexy to hypnagogic hallucinations and even temporal lobe epilepsy. But whatever its source or nature, it was real to Harriet.

Hard-Bitten

Harriet Tubman was one remarkably tough person. Any doubts about that will be dispelled by the story in which she found herself escorting a party of fugitives through the Maryland wilderness while experiencing an awful pain in her mouth, indicating tooth decay that had gone too far. Unwilling to keep going with so much agony, Harriet wandered off and knocked the rotting teeth out of her mouth with the butt of her pistol. The mission carried on as if nothing had happened.

LATE BLOOMER

The Combahee River raid in 1863 was one of the most famous events in Harriet Tubman's long, extraordinary life—a military success that secured the liberation of more than seven hundred slaves. Moreover, Tubman stumbled—literally—across a bit of warfare fashion wisdom that had escaped her until then. In the course of rescuing a slave mother with her children, Tubman's skirts got trampled and nearly tripped her up. The experience was unnerving enough for Harriet to write abolitionist friends in Boston, requesting (only half in jest) that they send her a pair of bloomers for the work that had yet to be done in South Carolina.

MOSES AND MARGARET

As far as we know, Harriet Tubman never bore any children of her own. She did, however, "adopt" a fellow Marylander named Margaret, a light-skinned girl of African descent. But Margaret was not a slave who'd been rescued. It seems likely (though a great deal of mystery surrounds the incident) that she was a free black girl living in relatively decent circumstances, and Tubman essentially kidnapped her during one of her trips south as if the little eight-year-old were unclaimed goods. As author Catherine Clinton recounts in *Harriet Tubman: The Road to Freedom*, Margaret is often referred to in reminiscences by friends and family as a niece of Tubman's, but this seems unlikely. Clinton even explores the remote possibility that Margaret was Tubman's biological child, a tantalizing notion that will probably never be proven one way or another.

THAT'S JUST PLAIN MEAN

Saddled with financial difficulties in the years after the war, Tubman was eager to entertain any possibility of acquiring a windfall to help her juggle her own debts with the burden of all the charity cases she had taken on. Unfortunately, in 1873, her vulnerability played right into the hands of a couple of con men. Their claim was straightforward: For $2,000 in paper money, they would hand over $2,000 in gold coin, a Confederate stash supposedly dug up in the chaotic final days of the war. The coins, they were quick to point out, belonged to the government, and so they were eager to unload such a burdensome treasure that could get them in hot water. It sounded like the opportunity of a lifetime. Unfortunately, when Tubman showed up with the money (loaned by a friend) on the night the exchange was to take place, the men showed up with chloroform—with which they proceeded to render her unconscious before stealing her cash and leaving her, bound and gagged, to be discovered by friends like a rabbit trussed for the pot. The incident, which sold a lot of papers, was a cruel reminder not only of Tubman's awkward situation, but also of her apparent financial naïveté—a bizarre exception to her otherwise canny survival instincts.

THE CONFEDERACY

14

JEFFERSON
DAVIS

June 3, 1807/1808–
December 6, 1889

HIGHEST RANK:
President of the Confederate
States of America

ASTROLOGICAL SIGN:
Gemini

NICKNAMES:
Sphinx of the Confederacy,
Banny (used by his wife, Varina)

WORDS TO REMEMBER:
"Never joke with a child or a
savage. They will not understand, and you will only destroy
their confidence in you."

anted: Chief Executive

*Exciting temporary position with excel-
lent chance for long-term employment!*

*Brand new, ambitious confederation is
looking for a bold visionary to fill the job
of president. Must be willing to delegate
authority, balance the need for assertive
executive power in a national crisis with
the firm injunction against sacrificing
states' rights, cooperate with an
entrenched and protective oligarchy,
develop new international relationships
and alliances from scratch, prepare to
match the challenge of competitors, industrialize a vast agrarian civilization virtually overnight without trespassing on regional autonomies (see "states' rights"*

When serving as Secretary of War for the United States in 1853,
Jefferson Davis imported camels for American soldiers in the
southwest. The experiment was not successful.

*earlier in advert.), and work flexible hours. Applicants should be able to show 10+
years military and/or legislative experience, infinite patience, proof that they are at
least 35 years of age, otherworldly self-sacrifice, statesmanlike deportment, and
ability to work with others. Some travel req'd. Slaveholder a plus. Position must*

be filled soon, as war is imminent—interested parties are urged to apply now. Base pay: $25,000*

*To be issued in a beautiful new currency whose dies have yet to be created.

OK, so this ad never appeared in a secessionist newspaper during those tension-filled days of early 1861. But if it had, Jefferson Davis would certainly not have applied. He knew how insanely difficult the job would be and harbored no ambition for political glory beyond that which he had already achieved. Nevertheless, the job was soon his—foisted upon him by a minority of his fellow Southerners and accepted by him in accordance with a blind and very deep sense of duty.

He knew that he wasn't the right man for the job. And in time everyone else knew it, too.

Not that his credentials weren't impressive. Indeed, he was one of the most respected public figures in America. Born in Kentucky, his early youth was spent moving with his family to Louisiana and then Wilkinson County, Mississippi. He acquired a good education at a series of institutions: St. Thomas College in Kentucky, Jefferson College and Wilkinson Academy in Mississippi, and back in Kentucky at Transylvania University. Though a natural young scholar in some ways, he once chafed at the idea of returning to school, whereupon his father sent him into the fields. There the heat and "implied equality with the other cotton-pickers" destroyed any remaining doubts about finishing his education. His father, Samuel, died in 1824, placing Jefferson under the nominal direction of his brother Joseph, a prominent lawyer in Mississippi. With his urging and influence, Jefferson—though not initially fond of the idea—got into West Point the very year of his father's death.

He got off to a good start at the academy, but things began going bonkers really fast. Combining ego, self-doubt, and a need to prove himself that often drew the wrong sort of attention, Davis became a hellion. That he graduated at all is quite remarkable, but graduate he did and commenced a brief career in the infantry. From 1829 through 1835, the young officer felt himself moldering in a series of frontier postings that fostered in him a growing distaste for the army life. His sole bit of excitement came in 1832 at the conclusion of the Black Hawk War, when Davis was charged with apprehending and escorting the great chief Black Hawk himself to St. Louis. He left the officer corps ignominiously three years later amidst a court-martial for insubordinate conduct. Though acquitted, a prideful Davis tendered his resignation.

By then he had developed a new occupation: loving Sarah Knox Taylor, the daughter of one Zachary Taylor, who would one day become the hero of Buena Vista and president of the United States. While still in uniform and under Colonel Taylor's command at Fort Crawford, Davis had fallen hard for "Knoxie," and she for him. Unfortunately, the colonel wanted something better for his daughter than he had been able to give her mother, and he vowed not to let her marry an officer. His rejection of Davis as a suitor for Knoxie only increased the young stallion's ardor, fostering a heightened emotional tension at the outpost that nearly exploded into a duel between Davis and Taylor. Cooler heads prevailed, however, and Taylor ultimately allowed that the two could marry in two years' time if they were still so inclined.

They were, and they did. Then, less than three months after marrying the woman of his dreams who had once seemed beyond reach, Davis had the evil fate of watching her die from malaria or yellow fever. He had been struck by the sickness as well, but had recovered a widower. Knoxie was just twenty-one years old.

His brother Joseph whisked him off to Cuba to recuperate and grieve, but Davis had turned a corner. After returning to the United States, he was instructed by his brother in the art and science of running a plantation that Jefferson christened Brierfield, a life that seemed as much refuge as livelihood. Demolished by Sarah's death and convinced of his own culpability in it (he had persuaded her to move to Mississippi in the midst of fever season), he aged visibly. Even in his teens, Davis was often described as "taciturn," "dignified," almost shackled with a formality beyond his years—characteristics that stood in striking contrast to his drunken hooliganism at the Point. But the last vestiges of youthful rebellion were banished in this new settled adulthood at Brierfield, where he indulged a love of details—whether in agriculture, bookkeeping, or architecture—and read up on local politics as a good yeoman planter should. And while he developed sharply delineated views on the important issues of the day, it wasn't until 1844 that he found an outlet for them as an elector from Mississippi for the presidential election. By that time he had met Varina Howell, an exceptional woman who was half his age and just as willful. They were married the following year.

His public career blossomed. He soon became a United States congressman from Mississippi and acquired a reputation for speaking, which junior representatives didn't usually do. And one of the bills he voted for was the one that presented Mexico with a declaration of war in 1846. Interestingly, it was a ballot that helped bring an end to his first successful adventure into politics. For he was soon chosen by his electorate to don a uniform and lead the First Mississippi Rifles, which he did in Mexico with conspicuous ability and élan. A capable combat officer, he was seriously wounded at the Battle of Buena Vista and was offered the rank of brigadier general. He turned it down, however, for reasons that exposed a strict adherence to states' rights that would one day compel him to break with the Union: Coming as it did from the president himself, the offer represented an interference by federal authority into state affairs (Davis had fought as a colonel of Mississippi militia, not as a regular officer in charge of national troops). He made a return to political life, aided immensely by his war exploits, and found himself in the United States Senate. Appointed secretary of war in the Franklin Pierce administration, he showed a capacity for hard work and attention to detail that awed and irritated his fellows in government by turns. After Pierce's single term, Davis was sent back to the Senate.

It was in that venue, on January 21, 1861, that Jefferson Davis said his farewells to the country against which he would soon lead a bloody four-year struggle. The address embodied all that he had become since scaling the heights of national power. Influenced by such states' rights advocates as the great John C. Calhoun, whom he viewed as a beloved mentor, Davis had consistently and fervently fought on behalf of the extension and protection of slavery and against the growing influence of free states on the federal government. Though a devout nationalist, his attachments to Mississippi and increasing antagonism toward what he perceived as a threat to Southern rights and, therefore, to the "balance of power" between the sections of the country compelled him to lend his eloquence in the Senate to the chorus of those who threatened secession in the years leading up to 1860. The speech itself reflected the exhaustion he felt at having failed in attempts at peaceful rapprochement and was filled with sorrow at the break he was making and the friendships he was severing. He had known for a week and a half about Mississippi's decision to secede and had put his hopes to avert a severing of the Union behind him. Rising from his sickbed against his doctor's recommendations (he was suffering at the time from a debilitating attack of neuralgia), he spoke under the duress of an awful head pain. After bidding "a final adieu," he strode out of the Senate chamber to emotional applause—from both sides—that nearly brought the roof down.

It was an American moment: A confluence of political tragedy and personal pathos that focused the nation's attention, North and South, on the unfolding secessionist drama that had acquired a dreadful momentum all its own. Not surprisingly, Davis's life would assume a momentum all its own, as well.

Nobody doubted that he was going to play a role in the embryonic Confederate States of America. Many began consulting him immediately on military matters, and Davis contented himself with the idea of donning a general's uniform. Indeed, without any real effort on his part, he was made a major general of the Army of Mississippi, and with characteristic energy and dourness, he began bugging anyone who would listen about the need for arms—lots of arms. Repeatedly told that he was being a trifle alarmist, Davis—like William Tecumseh Sherman, ironically—began to worry that everyone was underestimating the scale of the nightmare that awaited them all.

He was soon made president, giving him a lot more to worry about. Chosen as a compromise between the extremist fire-eaters and the border-state fence-sitters who had yet to back secession, Davis took the news like an accused felon takes a guilty verdict. His ashen-faced dread notwithstanding, there were plenty of things that recommended him to the job: He had been one of the nation's most effective secretaries of war; he had shown himself to be a clear-thinking, articulate defender of Southern liberties; he was a war hero and a patrician of national stature; and he had the ability to effortlessly put people on notice as soon as he strode into a room, as if everybody knew he was about to say something gravely important (not actually necessary in a chief executive, but it helps).

Unfortunately, there was one really important thing that he wasn't: a truly inspiring leader. His opposite in Washington wasn't either, but Lincoln soon became one and much more. Jefferson Davis, by contrast, seemed with time to become more of the things that get in the way of effective leadership, especially in wartime. Despite his years of debating experience in the Senate, he was incapable of compromise. People who didn't see his side of an argument after being carefully instructed in its merits were written off, almost as if they had dealt him a deeply personal blow. He was easily slighted, the result of a prickly pride that had always been there and that shaped every conflict, whether a disagreement with Varina over what to have for dinner or an argument over grand strategy with his generals. "I have an infirmity of which I am ashamed," he admitted. "When I am aroused in a matter, I lose control of my feeling and become personal." As a result, he played favorites, and he played them hard. He made a virtual habit out of latching on to subordinates because of personal loyalty rather than ability. He was aloof, unapproachable, "an icicle" who found it hard to become a man of the people or to exhort them to the sacrifices that confronted them. And he was by training more a bureaucrat than a chief, a fact that showed itself in Davis's relentless preoccupation with minutiae at the expense of the big picture for which he was ultimately responsible.

Overall military strategy for the Confederacy was of primary importance: Should the South concentrate its forces to deliver several overwhelming blows, or should they be dispersed along its (extremely lengthy) borders to meet whatever challenge the North throws down? Though attracted to the former by temperament, the new president deferred mostly to the latter on account of politics: Governors complained about being left unprotected in a bitchfest that Davis would have been foolish to ignore. Nevertheless, provisions were made to allow for some concerted offensives, resulting in a hybrid strategy whose wisdom has been the subject of considerable debate ever since. Such compromises exposed the inherent conundrum of the Confederacy: How on earth does a nation based on states' rights—i.e., the dispersal of political power—manage to triumph over a crisis that by its very nature requires the centralization of power to defeat? For the South to win, it was going to have to put on hold those very principles for which it had broken away from the Union in the first place.

To his credit, President Davis understood this. Others in power did not. So when his administration pushed through such scandalous measures as conscription (the first draft in American history), national taxation, and the commandeering of food, he drew splenetic criticism for being tyrannical, abusive—in fact, just like that power-grabbing bastard Lincoln! Whatever his hypocrisy, the bottom line is that, without Davis's willingness to embrace war measures that looked conspicuously like a rejection of Confederate dogma, the South would've been defeated much sooner.

In other matters, Davis performed less impressively. He treated his war secretaries like office clerks, lost countless hours in micromanagement, bickered with subordinates and generals needlessly, and made himself all but invulnerable to opposing points of view. Nothing illustrates his weaknesses quite like the way he fumbled things with his principal generals. To be fair, his decision to keep Robert E. Lee in charge of what would become the Army of Northern Virginia after Joseph Johnston's wounding was a stroke of brilliance. Lee ended up developing an understanding with his president that no other Southern general achieved, partly because Davis was bright enough to believe in him and give him a wide berth (as much, if not more, a credit to Lee's ingratiating manner as it is to Davis's vision). But in the west—the theater in which, as many historians argue, the war was truly won and lost—Davis simply blew it. P. G. T. Beauregard, the "little Creole" who opened fire on Fort Sumter and who was one of the South's best assets, was discarded like old fruit and banished to unimportant theaters, simply because the president didn't like him.

Braxton Bragg, by contrast, whose temperament and abilities were called into question by all of his principal officers, was allowed to remain in command long after he should've been kicked out, simply because Davis liked him and found it difficult to process awful opinions about him. Sure, Lincoln made some pretty lousy command choices himself. But Davis had better material to work with initially and simply wasted it.

Measuring Davis's role in the defeat of his infant nation will forever remain a subject of debate. It is even worth considering whether that nation had any chance of victory at all. By contrast, there is no doubt whatsoever about Davis's feelings as the war effort stumbled into futility. The old stubbornness flared, and he even believed that a scorched Confederacy devoid of life would be preferable to surrender. As Richmond fell and Lee surrendered, Davis and his cabinet went on the lam like criminals in a doomed cause . . . which, come to think of it, they had become. He and his wife and escort were surrounded by cavalry on May 10, 1865. Davis was apprehended while attempting to escape with Varina's shawl over his shoulders to make him look like a commoner fetching water.

It would take time for the South to accept Jefferson Davis into the pantheon of Confederate demigods. The North was far more expeditious in its judgment. Taken into custody like a common criminal, he was imprisoned in Fortress Monroe—manacled, until public outcry forced a change. He was now a feeble man who had suffered much during the war, from neuralgia, to recurring malaria and rheumatism, to an eye infected with glaucoma and herpes, to an abscessed tooth. For a nation mourning catastrophic mortality and destruction, he had become the war criminal of choice—a political figure, devoid of a "noble" uniform, who had deferred to treason and dared to make it stick. In the wake of so many corpses, his folly seemed more like murder. And he was slated to answer for it.

But that never happened. Perennially postponed, his trial became associated with a war that most folks increasingly wanted to forget. Davis never forgot, however, as was evident in his magnum opus, *The Rise and Fall of the Confederate Government*, in which others were still held responsible for the

South's defeat. It never occurred to him to have his citizenship restored, and he died unrepentant in 1889, probably of pneumonia. "Be obedient and good citizens," he had urged his fellow Southerners. As for Davis: When his casket was closed, a silken stars and bars was draped over it.

END OF THE LINE

Jefferson Davis never knew the precise year of his birth. He once observed, "Having once supposed the year to have been 1807, I was subsequently corrected by being informed it was 1808, and have rested upon that point because it was just as good, and no better than another."

Another story about his birth involves the origin of his middle initial, "F." Pregnant with Jefferson when she was forty-six years old, his mother, Jane, allegedly decided with husband Samuel to name him "Finis," in the hope that he would be the last of their ten children. It worked.

GREAT EXPECTATIONS

Raising hell was hardly unknown to the average West Point cadet in the early nineteenth century. But Jefferson Davis raised more than his fair share. It started early with a jaunt to Benny Havens's, a local tavern that offered food and drink to young cadets eager to supplement their horrid academy diet—a trip that was strictly forbidden. He was arrested and convicted of his crime, though he was granted a pardon.

A year later he somehow found himself there again. In the process of fleeing the establishment upon discovering the approach of a West Point instructor, he crashed some sixty feet down a wooded precipice, incurring wounds that landed him in the academy hospital for four months. A real trouper, he recovered in time for Christmas Eve 1826, when he and a friend procured the requisite drinking supplies to fuel an evening's insanity. The result was the notorious "Eggnog Riot," a gloriously inebriated breakdown of discipline that climaxed with the arrest and confinement of twenty-three cadets. Though most of them were dismissed entirely from the Point, Davis managed to escape that fate on account of testimony that placed him in his room before most of the damage had begun.

Just for kicks, on the verge of graduation, he was arrested for not being in his quarters after taps. Not surprisingly, he graduated in the bottom fourth of his class in conduct.

HUMPIN' IT

During his earlier Senate career, while serving on the Committee on Military Affairs, Jefferson Davis became convinced that camels would make an ideal mount and beast of burden for soldiers stationed in America's vast, arid Southwest. Others had been toying with the notion for a few years, but Davis was the first public servant to formally bring it to the government's attention. The idea was essentially laughed at. But in 1853, he found himself in a situation to act on the idea as secretary of war. Two years later, he arranged for the importation of fifty-four camels from Turkey and Egypt, and personally translated a French manual on handling the animals. Though they met all of the secretary's expectations and proved perfectly suited to the American desert, the camels proved anything but popular with soldiers, and the experiment ultimately died.

BYGONES AND SUCH

Born to the Davises in the midst of the Civil War, Varina Anne Davis— "Winnie"—was informally adopted in the postwar South as the "Daughter of the Confederacy." It was widely hoped that she would eventually wed someone appropriate to her status, such as a grandson of Stonewall Jackson or Robert E. Lee, and perpetuate a kind of "royal line" of Dixie. Needless to say, Jefferson Davis was taken aback when the man who came calling on Winnie introduced himself with a New York accent. Alfred Wilkinson was his name, and he had captured Winnie's heart during one of her trips to the North. While many diehards were scandalized, Davis apparently had had enough of grudges. In fact, he and Wilkinson grew to be fast friends. The young couple became engaged in 1889.

Sadly, Wilkinson lost his fortune a few years later, and the relationship fell apart. Winnie died a bachelorette at thirty-four.

IT'S NEVER TOO LATE

Jeff Davis never sought a pardon, because he never believed that he had done something to be pardoned for. His citizenship was restored, however—nearly ninety years after his death. On October 17, 1978, a joint resolution by Congress that was signed by President Jimmy Carter restored the old Rebel's citizenship, effective December 25, 1868. Davis probably rolled over in his grave.

15

VARINA HOWELL
DAVIS

May 7, 1826–October 16, 1906

HIGHEST RANK:

Confederate First Lady

ASTROLOGICAL SIGN:

Taurus

NICKNAME:

Queen Varina

WORDS TO REMEMBER:

"Would you believe it, he is refined and cultivated and yet he is a Democrat" (on Jefferson Davis).

Varina Howell Davis wasn't any happier at the prospect of her husband being president than he was. Jeff Davis was no politician, and she had no problem saying so. As for Varina herself, she felt unprepared for the role of a first lady, despite her years of experience in the drawing rooms of Washington; she would have a pretty hard time of it right along with Jefferson. Nevertheless, she was an extraordinary woman: whip smart, sophisticated, prepossessing, and loyal to her husband and his increasingly awful situation. The Confederates had only one first lady, and they could've done a lot worse than their Queen Varina.

When a hotheaded prison guard aimed his musket at Jefferson Davis (ignorant to the fact that he was challenging the president of the CSA), the level-headed Varina defused the situation by stepping in front of the gun.

By upbringing and temperament, she was better prepared than most to become a public woman. Varina grew up at the Briers, her parents' plantation in Natchez, Mississippi. Naturally bright, she devoured the excellent education given her by a tutor from New England and became quite a well-schooled, well-read young lady. Newspapers in particular drew her interest,

and it became common at the Briers to joke that young Varina knew more about the politics of the day than anyone else in the family.

And those politics were staunchly Whig, the party of choice for most of the area's landed aristocracy. One prominent exception was Joseph Davis, a close friend of Varina's father, and a Democrat. It is a testament to the closeness of the two households that Joseph was often referred to as "uncle" by Varina and her siblings. Joseph's younger brother Jefferson, however, was in self-imposed seclusion at his own estate, and remained something of a mystery. Varina was a grown-up, dark-haired beauty by the time she first set eyes on him; he had come to extend an invitation to his brother's house, and Varina's curiosity was piqued by the stern, older widower with the strange eyes and mellifluous voice. Curiosity in time grew into preoccupation, then courtship, and the two were married in February 1845.

The newspapers made a stir over the fact that Jeff Davis, a prominent Democrat on the verge of embarking upon a dedicated political career, had taken a Whig for a wife. And to be sure, the two did have their fair share of heated political arguments. But Varina's growing devotion to Jefferson led her to understand her role as ally in the struggles he faced. Her opinions would remain her own, but her politics, broadly defined, became more like her husband's. Washington beckoned.

If Jefferson's struggles were political, hers were quite a bit more personal. Almost from the beginning of their marriage, Varina found herself locked in a struggle for prominence in Davis's life with his older brother. Jefferson owed everything to Joseph: his land, his security, and his political prospects. He had grown up in the crook of Joseph's sheltering arm and had become accustomed to his assured, domineering presence. Varina, as tough and proud as she was literate and incisive, bristled at her brother-in-law's intrusions. The result was a not-so-subtle wresting match for Jefferson's soul, and it wasn't always pretty. Despite her intellectual maturity, Varina wasn't above acting out. During Jefferson's service in the Mexican War, her pining for his company literally laid her out physically, challenging him to forgo military honor (always a tricky thing) to visit her as she convalesced.

He acquired a sixty-day leave and made the trip, and she made a shaky recovery with him by her side. The sickness seemed born of stress from conflict with her brother-in-law, an issue that continued to fester. For his part, Joseph expressed his resentment at Varina by never giving his brother full ownership of Brierfield, the estate he had given Jefferson. The issue caused legal trouble years later.

These confrontations seemed to harden Varina for the life that was ideally suited to her. As a senator's wife, she blossomed in Washington, settling into capital society with an ease born of grace and confidence. At social occasions she compensated for her husband's officious rigidity with smiling wisecracks and bookish repartee. She became renowned as a natural organizer of events and an asset to Jefferson that went beyond gregariousness— Davis the politician depended on her insight and wisdom. They were a team.

Such a relationship could be as much a liability as an asset, as Varina and her husband discovered eventually. In the wake of secession and the choice to make Jefferson Davis president of an infant republic, the Confederacy got a seasoned drawing-room campaigner as first lady. She seemed a bit overwhelmed during the early days, when the new government was struggling toward self-realization in Montgomery, Alabama. After all, she was the first of her kind, just as much as her husband, and her earnest desire not to screw it up lay plainly in her forced expressions of confidence. But not long after relocating the capital to Richmond, Mrs. Davis came into her own, manifesting in greater relief all the qualities that had defined her and her link to Jefferson. To a society that prided itself on the quality of its cultured womanhood, Varina's educated polish was plain to see. She shined in public. Even her husband's critics were taken by her; indeed, Varina was much better at feigning goodwill than the president was and did him many a service by smoothing over rifts in the government. She shared his ambition, but none of his excruciating sensitivity—in fact, she may have been a better politician than he was.

And eventually everybody knew it. Though Jefferson had always shined as a legislator, his ability as an executive was anyone's guess. In time, that question was answered and not very flatteringly. Varina, on the other hand, had a facility with people that made her useful and dangerous. The women of Richmond felt it keenly and were acutely divided on their opinion of her. But the men were mostly won by her nature, which could shift from motherly to seductive to literary to sanguinary in a heartbeat. She was an intellectual with a mean streak, a ready tongue, and an ability to manipulate. But whatever she did, it was always with the president's welfare in mind, for she loved him unconditionally.

In such an environment, fed by wartime drama and tension, arose the court of Queen Varina. Presiding over it along with the matriarch herself was Mary Chesnut, the great diarist and a close friend. They and their circle created a mild perversion of Southern refinement: an environment of keenly intellectual snappishness, whose polite melees made and dashed Rebel fortunes, presenting an effete twist on the destructive epic unfolding around them. The first lady's direct impact on Jefferson Davis's decisions was always subtle; but everybody seemed to know that she spared no effort in the attempt to influence. In fact, the president was deaf to the advice of everybody. But the knowledge that a woman had even mild sway over decisions—especially military ones—caused no shortage of agita. The fact was that, whatever remarkable processes fueled Varina's mind, her primary impulse was always loyalty: she despised those who didn't adore Davis.

That she was so eloquent and crafty made her a subject of hostile scrutiny. Varina was much shrewder in her judgments of those who surrounded her husband than he was, but just as careless in leaking her opinions. The generals under her husband's command came to understand how she felt about them: Joseph Johnston was despised, Beauregard was useless, Lee was worthy of respect, etc. This stuff sowed the sensation of intrigue where none was welcome. And maybe it wouldn't have made a difference, but for the fact that Varina was open-minded in her associations. Her enduring friendship with Margaret Sumner McLean, a Union sympathizer and daughter of a Northern officer, for instance, did nothing to warm her to people who were looking for ammunition against her and her husband. Varina openly maintained her Northern associations, damn the consequences. Other, perhaps more inevitable, factors made things worse. Though her wardrobe was famously plain, she continued to set a relatively decent table when everyone else in town was scrounging for the simplest of amenities. She got appointments for friends and family that they didn't always merit. And she did not restrain herself from sarcasm—Varina's merciless sneers to friends and foes alike were often the subject of Richmond gossip.

In the final year of the war, as hope of victory faded, Varina became the realist of the relationship—Jefferson couldn't imagine absolute defeat, but his wife wasn't nearly as stubborn and began to see the writing on the wall. As the Confederacy fell apart around them, she was burdened with standing by Jefferson in a cause whose hopelessness was apparent to everyone except him.

She probably would've welcomed a swifter end. Instead, when the fall of Richmond seemed imminent, the president sent her packing after giving her a lesson in loading and shooting a pistol he insisted on giving her. She headed south as he and his cabinet, in a separate party, did the same. The two exchanged frantic letters on the run in an attempt to meet up as the final moments of the war played out. When they finally reunited in Georgia, it was just in time to get nabbed by Federal cavalry.

In addition to all the extreme physical discomforts and moments of terror, the trip had been a humiliating one. Queen Varina had been able to shield herself from opponents while ensconced in her Richmond home. But now, as a refugee on the run, she was sometimes confronted with hostility by those whose feelings of propriety had fallen with the cause. Mocked openly by many who encountered her on the road, she was taken in by stalwarts who risked life and limb by doing so. Caring for her family had become her sole purpose in life.

Final surrender ended one kind of suffering and began another. Living in postwar Savannah, Varina read newspaper stories about Jefferson's imprisonment at Fortress Monroe and seethed. Upon hearing that he'd been shackled, she fell into hysterics, barely controlled by a liberal regimen of opiates. She sent her children to exile in Canada and began one of the most important efforts of her life: a letter campaign to ease her beloved husband's suffering. Though the couple was granted the right to correspond by letter (all of Jefferson's were screened by the attorney general), it wasn't until the spring of 1866 that she was given permission to visit him in Fortress Monroe, and then only because he appeared to be dying. She soon secured his release from a government that had long since stopped caring about Davis's capacity for mischief, saving him from a grisly wasting death that no doubt awaited him in his incarceration.

Varina cared for him until his death in 1889, though the two often lived apart. At the funeral she stood like a quavering symbol of dreams long past, drawing a flood of tears from soldered gray warriors who had tried in vain to put the past behind them. In a strange sort of way she was now free. She had been railed by her detractors during the war for her Northern connections; now she would set tongues to wagging yet again by moving to New York City.

The reasons for the move were straightforward enough. Her doctors recommended a cooler climate in which to live, far from the malarial heat of Mississippi. And Varina's finances were dismal in the wake of Jefferson's death; by relocating to the publishing capital of North America, she could foster her daughter Winnie's literary aspirations and perhaps earn a living herself. There, like an eccentric museum piece, she held court once again, the wizened and regal symbol of a dead cause that everyone wanted to remember as noble and romantic. She wrote articles, made appearances at all the right occasions, and became an unlikely fixture in the city's publishing elite. It was the return of Queen Varina—in the most ironic of venues.

She had changed her name to Mrs. V. Jefferson Davis, galvanizing the association with history that gave her a place and an income. Her twilight years were never free of financial worry, but they were at least worthy of the witty belle from Natchez who had become a living curiosity. In October 1906, as she lay on her deathbed, Varina rasped to her attending daughter, "My darling child, I am going to die this time but I'll try to be brave about it. Don't you wear black. It is bad for your health and will depress your husband."

New York City mourned her passing, but Dixie got her back in the end. Given a military funeral, she was buried in Richmond's Hollywood Cemetery. A local paper called her "one of the last living mementoes of the Confederate Government, one of the last of all to die."

BAPTISM OF FIRE

Varina was only eight years old when she was put rather dramatically in harm's way, giving her a taste of the tumultuous future that awaited her. When the house in which her family was staying caught fire, little Varina found herself without much help—the adults were off on a social occasion, and the young servant placed in charge took off for help as soon as she saw the flames. Varina, showing remarkable composure for a tyke, gathered up her siblings—one of whom was just an infant—and herded them out of harm's way. The structure burned to the ground, but not a single life was lost, thanks to the little eight-year-old who'd found her grace under pressure.

Grave Circumstances

Jefferson Davis had been deeply in love with Sarah Knox Taylor, his first wife who died under tragic circumstances, and Varina knew it. Davis's first love seemed to be his most passionate. Whatever the truth, Varina was kind to Knoxie in her memoirs and with regard to the children, who were taught to remember their father's first spouse fondly.

That said, Varina was put through what can justly be called an unfair trial almost as soon as she became Mrs. Jefferson Davis. On their honeymoon, the newlyweds made a stop at the home of Jefferson's sister—the very place where Sarah Taylor had died. Varina accompanied her new husband to his first wife's gravesite to lay flowers upon it. Though some speculation remains as to Varina's true feelings on the subject, it seems that she had given in to Jefferson's impulse to venerate one wife on his honeymoon with the other—not exactly a serenade by moonlight, to say the least.

DINNER THEATER

As first lady of the Confederate States, Varina Davis had a habit of making remarks and gaffes that many thought offensive. It's as if she simply didn't feel the same social restraints as others. One of the most celebrated examples of her impropriety involved the wife of Bradley Johnson, a Marylander who had taken the trouble to raise and organize a regiment of soldiers from his native state for the Confederacy. While dining with the Davises one night, Mrs. Johnson recounted the nasty pitfalls involved in procuring the proper clothing for such a unit. According to her, the seamstresses enlisted to create the soldiers' garments had made a disastrous miscalculation that required the procurement of more material to do the whole process over again: the men's underwear had been stupidly, totally botched. As they listened to Mrs. Johnson's tale of sartorial woe, the diners dutifully responded with expressions of grief—all except the first lady, who shamelessly laughed her head off.

FIREWALL

Varina did her best, day after day, to buttress her husband's waning support. But on one occasion she did much more than just save his reputation—she saved his life. In November 1863, when returning to Richmond one night after a visit to Drewry's Bluff, President Davis and his wife were challenged by a guard in front of Libby Prison. When Davis responded that he was Jefferson Davis, the tense young man called him a liar. Incensed, the president raised his cane in a threatening motion, and the guard responded by leveling his musket. It seems entirely possible that the executive branch of the Rebel government could've been beheaded there and then, but for the alacrity of the first lady. She literally interposed herself between the cane and the rifle and assured the sharp-eyed sentinel that her companion was indeed the president, bringing the conflict to a peaceful conclusion.

16

ROBERT E. LEE

January 19, 1807–October 12, 1870

HIGHEST RANK:

Confederate General

ASTROLOGICAL SIGN:

Capricorn

NICKNAMES:

Granny Lee, King of Spades, Marse Robert, Uncle Robert, Bobby Lee

WORDS TO REMEMBER:

"I must say that I am one of those dull creatures that cannot see the good of secession."

In April 1861, the highest-ranking soldier in America, Winfield Scott, needed a ringer. Since the shelling of Fort Sumter, he was facing a lower South in open rebellion and a handful of other slave states on the verge of going the same way, including his native Virginia. President Lincoln, his new superior, had authorized the mobilization of an army of volunteers to deal with the crisis. But in his mid-seventies, Scott himself was too old to take the field at its head. What he needed was a younger, experienced officer of sterling reputation, unimpeachable character, and consummate ability.

And he had just the guy: a colonel in the regular army who had been on Scott's staff during the latter's world-famous conquest of Mexico City in 1847, and who had emerged from that conflict as one of the most respected officers in the military. Since then, Scott had taken the dashing officer—a fellow Virginian—under his wing and embraced him as a friend. No one was held in higher esteem by Scott, who planned to make his estimable protégé an offer he couldn't refuse: commission as a major general and command of an army that could conceivably grow to 100,000, a host of historic proportions. As for the candidate's loyalty, there was little question: "I wish to live under no other government," the fellow wrote to a relative in the midst of the secession crisis. "I wish for no other flag than the 'Star spangled banner.'" Was this guy perfect or what?

He sure was. But Robert E. Lee wrote something else in a letter to his family: "I am willing to sacrifice everything but honor for [the Union's] preservation." Everything but honor. And that's why he turned down Winfield Scott's proposition, turned his back on the sort of opportunity that every ambitious West Pointer lusted for. Shortly after Scott tendered the offer, Virginia seceded; Lee was now bound by sacred duty to defend it with all his ability, whatever his opinions on slavery, states' rights, or Abraham Lincoln. To Robert E. Lee, honor was everything.

Handsome, urbane, of old Virginia blood, Lee embodied the chivalric aristocracy of America's South. Even his ancestry fit the bill. His father, Henry "Light Horse Harry" Lee, had been one of George Washington's most effective fighting officers during the Revolution and a legend in his own time. In fact, Harry's tactical gifts were matched only by his astounding financial incompetence—he ultimately went through the inherited fortunes of two wealthy wives, mostly in idiotic land speculations, as easily as he had scattered terrified redcoats during the war.

> At the conclusion of the Civil War, Lee signed an oath of allegiance to the Union—but the document went misplaced for more than a century. Lee died having never reaffirmed his loyalty, at least in a clerical sense.

Harry had numerous children. Robert Edward, destined to be the most famous, was born by Lee's second wife, Ann Carter Lee, descended from a hoary clan that stretched back across the Atlantic and into English history. (An ancestor on her mother's side, Alexander Spotswood, had been with Marlborough at the Battle of Blenheim in 1704.) Robert's illustrious father died, broken and shamed, when the boy was just eleven. Though the youngest of Ann Carter Lee's sons, Robert was to take care of his dying mother with a sincerity and attention to detail that marveled neighbors and acquaintances. He became the young patriarch of his mother's household—

a household that, though nearly penniless, was still established by connections to the Fitzhughs, Randolphs, Custises, and other prominent Virginia
families. Robert, an intensely dedicated son, of extraordinary intelligence
and deportment, was everything that West Point was looking for (and, best
of all, the academy offered a free education). Like many of Virginia's finest,
he was off to that idyllic bastion on the Hudson in 1825.

With such sterling qualifications, it was hardly surprising that Lee graduated four years later ranked second in his class. But the fact that he did so
with no demerits whatsoever on his record—well, that was just spooky. Lee
was like some sort of martial ideal. Scooped up by the Corps of Engineers,
he commenced a truly enviable military career. After constructing fortifications and harbor works around the country, he served on Winfield Scott's
staff during the war with Mexico, earning the great commander's enormous
respect, three brevets, and a wound, incurred at the Battle of Chapultepec.
He went on to serve as a very highly esteemed superintendent of West Point,
and took a lieutenant colonelcy in the cavalry, patrolling the desiccated,
interminable wastes of the Texas frontier. As for his finances, things were
looking up. In 1831, this impoverished son of discredited nobility had married a very wealthy, very beautiful, very difficult young lady named Mary
Custis, daughter of George Washington Parke Custis, who was Martha
Washington's grandson and George Washington's adopted son. Upon his
father-in-law's death in 1857, Lee found himself taking extended leaves to
go back east and settle the estate that his wife had inherited—which included
a vast, gorgeous estate overlooking Washington, D.C., called Arlington.

It was in the midst of one such sojourn that the colonel found himself
summoned by President Buchanan in 1859 to do something about the raid
on Harpers Ferry by John Brown and his squad of radicals. Dressed in civilian clothes, with James Stuart by his side (a younger acquaintance made
during the West Point superintendency, who would one day make history as
the flamboyant "Jeb" Stuart), the colonel directed a detachment of marines
to storm Brown's garrison inside the town's fire engine house, bringing the
tense standoff to a close. The incident further secured Lee's reputation as a

dependable and loyal servant of both the federal government and the Commonwealth of Virginia—two authorities that would soon be pitted against each other, forcing him to make the defining decision of his life.

Few who faced that decision made it so reluctantly. "You have made the greatest mistake of your life," said Winfield Scott to the man he had hoped would end the rebellion. Instead, Robert E. Lee would draw it out into a ghastly, murderous marathon, and all because of the qualities that had made him Scott's first choice as pacifier of the South.

Those days were far off, however. In the meantime he was made a major general in his home state's military, burdened with organizational responsibilities. The Confederate government immediately understood his value, and made him a brigadier general in the C.S. Army. Field command soon followed in northwest Virginia, where Lee—er, blew it. At Cheat Mountain and Laurel Mountain, his Rebel force was held off by determined Union resistance, earning him the sobriquet "Granny Lee" for his apparent lack of audaciousness. Reassigned to South Carolina, he oversaw the construction of coastal defenses. Then it was back to Richmond, where he assumed his place at President Jefferson Davis's side as military advisor.

It was in this capacity that Lee found himself with President Davis at the dawn of June 1862, watching Joseph Johnston lead his troops against George McClellan's bluecoats at the Battle of Seven Pines. Soon reports filtered back that Johnston, son of a man who had fought under Robert E. Lee's father in the Revolution, was wounded. The Rebels defending Richmond were leaderless. Gustavus Woodson Smith, Johnston's nonplussed, jabbering second-in-command and successor, rode up and filled Lee and Davis with fear at his obvious lack of command potential. (Smith soon suffered a nervous breakdown.) The Confederate capital was in danger, and Davis did what he needed to—he placed Lee in command of the defenders of Richmond.

And so the seeds of a legend were sown. Up to now, Lee had been known as a "Granny" and, for his insistence on defensive earthworks, the "King of Spades." But he was about to give the world a lesson in brazen generalship. Assuming command of a hopeless situation (for it surely seemed like one to any sane observer), Lee managed to stem McClellan's advance on Richmond just long enough to hatch a crazy plan. Leaving a weakened screen in front of Richmond, he gathered the strength of his force—now called the Army of Northern Virginia—for a blow on McClellan's right flank, where a single corps was separated from the rest of the Federal army by the swollen waters of the Chickahominy River. It was so bold that McClellan fell for the trap: unwilling to test the Confederate lines before Richmond (where Lee was weakest), the Union commander interpreted the storm of enemy activity on his right as an indication that the Rebels outnumbered him and threatened his army's very existence. He fell back, and back again. For a week of clashes known as the Seven Days, Lee thrashed against his enemy's greater strength, each time receiving better than he gave, but forcing McClellan further back toward the James River. Even as they continued to deal telling blows on their Confederate attackers, the more numerous Union forces, relentlessly pressed, continued to retreat from the goal that had so recently been within their grasp. McClellan ultimately withdrew to Harrison's Landing and evacuated his army. Lee had saved the Confederacy.

Frankly, it was a miracle. At no time was McClellan outnumbered—indeed, at no time did he lack the men or resources to smash through to Richmond. Lee had gambled everything and won, like a poker player who had bagged the whole pot with a deuce, a three, a six, and a set of balls the size of Hippity Hops.

This was to be Robert E. Lee's methodology for much of the war. He stood out not only because he understood the Confederacy's very precarious situation, but also because he knew how that situation could set him free. When you have unlimited resources and men to draw on, you had better not risk them foolishly. But when you're hampered by a paucity of matériel, and you're hoping to pummel your much wealthier opponent into a state of dizziness and despair, you had better risk big or not show up at all. Hell, you're certainly going to lose if you don't give it a try. And this is what Lee understood: gamble or lose.

So he kept gambling. It worked at Second Bull Run, where he sent Stonewall Jackson up and around the Federals in a huge flanking maneuver and then finished them off by marching north with Longstreet and uniting the Army of Northern Virginia in time to deal a devastating defeat. So devastating, in fact, that Lee decided to take the army into Maryland, where—it was expected—they would be met as liberators. But there his gambling produced trouble. Determined to take the Union garrison at Harpers Ferry, which would be in his rear during a thrust into Maryland, Lee split his army into several columns that were to converge on the target. Risky? Quite—especially when your opponent gets his hands on your plans. Left carelessly by a subordinate as a wrapper around a few cigars, Lee's elaborate orders regarding the advance on Harpers Ferry fell into McClellan's possession, handing him the opportunity to strike at an Army of Northern Virginia that was divided rather than united. The result was the bloodiest single day in American history.

McClellan, alerted to his opponent's weakness, moved west to intercept him. Slowly. Made even slower by the Army of Northern Virginia's delaying actions, McClellan was unable to confront his nemesis before Lee had the opportunity to gather most of his strength. Still, the Southerners were radically outnumbered, the Potomac River barring their path to safety. Should their position prove untenable, they would have nowhere to retreat to, producing either a mass surrender or a slaughter. This was the price of Lee's gambling writ large: He had concocted a scheme that would've worked under ideal circumstances but that had fallen apart under the realities of campaigning.

The epic fight that resulted was called Sharpsburg in the South, after the nearby town, and Antietam in the North, after the creek that meandered between the opposing armies. The clash was intended to be Lee's destruction and nearly was. Throughout a day of unprecedented carnage, Lee and his lieutenants desperately made the most of their meager numbers, strengthening challenged sections of the line by weakening others and praying for some sort of deliverance. Interestingly, they got it in the shape of A. P. Hill's Light Division, which had raced some seventeen miles from Harpers Ferry to answer Lee's summons. Hill's appearance was the Army of Northern Virginia's salvation.

Having escaped annihilation by a whisker, Lee was content to leave Maryland (which hadn't been very welcoming after all). Regrouping and refitting after the slaughter of Antietam, he next met the Army of the Potomac at Fredericksburg. There, in December, he awaited the crossing of Burnside's forces and watched, awestruck, as waves of enemy troops broke against his entrenched infantry in bloody futility. "It is well that war is so terrible," he famously remarked while watching the spectacle, "or we should grow too fond of it." A staggering Union defeat, it was shocking proof that the Confederacy's principal army was more than a match for the North's overwhelming material superiority. Lee was literally getting away with murder.

And so dawned 1863, the year of reckoning that was to witness the Army of Northern Virginia's greatest success and its most ignominious failure. When Joseph Hooker stole a march on his enemy and managed to bring much of the Army of the Potomac across the Rappahannock and the Rapidan to advance on Lee's flank from the north, the resulting clash at Chancellorsville saw Lee the gambler at his greatest. Leaving part of his army at Fredericksburg to guard the back door, as it were, Lee moved west to intercept Hooker in the thickets of the Wilderness. Already outnumbered, Lee once again ignored military sanity and further divided his army, sending Stonewall Jackson on a long, circuitous flanking maneuver while he himself risked getting smashed to pieces by a force that dwarfed his own. Hooker never caught on, however, allowing Jackson to creep up on the Union right flank and shatter it with a brilliant surprise attack. Once again, Lee had gambled—on his enemy's caution, his subordinates' surpassing skill, his infantry's resilience, and his own lucky streak.

But the war was already two years old—how long could this go on? He needed to force a decision—to win foreign support, to undermine Northern resolve, to buy time for his army and his cause. The Army of the Potomac, whatever the relative quality of its commanding generals, was only getting stronger. By contrast, Lee's men already had trouble finding shoes and often subsisted on green corn. Something dramatic had to happen soon. Though he had trounced the enemy at Chancellorsville, he had failed to destroy him.

And so he went after them—"those people," as he always referred to the Army of the Potomac. He went north to draw them out and crush them and also to live off the fat of the Pennsylvania countryside, to find those shoes his men needed so badly. But when the battle came, it wasn't on ground of Lee's choosing. At the town of Gettysburg, the Federals held on to the high ground and dug in. Lee was advised by James Longstreet, his "old warhorse," to shift the army southeast and draw the enemy off its ridge by threatening the road to Washington. But the commander demurred. The Army of the Potomac was here, and it was here that he would destroy it.

Or not. Gettysburg was a Rebel defeat that could be laid squarely at the feet of Robert E. Lee. Having snared the Army of the Potomac, he would not let go. For three days he threw his splendid infantry at George Meade's blue-coats: initially on the enemy flanks and finally—most spectacularly—right up the middle. Meade's men were happy to oblige their eager assailant with devastating, heroic defiance. Lee had finally gambled and lost.

Now the Federals had the initiative, and they would not surrender it. The following year, 1864, saw Lee pitted against Lincoln's last best hope: Ulysses Grant. That the newly minted lieutenant general took as long to defeat the Army of Northern Virginia as he did is a testament to Marse Robert. Wily to the end, Lee negated his opponent's superior numbers by attacking him in the Wilderness; gave Grant a hot welcome at Spotsylvania by divining his decision to go there; and lured him into a slaughter pen at Cold Harbor. He might well have been able to do much more had his army not been encumbered by the millstone of Richmond, whose defense shaped the coarse of events that blood-soaked summer. By the time he felt desperate enough to consider abandoning the capital altogether, it was too late. Grant, though unable to annihilate his nemesis, had finally managed to fix him in the works of Petersburg.

And so the thing that kept Lee going was the quality that got him into this mess in the first place: honor, a thing of itself, innate, intangible, and unassailable because of its sublime ethereality. He was buttressed by responsibility to his men and the fact that he was fighting on his own

Virginia soil, and duty gave him the raison d'être that a crumbling Confederacy could not. He was far from perfect. His most acclaimed successes, from the Seven Days to Second Bull Run to Chancellorsville, all came at a sickening cost in lives. Seemingly unaware of the technological changes that had rendered the battlefield so lethal to massed infantry, he never perfected a fashion of warfare that compensated for the South's paucity of manpower and kept feeding his dwindling ranks into a quest for decisive victory that never came. And his preference for broad, generalized directives that left so much initiative to his principal subordinates had sometimes led to confusion. Nevertheless, his nation had already begun to fixate on him as an idealized personification of all they were about to lose—the poised and proud representative of Southern gentry. As if to confirm this, the government, in the final January of its existence, named Lee commander in chief of the Confederate armies.

Whether or not he really was all that Southerners claimed, Lee certainly looked the part at Appomattox when he surrendered to Grant. Only after sitting down and patiently, thoroughly seeing to the fate of the men he had led for what seemed an eternity did he allow something else to stir—a quickening rage at having fallen from such heights. Red-faced and wound-up, he paced beneath a tree, interrupted now and then by Federal officers, who had of late been his mortal enemies, coming up to greet the great battle chief with pleasantries that must have struck harder than minié balls.

But the new status quo would require such sacrifices. He was to prove nearly as influential in peace as he was in war, submitting quietly to the new order and urging others to do the same. While he himself helped reinvigorate Washington College by serving as its president until his death in 1870 from heart disease, many of his former subordinates started fanning the flames of his reputation into the myth of the "Lost Cause," a phenomenon whose endurance spoke volumes about Lee. He remains one of the most esteemed military figures in history—a fate any victorious general would kill for.

MARY, MARY, QUITE CONTRARY

Robert E. Lee came from the social equivalent of an excellent claret with too many cork bits floating in it. One of them, of course, was his father, whose disgraceful downfall and stints in debtor's prison more than tainted his sterling Revolutionary War record. But there was another smirch on the Lee name: Robert's half brother Henry, the oldest son of Light Horse Harry. A clever wordsmith who, like Robert, married up, Henry lost his two-year-old daughter to a fall down the stairs of the family manse, Stratford Hall. Anne McCarty Lee, his wife, fell into mourning that evolved gradually into a devastating morphine addiction. With his household and marriage a shambles, Henry did what any dissolute middling patrician would do under the circumstances—he took to sleeping with his teenage sister-in-law, who soon grew large with child.

With relatives like this, it was hardly surprising that Robert, despite his obvious intelligence and good looks, should have trouble in the courting department. Family reputation counted for much in planter society. Nevertheless, he managed to catch the eye of a young lady who was witty, attractive, and rich. Mary Custis's father did his best to shoo away the impoverished son of a feckless spendthrift, but to no avail. With his own fortune in mind, Custis no doubt recalled the old chestnut about falling apples, trees, and their relative proximity. Mary's mother, on the other hand, thought they made a good match. Mrs. Custis even did her part to hurry things along when, during one of his visits to Arlington, Robert read Sir Walter Scott aloud until he grew positively weary. (Always a risk with Scott.) Mrs. Custis suggested that Mary take him into the other room and offer him some of the fruitcake on the sideboard (wink, wink). There, concealed from older eyes, the officer worked up the courage to propose and was rewarded with an answer in the positive.

In a whirlwind courtship, Robert E. Lee had pulled off what his fiancée's adoptive grandfather, George Washington, had himself done: secure land

and a future by marrying into wealth. But it came at a price—specifically, his wife. Mary was everything her deliberate, assiduous, and disciplined husband was not. She was tardy, irreverent, sloppy, and a little lazy, all qualities she had inherited from her father, who had risen to become one of Virginia's most famous dilettantes. She was spoiled and supercilious. Most troubling of all, she found army life and army families a dreadful bore. While Robert adored his children, his wife chafed at the responsibility. All of these differences proved difficult enough without anyone's getting sick. But then someone got sick. By 1857 it had become terribly obvious that Mary suffered from rheumatoid arthritis, confining her to a wheelchair essentially for the rest of her life. And so Robert E. Lee would live out the rest of his life—when he was able—caring (as he had done for his mother) for his invalided wife.

DEAD AND BURIED

Robert E. Lee never owned Arlington, the gorgeous estate inherited by his wife, Mary. He did, however, restore the grounds and its 250 slaves to profitability after marrying into the Custis clan. Designed by George Hadfield, the English architect who had a hand in designing the national Capitol, the house of the property was a beautiful Greek revival showpiece. It dominated 1,100 acres of pristine property that would ultimately be used against Lee and his wife in ways they could not possibly have foreseen.

Abandoned in the face of war, Arlington was seized when taxes levied against it were not paid by Mary Custis Lee. When it was offered for public sale, the government bought it in January 1864. General Montgomery Meigs, quartermaster general of the Unites States Army, turned the grounds into the greatest possible insult that its onetime owners could imagine: a cemetery for the nation's war dead. Its first permanent residents arrived because the cemetery at the Soldiers' Home in Washington had become full. From there, it filled up at a pace that, in large part, was determined by the rate at which its former caretaker, Robert E. Lee, could kill enemy soldiers. And so began America's national cemetery—as an act of calculated revenge against the man whose military genius supported secessionist rebellion for four bloody years.

Have Gun, Will Traveller

In early 1862, Robert E. Lee paid a fellow officer named Joseph Broun $200 for an extraordinary horse. Soon named "Traveller," the beast went on to become famous as Lee's treasured horse. But the general had a few others, as well. During the Maryland campaign in 1862, Lee was holding Traveller by the reins when the animal started at some disturbance nearby. In an attempt to seize the bridle and control his mount, the general fell, breaking one hand and badly spraining the other. Eager to give Lee another horse that might not be so high-strung, Jeb Stuart sent his chief a little sorrel mare named Lucy Long, whom Lee rode until she became pregnant two years later. As for Traveller, he remained the general's primary horse until Lee's death. Interestingly, the great warhorse that had carried one of the greatest military leaders of the age through one of the bloodiest conflicts of all time came to a sad and silly end. Shortly after Lee's death, Traveller was grazing one day when a nail punctured one of his forefeet. The animal got lockjaw and died soon after.

MISPLACED ALLEGIANCE

Robert E. Lee believed firmly in reestablishing accord between the North and South after the war. Part of the process of being reinstated as a citizen was signing an oath of allegiance, which Lee eagerly did. The process went no further, however, because the oath was . . . er, misplaced. Lee died having never reaffirmed his loyalty, at least in a clerical sense. A century after his death, the missing document was discovered with some other papers in the National Archives. And in 1975, citing the general as a "symbol of valor and duty," President Gerald Ford signed Senate Joint Resolution 23, restoring to Robert Edward Lee all the rights of citizenship. Everyone knows that government wheels grind slowly, but really . . .

17 JAMES LONGSTREET

January 8, 1821–January 2, 1904

HIGHEST RANK:
Confederate General

ASTROLOGICAL SIGN:
Capricorn

NICKNAMES:
Bulldog, Dutch, My Old Warhorse (by Robert E. Lee), Old Pete, Peter

WORDS TO REMEMBER:
"This is a hard fight, and we had better all die than lose it" (at the Battle of Antietam).

History has handed down to us two James Longstreets. The first is a likable military Übermensch, routinely referred to by historians as the finest tactician on either side of the Civil War, whose simple charisma and sublime instincts earned him the most intimate place in Robert E. Lee's circle. The second, on the other hand, is a regular Mr. Hyde: an unkempt, boorish, calculating opportunist whose incompetence and perfidy cost the Confederacy the war and who defected to the winning faction after the war in a gutless, unforgivable breach of faith. In the popular consciousness, he has been revered, reviled, and forgotten by sharp turns. Indeed, so much emotion has been heaped onto attempts to discover whether either storyline is true that seeing the fellow himself has become nearly impossible.

Due to an inflamed wound on his foot, James Longstreet was incapable of wearing boots during the Battle of Antietam. He fought one of the war's bloodiest battles while dressed in carpet slippers.

One thing is for sure: There wasn't much cause to expect that James Longstreet would grow up to become one of the most controversial men in American history. Born in South Carolina, he grew up in Georgia and

secured a spot at West Point from Alabama, where his mother relocated with the family after his father's death. The military academy proved an ideal environment to make friends and pull pranks; it was hardly surprising that Longstreet graduated in 1842 near the bottom of his class academically. Nicknamed "Peter," connoting toughness and dependability, Longstreet had spent his late youth under the eye of Uncle Augustus, a brilliant educator and judge who went on to hold the president's post at several colleges. But Pete was no bookworm, and it was in the Georgia wilds that he had discovered his principal loves: physical activity and the outdoors. For this energetic and gregarious jokester, classwork was to be endured.

Fortunately for "Old Pete," classwork had nothing to do with staying cool under fire and killing enemy soldiers, both of which he did quite well in the Mexican War. Wounded and awarded two brevets for bravery, he served in the postwar frontier army as a popular and respected young officer. He was an army paymaster when war broke out between the states in 1861—a fact that, in the wake of imminent events, would seem incredible.

He proved soon enough that he was better at leading men than counting change. When Union general Irvin McDowell made a thrust across Blackburn's Ford in the prelude to the First Battle of Bull Run, he ran up against a brigade of Rebels led by a newly minted brigadier general named Longstreet. Peter inspired his men by calmly sitting on his horse in civilian clothes and taking in the spectacle of advancing Federals as if they were a pretty tableau in a history book. His troops repulsed, McDowell ended up changing his strategy for getting across Bull Run—a decision that led to Union disaster three days later, when the main clash came. This kind of stolidity, along with Longstreet's prewar reputation, endeared him rather quickly to the guys who mattered most—particularly Joseph Johnston, the commanding general running things in Virginia. Longstreet took the faith placed in him and blew it all to hell in the spring of 1862, when, at the Battle of Seven Pines, he misinterpreted his orders, marched his troops down the wrong route of attack, and undermined the entire Confederate plan. It was a conspicuous failure by a man who, though trusted in important circles, had yet to secure tenure for himself in the Rebel army. Nevertheless, Longstreet's reputation survived the debacle, not least because Johnston's wounding at Seven Pines placed the defenders of Richmond in a state of chaos that abated only with Robert E. Lee's arrival as Johnston's replacement.

Throughout the first months of the war, many of Old Pete's intimate friends had come to look on his tent as a second home, where whiskey, poker, and ribald conversation were always in fashion. Then a scarlet fever epidemic struck Richmond in January 1862, claiming three of his children. Longstreet and his wife, Louise, were simply destroyed. From this point onward, something of the spirit that had fueled those long nights of cards and drinking disappeared. But Peter retained much of the robust amiability that had become his trademark—enough to coax Robert E. Lee into joining those who continued to feel drawn to his company. Beginning with the Seven Days' campaign that followed, Longstreet endeared himself to the commander of the new Army of Northern Virginia.

The bond between the two, however, was based on professional trust. To build the Army of Northern Virginia into an effective force, Lee needed officers he could depend on, and no one proved more dependable in the Seven Days' Battles than Longstreet. Lee ended up dividing his army into two wings, giving the smaller one to Thomas "Stonewall" Jackson. To Old Pete went the majority of the army and the commanding general's highest confidence. The result was an operational structure that, in practice, was not unlike a hammer and anvil. Despite an utterly lousy performance in the Seven Days, Jackson—with his Shenandoah Valley exploits still on everyone's lips—was made the hammer, a role suited to his innate boldness. Longstreet, conversely, became the ballast of the army and the foundation of its strength. Lee considered his counsel invaluable.

The feeling wasn't mutual—not completely, anyway. Though taught like every other West Point grad to appreciate the aggressive mentality, Longstreet had become an ardent fan of the strategic offensive combined with the tactical defensive. That is, seize and maintain the initiative in war to steer the course of events, but when battles are joined, always find the most defensible ground and invite the enemy to make attacks upon your position that are doomed to failure. A fundamentally conservative stance, it was increasingly at odds with Lee's impulsive need to attack and incur casualties that Longstreet, at least, felt certain the Confederacy couldn't afford.

At first the difference remained in the background of a friendship that blossomed amidst the tremors of war. Through the campaigns of Second Bull Run, Antietam, and Fredericksburg, Old Pete solidified his role as the stout, sarcastic, tobacco-chomping bulwark of the Army of Northern Virginia, earning his men's devotion for his solidity and concern for their welfare, and the respect of his fellow officers for his outstanding ability to handle vast numbers of men as if they were a small marching band. Though he missed the fireworks of Chancellorsville (he had been sent temporarily to southeast Virginia on an independent command), Longstreet was back at Lee's side for the invasion of Pennsylvania. And there, in the most pivotal campaign of the war, their differences collided in a Confederate disaster that—to Longstreet's terrific misfortune—refused to die.

Pete picked up his most famous nickname in the wake of Antietam, when Lee, elated to find that Longstreet had survived the bloodletting, enthusiastically referred to him as "my old warhorse." It was an apt description. Longstreet even looked the part, with his thick physique and burly beard. If Jackson—killed at Chancellorsville—had been Lee's right arm, Old Pete was his heart and soul. But when Lee turned to his warhorse for input on the grand idea of striking deep into Pennsylvania, the steed reeled. For Longstreet, the war's fulcrum had shifted west, where Ulysses Grant threatened Vicksburg like the Angel of Death. Pete the strategist understood that losing the Mississippi River meant losing the war, and he didn't understand why his superior wanted to go gallivanting off into the pastures of Pennsylvania. In language that many historians claim is proof positive of Longstreet's insatiable ambition, he had been suggesting that he be allowed to go west with a good chunk of the Army of Northern Virginia in order to resolve the question that loomed over the fate of the western theater; i.e., defend in the east and go over to the offensive in the west. Lee was having none of it, however, and he needed his old warhorse to pull off the northern invasion. And so it went.

Hence Gettysburg. By the time Longstreet arrived at the battlefield, it had turned into precisely the sort of situation that he thought must be avoided at all costs: The Army of Northern Virginia was on the tactical offensive against a foe of unknown strength on the tactical defensive (and on easily defensible ground). The battle lasted three days, as Lee strove to find a weak point in his opponent's lines. And Longstreet's First Corps was his blunt instrument.

Longstreet didn't even like fighting on the ground in question; now he was supposed to carry the day. Despite his sanguine pleas to abandon the madness of assaulting heavily defended high ground, Old Pete was ordered by Lee to attack the enemy's left flank on July 2 and drive it from its advantageous position, thereby rendering the rest of the Federal works either useless or doomed. What happened next depends on which historian you ask. It seems that Pete, angered by his superior's insistence on attacking a formidable position without all of the First Corps present (a division under George Pickett had yet to arrive), carried out his orders with less than the usual aplomb. Indeed, some accounts insist that he dithered like some sulking child faced with a chore. His subordinates made things more complicated by protesting the planned deployment and insisting that a flanking maneuver be executed instead of a head-on test of grit. By the time Longstreet's men were ready, it was late afternoon. The attack that ensued produced much heroism and a lot more blood, but no victory.

But it gets better. Longstreet, torn between vindication and horror, was supposed to direct the following day's shenanigans as well. The division under Pickett that Pete had been waiting for had one hell of a welcoming party: Accompanied by divisions from A. P. Hill's corps, it was to throw itself across the vast flatland that separated the opposing armies from each other in a last-ditch assault against the center of the Union line. This made the previous day's folly seem like a cakewalk, and Longstreet knew it. When the time came to send his old friend Pickett forward, all Pete could do was nod, his disgust at the task having rendered him speechless. Pickett's charge was an unmitigated catastrophe.

In the wake of the Gettysburg reverse, Longstreet's western schemes found favor. The resultant sympathetic mood in high places put him on a roundabout journey by rail with thousands of his men toward the battle that would witness his finest hour: Chickamauga, in his home state of Georgia. Debarking from the train into the chaos that typified General Braxton Bragg's area of command, he followed the sounds of battle until he found Bragg and helped to hatch a plan that would make history. What ensued was the sort of Union rout that hadn't been seen in those parts since the Battle of Shiloh.

Chickamauga was the zenith of Longstreet's career, earning him the nickname "Bull of the Woods." He had arrived with almost no intelligence about the enemy, found his fellow commander's camp with no help from Bragg, and dealt a blow to the enemy that left no doubt whatsoever as to the truth of his ability. And this at a time when the Confederacy's star was falling on all fronts. Infighting and a lack of cooperation, however, prevented the Confederates from properly exploiting the extraordinary victory they'd achieved. The western theater continued to slip further into Union hands. And Old Pete did nothing to help: After advancing his men far enough to besiege Ambrose Burnside in Knoxville, Tennessee, he was eventually driven away, exposing his weakness for independent command. He went back to the Virginia battlefields that had made him a legend.

But there's the rub: Those fields hadn't earned him the laurels he deserved. Despite the gravitas of his position and the significance of his achievements, Longstreet remained the least popularized of the Army of Northern Virginia's lead players. Why? For one, he was a Georgian (or Alabamian or South Carolinian) in an army whose aristocracy was almost entirely from Virginia. And it didn't take a genius to spot the difference between Old Pete the backwoods hick and all the Old Dominion aristocrats. Longstreet could hold his own in a drawing room soiree, but not without giving away a certain impatience with Victorian fustiness. Nothing about Old Pete's martial certitude was romantic—he didn't exhibit the breeding of

Robert E. Lee or the dash of Jeb Stuart. And he certainly didn't ooze Old Testament rectitude like that quintessential Southern favorite, Stonewall Jackson. Pete's coat was often undone, his speech was unadorned, and he ate like a boar. Simply put, he didn't make very good copy. Ironically, the very press that irritated Longstreet for ignoring him during the war would infuriate him years afterward for doing precisely the opposite.

In the meantime, the old warhorse threw himself into the final act of the doomed experiment to which he'd pledged his sword. In the murky, labyrinthine hell of the Wilderness, he nearly lost his life when he took a shot through the throat from friendly troops in a near-deadly moment of confusion. By the time he returned to the First Corps the following autumn, the stalemate around Petersburg had begun, Sherman had taken Atlanta and stood poised to eviscerate Georgia, and everybody with more than four brain cells knew that the fat lady was warming up her voice. Longstreet, stalwart to the end, stuck with the Army of Northern Virginia right through Lee's surrender at Appomattox.

And then the real fighting began.

But not at first. As Lee's principal lieutenant and a man who had inspired thousands of soldiers during the war, Longstreet entered the chaotic Reconstruction era as a venerated Southern hero. Indeed, he even had notoriety going for him: Along with Jefferson Davis and Robert E. Lee, he was considered by President Andrew Johnson to have been too much trouble to pardon. But Lee's ex-warhorse had a practical, canny side to him that saw the end of the war as a new beginning for anyone smart enough to realize it. He was a survivor, and he had a household to support. It was time to put the rebellion behind him and become part of the future.

There was nothing unique or particularly brash about that. But central to Longstreet's plan of action for success was joining that most despised institution of Northern aggression: the Republican Party. This heresy, perpetrated by one of the most esteemed officers to wear gray in the late rebellion, hit most Southerners like a vigorous kick in the groin. In fact, virtually everything about Longstreet was beginning to piss people off. He refused to wax indignant about black suffrage, accepted a series of political appointments from the occupying Republicans, and warmly embraced associations and friendships with his erstwhile enemies—not least Ulysses Grant. This was a friendship that had existed since West Point and was solidified by marriage: Old Pete's mother was a cousin of Julia Dent, Grant's beloved wife. Friends and kinsmen, Grant and Longstreet shared a sincere affection for each other that personified the nation's slowly healing wound. To the average defeated secessionist, it had the effect of a belly full of castor oil. (Another friend was Dan Sickles, drawn to Longstreet as a fellow hard-drinking scoundrel attacked for his unpopular decisions at Gettysburg.)

This might have remained what it was—one man's bold, abrupt transformation in the face of circumstances beyond his control—were it not for the fact that greater schemes were afoot. If Longstreet worried about the future, a bunch of his fellow Confederates were obsessing over the past. To men like Jubal Early, a former corps commander in the Army of Northern Virginia, the fall and occupation of the South was a tragedy too enormous to explain without recourse to fantasies. Dixie's finest, each of whom had been worth three Yankees in a fight, must have been sold out. Fortunately for the "Lost Cause" enthusiasts, a scapegoat already existed—and, incredibly, he stood passively amongst them like a sacrificial goat, his throat casually exposed.

It was Early himself who sliced first, publicly casting Longstreet in the role of a Judas who had deliberately squandered victory at Gettysburg, the war's turning point, by allowing his differences of opinion with Lee to affect his decisions. This theory made headway with the help of several congruent myths: first, that Robert E. Lee was all but infallible; second, that Union armies were incapable of scaring up some sort of victory on their own; and third, that Longstreet was petulant and puerile enough to risk the fate of an army in order to prove a point. The decades of strife that followed sickened Longstreet, affecting even his religion: He left Episcopalianism and its association with American soldiery for Catholicism.

When the Lost Cause assumed the dimensions of a religion (which it did in due time), any attempts at resistance by Longstreet doomed him as surely as the pleas of a witch before the medieval Inquisition. Unfortunately, Longstreet did the one thing that could make his situation worse: He stooped to the level of his accusers. Old Pete's rebuttals, both in journals and in his memoirs, showed him to be a vain and supercilious agitator, no more concerned with setting the record straight than the men who methodically attacked him. Blatantly setting himself up as the brains behind Lee's operation, Longstreet came off as a braggart and made the unlikely accusations against him seem more plausible.

He died of pneumonia in 1904. He is a man who continues to personify the passion with which Americans choose to look back at the war that once divided them. As the most controversial of Lee's lieutenants, it is strangely fitting that he was the last of them to go.

INGRATE

James Longstreet was seventy-six when he married Helen Dortch, thirty-four, in 1897, in his second marriage. Maria Louisa, known as "Louise," had been Longstreet's beloved wife for more than forty years. In addition to bearing up under the strain of being the spouse of a military man in wartime, Louise had borne ten children with Peter, only five of whom made it to adulthood. It was a long, close, and emotionally intense marriage by any standard. And Longstreet never mentioned her in his memoirs.

FIGHTING IN STYLE

Robert E. Lee never needed the steady professionalism of James Longstreet more than he did on September 17, 1862. Little wonder that Lee ended up calling Old Pete a warhorse after the Battle of Antietam. The Georgian showed his sense of black humor during the beginning of the fight when the mount of fellow Confederate general D. H. Hill lost its forelegs to a Union cannonball. As Hill tried to dismount the swaying animal, Longstreet teased his distressed friend, telling him to come down one side, then the other, "get off over his head, Hill," and so on, making light of the gruesome spectacle. (Hill ultimately made his escape and put the beast out of its misery.) But later in the day, Longstreet gave evidence to support his reputation as one of the calmest of fighters in the thickest of scrapes. At one point, virtually the only thing that stood against a Union advance on Longstreet's end of the line was a Confederate battery that had been savagely denuded of artillerists by enemy shells. Old Pete ordered his personal staff to the rescue, as they took over the guns themselves and started pouring canister shot, per Longstreet's orders, into the oncoming Federals. The general himself directed their efforts from the back of his horse while calmly chewing a cigar, the air around him popping with enemy bullets. It became one of the indelible images of that bloodiest of days and one of the moments that secured for Longstreet a beloved place in the hearts of his men.

But the best part of it all was that, owing to an inflamed scraping wound on his foot, Longstreet was incapable of wearing his boots that fateful day. He fought the entire Battle of Antietam wearing carpet slippers.

PARTY ANIMAL

On the second day of Gettysburg, Longstreet threw himself into the maelstrom around the peach orchard, personally leading a brigade of Mississippians by riding in front of their ranks and waving his hat in his hand. A captured Union officer who had witnessed the display later remarked, "Our generals don't do that sort of thing." Despite antics like this, Old Pete managed to get through the Civil War without being captured. Ironically, it was in his postwar career that such a humiliating fate befell him.

Having settled in New Orleans after the war and allying himself with the governing Republican faction, Longstreet found himself at the flashpoint of violence that engulfed that city over politics gone mad. In the autumn of 1874, Longstreet—appointed leader of the state militia forces stationed in New Orleans—was ordered to confront mobs of agitators convinced that the

Democratic Party was being shafted and that the only way to stop radical Republican abuse was through a street war. Calling themselves the White League, the ranks of anti-Republican demonstrators included a large number of Confederate veterans. On September 14, they marched on the State House, only to be intercepted by policemen and militia, many of whom were black, led by none other than James Longstreet—a man whom many of the White Leaguers had once saluted as general. When he rode out to parlay with the League's leaders, it proved a mistake. They pulled him from his horse, took him prisoner, and opened fire on the troops under his command. Held captive until the struggle was concluded by the intervention of federal troops, Longstreet found his reputation throughout the South further smeared by the fact that he had led black troops against white Southern veterans. For Lee's old warhorse, it was a humiliating moment indeed—especially when a White League leader later admitted that he had had to prevent his men from "firing particularly at Longstreet."

Burnt Offerings

Longstreet eventually left Louisiana behind for the Georgia he called home, settling on a farm that his hostile neighbors derisively dubbed "Gettysburg." Perhaps aware of the fact that his fellow Georgians held him in contempt, he guarded his fields and vineyard with a shotgun, with which he was widely believed to be deadly accurate. Unfortunately, it wasn't trespassers he needed to worry about, but fire. In 1889, the house burned to the ground, taking several invaluable artifacts with it—including his uniform and sword, as well as a sash that Jeb Stuart had given him. But the greatest loss may have been all the papers he had been gathering to defend his conduct during the war. Their loss only made his fight to save his reputation that much harder.

THOMAS JONATHAN "STONEWALL" JACKSON

18

January 21, 1824–May 10, 1863

HIGHEST RANK:
Confederate Officer

ASTROLOGICAL SIGN:
Aquarius

NICKNAMES:
Old Blue Light, Old Jack, Stonewall, Tom Fool

WORDS TO REMEMBER:
"The moment a grain of black pepper touches my tongue, I lose all strength in my right leg."

Barnard Bee, a brigadier general from South Carolina, gave his life to the Confederate cause in the first major engagement of the Civil War. But he secured a place for himself in the history books by christening a legend. Desperate to rally his hard-pressed men at the First Battle of Bull Run, he looked to a prominence behind him known as Henry House Hill, where a Virginia brigade under former science professor Thomas Jackson stood stoic and immovable before the Union onslaught that was crashing upon it. "Look, men," Bee cried, "there is Jackson standing like a stone wall! Rally to the Virginians!"

A notorious hypochondriac, Jackson was convinced that one of his arms weighed more than the other. His solution: Raising the heavier limb above his head so the blood could drain from it.

Bee, who lay mortally wounded by the end of the day, had given America one of its most exalted nicknames—and one of its most ironic, as the world would learn soon enough. A preternaturally gifted exponent of surprise and maneuver, Jackson bore as much resemblance to a stone wall

as a tornado does to the structures it decimates. And it wasn't just his tactics that set him apart: The fact is, few figures in American history have been at once so lionized, so elusive, and—frankly—so damn strange.

He was born in the rugged northwest quarter of Virginia to parents who died by the time he was seven. If he had anything like a mentor, it was an uncle named Cummins Jackson, an industrious and rather unscrupulous businessman whose milling operation put the clan in good stead both financially and politically. At seventeen, young Thomas was deputized a constable to the Lewis County court, in which capacity he collected outstanding debts, enforced judicial decisions, and impressed the community with his honesty and hard work. Such service in the public interest was an ideal outlet for this straitlaced, earnest youth looking to better his prospects. West Point beckoned when an applicant from his state ended up bowing out of the program, securing Jackson an appointment if he passed the entrance exams.

He passed, but by the slimmest of margins. It was the inglorious beginning of a relationship with academics that occupied much of Jackson's life. Raised on the wooded slopes of western Virginia and accustomed to hard physical labor, Jackson was no intellectual. But his aspirations of becoming one helped him develop one of his most outstanding qualities: intense, single-minded concentration. Determined to exploit his West Point opportunity for all it was worth, Jackson set goals for himself and pursued them with the discipline of a religious ascetic. It was obvious to him that he had a lot to learn, and he would learn it at any cost. When the course work became confusing, he simply waded through it for however many hours it took to acquire a rudimentary grasp of the subject. Then he would set about memorizing it all, sitting perfectly erect for hours in a straight-backed chair, staring blankly at the wall, lost to a universe of laboring brain cells.

With neither the time nor the patience for frivolity, Jackson struck his fellow plebes that first year at West Point as an awkward eccentric with about as much charisma as a railroad tie. He couldn't have cared less, and he continued his daunting study regimen. Unduly modest, he sought academic help from whomever would give it and made the most of his time with fellow cadets by asking questions to expand the inventory of data he was amassing in his head. While nothing came naturally to him, seemingly nothing was beyond his grasp once he'd started sweating over it. In 1846, he graduated seventeenth in a class of fifty-nine.

He didn't have long to wait to put all his hard-earned studying into practice. War with Mexico came as soon as he graduated, and Jackson—now an artillery officer—went south in search of glory. He found it the following year at the pivotal Battle of Chapultepec, where he efficiently manned his gun in the face of a veritable hailstorm of enemy fire, to which he seemed oddly oblivious. The performance played a leading role in the American victory that day and was soon the subject of countless campfire conversations. A hero was born.

For Jackson, the moment at Chapultepec was all-important. Not for the fame or admiration that came with it, but because it had validated the choices he'd made, the hard work he'd done. And he liked it: The mortal danger, the gravity of the moment, the honor and solemnity of following orders all made him feel more alive than he'd ever felt before. He had also survived against all the odds, galvanizing something that had been stirring in him since before his West Point days: religion. Awarded two brevet promotions for his service in the campaign, Jackson was truly content to look upon the army as his home.

Or so he thought. After returning to the United States from occupation duty in Mexico (during which he began a lifelong love affair with the Spanish language), Jackson endured various uneventful postings until, in 1850, he was transferred to Fort Meade in the wilds of Florida. There he encountered the one thing that could spoil his attachment to the army: an intolerable commanding officer. He was Captain William French, a fellow veteran of the Mexican War, and the two seemed to grate on each other's nerves right from the beginning. Things got rough when French called Jackson's ability into question during a series of scouting missions, then came to a boil over the construction of new fortifications; searing tension led to accusations and recriminations. If the two sparring officers believed themselves locked in an epic struggle of wills, the army seemed more irritated than anything else. The whole thing came to nothing.

By the time things at Fort Meade went really haywire, Jackson had received an offer to become a civilian teacher at Virginia Military Institute. Disillusioned with the swamps of Florida, he now accepted it. Any regrets he may have had about leaving the army would be offset by joining a regimented community designed on the West Point model. It was a highly regarded school with a deep sense of tradition and attachment to his native Virginia, and it afforded him an opportunity to make a good living by passing his experience and sense of duty on to the next generation.

All well and good. But Jackson had nothing to recommend him to the position beyond a heroic reputation and a respectable record at West Point, neither of which can be said to make a great teacher. So, not surprisingly, he wasn't. Lanky and graceless, with unnaturally large feet and a high-pitched voice, he did not exactly inspire awe in his students. When he inspired anything, it was usually confusion. Jackson's subject, called "Natural and Experimental Philosophy"—a heady brew of physics, optics, mathematics, and a few other intimidating "-ics"—was considered central to the VMI curriculum, if only because it separated the men from the boys. Jackson got by in the only fashion he knew: hours of rote memorization. As a result, his students were presented with a human tape recorder rather than a teacher—a man whose classroom style was limited to the regurgitation of data that had been stuffed into his head the evening before. Any deviation from the textbook, however minor, was simply impossible to grasp. Biographer James I. Robertson Jr. relates a story that says it all: "What are the three simple machines?" Jackson once asked a cadet in class. "The inclined plane, the lever, and the wheel," replied the student. "You are wrong, sir," Jackson said. "The lever, the wheel, and the inclined plane."

The cadets usually had a blast at their teacher's expense, making jokes about his ungainly walk, his humorless manner, and his awkward lectures. But it was a different story when they were on the firing range. As the artillery instructor, Jackson showed an impassioned, electric energy that was missing from his philosophy classes. There, amidst the thunder of the guns, was where he belonged.

In April 1861, VMI's cadets found themselves following that stern, blue-eyed gunner to Richmond on a march to war. And while many of them still razzed him as their endearingly peculiar "Old Jack," they would soon come to regard him with unqualified awe. Like many of his fellow Virginians, Jackson's stance on the stresses that divided North and South was straightforward: Secession was wrong, but Federal tyranny was worse. Now, as the nation broke apart, he sided with the Old Dominion. But it was more than a civil war to him: It was a crusade. A Presbyterian whose religious devotion bordered on the fanatical, he prayed feverishly in the weeks following Abraham Lincoln's election for some divine solution that would avert a call to arms. But once the fight began, Jackson sincerely believed that his beloved South was being oppressed by a mongrel Yankee culture whose soulless, hivelike modernization threatened the very foundations of God's earthly realm. Such a fight required bold action on a whole new level, and not just for spiritual reasons. With its material abundance and massive population, the North must be stunned into capitulation through constant, relentless defeats. The Confederacy must go on the offensive, never surrender, and pummel the Federals with a series of merciless blows that occur too quickly in succession to allow them a moment's peace.

Jackson even suggested that no prisoners be taken, a notion that struck virtually everyone who heard it as quite dangerous and perhaps insane. But outrageous audacity would come to define Jackson and his greatness. After delivering VMI's finest to Richmond and offering his services to the Rebel army, he was sent north to organize the defense of Harpers Ferry, then rushed to Manassas Junction and immortality at the Battle of Bull Run, where Barnard Bee made his famous pronouncement. Thereafter known throughout the Confederate army as "Stonewall" Jackson, the former VMI professor was given the command that turned him into a phenomenon. Toward the end of 1861, Jackson was sent to the Shenandoah Valley, where, the following spring, he was ordered to stir up enough trouble to keep the Union troops stationed there from reinforcing McClellan's drive on Richmond. During the ensuing two and a half months, Jackson force-marched his "foot cavalry," as his men became known, down and up the valley in a furious, lightning-fast campaign. They trudged hundreds of miles on substandard rations and won several major battles. Collectively, Union forces in the valley always outnumbered Jackson's total command, but time and again he was able to deliver a greater force onto the battlefield. He did it through stealth, speed, familiarity with the terrain (he'd grown up just beyond the mountains to the west), and sheer trickery—a virtual recluse who kept his elaborate plans even from his closest subordinates, he once transferred a bunch of his troops out of the valley by train, then brought them back again, just to confuse Federal spies. Ultimately, Jackson had turned what was intended to be a diversion into one of the most outstanding examples of generalship in the history of arms. His Shenandoah achievement is still studied today as a model of how to defeat a numerically superior opponent through maneuver and deception.

Jackson was summoned east again to help Robert E. Lee drive the Federals away from Richmond in the effort that came to be known as the Seven Days' Battles. Marred by misleading intelligence, Union resourcefulness, lousy maps, and the fact that Lee was working with an incomplete and untried staff structure, the Confederate offensive had trouble right from the start. Jackson didn't help matters, performing with none of the dash or ingenuity that had defined his valley triumph. In fact, the chaos of the Seven Days pointed to Jackson's greatest weakness: his inability to compensate for an unforgiving, hard-driving style of command. Stonewall, to put it simply, was exhausted. During one evening mess, the general's head was seen falling forward in slumber, a biscuit clenched between his teeth.

No matter. McClellan's Federals were pushed off the Peninsula anyway, and Jackson was soon on to more remarkable feats, all of which he piously claimed to be the work of Providence. His vaunted troops won a close battle at Cedar Mountain, performed a daring end run around the Union right before the Second Battle of Bull Run (another incredible feat of his foot cavalry, some of whom marched approximately fifty-four miles in two days), endured the appalling slaughter of Antietam, and turned back a potent Federal assault at Fredericksburg. He had weaknesses, to be sure. It was said that Stonewall put more officers under arrest than all other Rebel generals combined, a testament to his unyielding need for absolute discipline. And his refusal to share his plans with prominent subordinates led to a needless amount of confusion—in an effort to keep things from the enemy, he often succeeded in keeping them from his own men. But Jackson had become the toast of spectators across the globe. Northerners read of his exploits with a mixture of alarm and grudging admiration. To Robert E. Lee, he was indispensable—the bold, visionary lieutenant who could be relied upon to deliver the coup de grâce in every battle that mattered.

And it was in that capacity that Jackson made his final—and most amazing—performance. In May 1863, Lee faced somewhere around 70,000 Union troops under Joseph Hooker with only 40,000–50,000 of his own near Chancellorsville, Virginia. Ever the gambler, Lee divided his smaller force, betting on Jackson's ability to pull off another miracle. It was a good bet. Jackson and his corps of 26,000 Rebels were dispatched on a tortuous twelve-mile march through a densely wooded thicket called the Wilderness to emerge on Hooker's far right flank. Moving such a large body of men and artillery such a considerable distance along narrow, vine-choked footpaths on an oppressively hot day was no easy feat, and it took Jackson nearly all of May 2 to pull it off. Late that afternoon, he sent his men howling out of the trees to slam into the enemy's exposed flank. Having achieved complete surprise, they rolled up the Union Eleventh Corps like a carpet, eventually advancing three miles before darkness brought the rout to a halt. Furious Rebel attacks the following day further shrank Hooker's perimeter. He pulled the Army of the Potomac back across the Rappahannock by May 6. Chancellorsville was an astounding Confederate victory.

But by that time, the man who had orchestrated it was fighting for his life. At around 9:00 on the evening of May 2, Jackson and his staff were reconnoitering the lines when, in the confusion of the night, they were mistaken for Union soldiers by a unit of North Carolina infantry and cut down in a fusillade of musketry. Two balls tore into Jackson's left arm and a third lodged in his right hand. He was rushed to a rear area field hospital amidst the terrific violence of a nighttime artillery duel, and his left arm was later amputated. In the wake of his surgery, pneumonia settled in and took him on May 10.

In addition to the Second Corps, Jackson left behind a small family (Mary Anna Morrison, his second wife, and the mother of his only surviving child, Julia; his first wife, Elinor Junkin, died in 1854), a tough, dwarfish steed named Little Sorrel, a deeply bereaved Confederacy, and an outsized reputation that has only grown in the ensuing century and a half. It is telling indeed that Robert E. Lee never again attempted the daring flanking maneuvers that his favorite general performed effortlessly at such conspicuous Southern victories as Second Bull Run and Chancellorsville. "He has lost his left arm," Lee famously remarked upon hearing of Jackson's amputation, "but I have lost my right arm."

GIBSON WHO . . . ?

Thomas Jackson may not have made it through his first year at West Point had it not been for a whiz kid named W. H. Chase Whiting, one of the academy's best students at the time. When Jackson beseeched Whiting to be, in effect, his tutor, Whiting accepted and steered the hapless plebe through examinations (barely). But there's another figure without whom Jackson would never have graduated and become a legend—or, indeed, have even gotten into West Point at all. When Congressman Samuel Hays appealed to his fellow northwest Virginians to give him two West Point applicants, Jackson was one of several who answered the call. But he was bumped by Gibson Butcher, who eased out Jackson in the preliminary interviews. Though Jackson was crestfallen, he would get another chance—when Gibson Butcher came wandering back to Virginia from West Point, a victim of the academy's harsh standards.

He had realized that the Point was not for him and had experienced a change of heart. Had it not been for Butcher's laziness, the South might never have gotten its most celebrated tactician.

GOD'S INSTRUMENT

At some point in 1862, Stonewall Jackson stopped reading newspapers. He had become the subject of countless front-page stories, and it bothered him. To Jackson, God was the prime enabler of the Confederate army's success, and he was merely His instrument. This may seem like so much false modesty, but to Jackson it was very serious. In fact, few—if any—general officers of either side during the Civil War were as profoundly religious as Stonewall Jackson. Baptized on April 29, 1849, at age twenty-five, Jackson the seeker became Jackson the evangelist, commencing a life given over almost completely to the veneration of God. The officers on his staff were selected as much for their piety as for their ability. Jackson prayed intermittently throughout each day, whether there was a battle or not. He gave ten percent of his pay to the Presbyterian Church. To him, spreading the faith was mandatory. He pleaded with his only remaining sibling, Laura, to become a more heartfelt Christian, and during his years as a VMI professor, he taught a Sunday school class for slaves. Jackson was so serious about not conducting secular business on Sunday that he refused even to read mail on that day or, until leading troops in battle during the Civil War, to discuss secular issues. Such committed faith could be a dangerous business: As Jackson himself once remarked about the walks he was fond of taking in the woods to pray, "I was . . . annoyed that I was compelled to keep my eyes open to avoid running against the trees and stumps."

In His Dreams

Here's a supreme irony for you: Thomas Jackson had a notorious habit of falling asleep in church.

SICK AND TIRED

Stonewall Jackson is one of the most famous hypochondriacs in American history. Seemingly everything was wrong with him at one point or another, often all at once: rheumatism, neuralgia, dyspepsia (the bane of his existence), consumption, and ear infections. His vision was bad and got progressively worse (though he staunchly refused to wear spectacles), and his eyes often caused him pain. A believer in self-diagnosis, he read widely on human anatomy, but reached some dubious conclusions. He was convinced, for example, that one of his arms was heavier than the other, requiring him to raise the offending limb for long moments at a stretch to let the blood and humors run down into his body and even things out (!). Jackson always sat up straight as a board—because he thought slouching compressed vital organs, disrupting their ability to function. Of course, he admitted in correspondence to his sister that his afflictions were probably "decreed by Heaven's Sovereign" as punishment for his sins.

Not surprisingly, Jackson's remedies were often just as eccentric as his "ailments"—such as inhaling the smoke of burning mullein, an herbal remedy for respiratory ailments. His favorite nostrum was hydropathy, or "taking the waters" at one of the popular spas of the time. He also espoused calisthenics, which, though based on sound thinking, typically involved some very strange antics: Friends and associates grew accustomed to seeing him hopping in place or furiously pumping his arms to get his heart going.

BON APPÉTIT!

Though Stonewall Jackson insisted on getting the same rations as his men, it couldn't have been that much of a sacrifice. Mindful of the illnesses that seemed to dog him, he fixated on diet as an obvious solution to any physical issue. As a result, his menu was nothing if not bland: unseasoned meat, lots of tea and water, and stale bread (he was known to leave bread out in the open and time its aging so as to acquire the precise degree of staleness). Tobacco and liquor were out of the question, though he did request whiskey on the evening of his amputation at Chancellorsville (one can hardly blame him). He loved fruit, lemons most famously, sections of which he was often seen sucking. Food was too important to leave to chance: Jackson typically showed up at social occasions with his own food in hand.

JOHNNY CASH

The 1864 series of the Confederate $500 bill featured Stonewall Jackson's likeness. He was the only Confederate to die during the war that was featured on Confederate currency.

JUDGING A BOOK BY ITS COVER

"The Old Dominion must be sadly deficient in military men, if this is the best she can do," wrote one Southern news correspondent in 1861 upon setting eyes on Thomas Jackson. "He is nothing like a commanding officer." This observation was made in the weeks before Jackson rose to prominence as the legendary "Stonewall." But his appearance would always be, to put it mildly, underwhelming. To begin with, his feet were simply gigantic, the feature that always and instantly set him apart in a crowd. And while his boots were custom-made, the rest of his clothing was egregiously ordinary. He began the war in his plain blue VMI uniform and kept the kepi long after the rest of the outfit began falling apart. The faded, crumpled cap became his hallmark, its visor pulled down so low over his eyes that he was forced to tip his head up just to see forward. Even his horsemanship was goofy: When riding Little Sorrel at a gallop, he leaned so far forward that observers often worried he would pitch over the animal's head at any moment. His men learned to spot his approach on horseback at long distances from the maladroit profile of the rider.

WITH ENEMIES LIKE THESE . . .

During the Seven Days' Battles, Stonewall Jackson once captured a handful of confused Federals. Upon learning the identity of their esteemed captor, one of the soldiers was heard to exclaim, "Gentlemen, we had the honor of being captured by Stonewall Jackson!" It was an honor indeed. The fact is, Jackson had virtually as many fans in the North as he did in the South. In February 1863, a Confederate pilot boat was captured by Union forces and assigned by the United States Navy for service out of Key West. Her name? The *Stonewall*. Her captors never renamed her out of respect for the vessel's namesake. She even captured a blockade-runner in January 1864.

"I Sing of Arms and the Man . . ."

Stonewall Jackson's amputated left arm is probably the most famous limb of the Civil War. A day after the removal of Jackson's arm, his friend Beverley Tucker Lacy—the chaplain whom Jackson had chosen to oversee the spiritual matters of the Second Corps—buried it in the family plot of his brother's estate, Ellwood, not quite a mile from the field hospital. Almost exactly one year later, during the Battle of the Wilderness, Federal troops dug up the arm and reburied it. In 1903, James Power Smith, one of Jackson's wartime staff officers, placed a small monument over the spot to mark it for posterity. The actual remains of the limb, however, have never been seen by anybody since those violent days in the Wilderness in 1864—except, allegedly, by Smedley Butler, a major general in the United States Marine Corps who is believed to have exhumed it during Civil War reenactment maneuvers in 1921 and to have reburied it in a metal box, though there is some debate as to whether or not this really happened. Whether the arm is precisely beneath the marker that stands in the burial plot now is open to question, though there's little doubt that it resides somewhere in the cemetery. Interestingly, Jackson himself would probably have dismissed all the fuss over his arm as so much impious idolatry.

19 RICHARD STODDERT EWELL

February 8, 1817–January 25, 1872

HIGHEST RANK:

Confederate General

ASTROLOGICAL SIGN:

Aquarius

NICKNAMES:

Dick, Old Bald Head, Old Baldy

WORDS TO REMEMBER:

"It don't hurt a bit to be shot in a wooden leg."

July 5, 1863. As the Army of Northern Virginia retreated south from its defeat at Gettysburg, Lieutenant General Richard Ewell was conferring with Robert E. Lee and James Longstreet when enemy artillery rounds began wreaking havoc with the slowly moving column. Enraged, Ewell begged his superior for permission to wheel his corps around and strike the Federal pursuers. Lee refused, however, insisting that now was not the time. And though he didn't voice it, there must have been another thought going through Lee's head at the moment: a wish that Ewell had felt this aggressive four days earlier, when it really mattered.

Such inconsistencies had once been unheard of in Dick Ewell. In the Shenandoah Valley, he had been Thomas "Stonewall" Jackson's sturdy right hand, and he had gone on to inherit the Second Corps when Jackson fell. But that was the problem: Who could fill Stonewall's shoes? Someone had to do it, and Ewell was as good a choice as any. But it wasn't long before the inevitable comparisons began to be drawn—not least at Gettysburg, where many Southern men found themselves wondering aloud, "If only Jackson were here . . ."

Born in Washington, D.C., Ewell grew up in Virginia. His family was poor and his father was drunk, then dead. Ewell never really knew him. After his older brothers went off to make something of themselves, Ewell helped to run his mother's denuded household, becoming precisely the sort of honest, industrious fellow that had "West Point bound" blazoned across his

seamless brow. He graduated from the academy in 1840, a good student—though rough-hewn—who drew snickers with his lisp but impressed everyone with his unmistakable potential. What followed was a long, arduous affair with America's colorful Southwest, replete with Indian strife, otherworldly boredom, and intermittent droughts. During the Mexican War, he caught malaria and lost a brother to enemy fire. He was awarded a brevet to captain for his troubles. Life on the frontier suited him; he earned respect from soldiers and fellow officers alike for his brusque, can-do manner and supplemented his income with shrewd speculations in cattle and silver mining. He was smart, mindful of the ladies, tough when he needed to be, and incorruptible. Such qualities made military careers in those days, and Ewell's was no exception.

> With his bulging eyes, beaklike nose, and a habit of cocking his head to one side, it's no wonder so many people compared Richard Ewell's appearance to that of a bird.

Siding with his native Old Dominion at the outbreak of civil war, "Old Baldy," as he quickly became known, was a Confederate asset—an officer of dragoons with combat experience and plaudits from some of the most important soldiers in the country (the great Winfield Scott had commended Captain Ewell's ability during the Mexican War). Material like this was not lost on Southern authorities, but Ewell became the butt of war's bad joke at First Bull Run, where a confusion in orders rendered him and his brigade on the right flank while matters came to a decisive head on the left. It was a bad start, to be sure, and one for which poor Ewell drew no small amount of press attention.

But what do the papers know? It wasn't long before General Jackson was being sent west to the Shenandoah Valley, and Ewell went with him. There Ewell learned several things: first, that the nickname "Stonewall" may have had more to do with Jackson's penchant for withholding information from those around him than any gift for standing firm against assault; second, that this could be profoundly frustrating; and third, that Jackson was either a genius or a lunatic. Ewell proved his worth by keeping up with Jackson's lightning pace, providing a tough, reliable counter to the latter's shamanistic excesses. Jackson was in charge, though, and that suited Ewell just fine; with precise orders (when they were forthcoming), Ewell was in his element, comforted by the assurance that the greater course of things was somebody else's problem.

Ewell handled his division ably during the Seven Days' Battles, during which so many other Confederate leaders bungled, foundered, or—in Jackson's case—slept. The next campaign, however, witnessed the defining tragedy of his life. At the beginning of the Second Battle of Bull Run, on August 28, 1862, Ewell was gravely wounded in his left leg during a hot fight near Groveton, Virginia. Rushed to a house several miles from the battlefield, the general was put under the saw the following day. The amputee's survival was in doubt for some time, as Ewell's health had never been very good since his malarial days before the war. But ensconced at Dunblane, the home of his cousin Jesse Ewell, Dick made a gradual and impressive comeback.

The question was: a comeback to what? Jubal Early had taken over his division and would probably retain the post. Besides, Early was a friend, and Ewell didn't cherish the prospect of testing their relationship. That some sort of place would be found for him, however, was not in doubt. Ewell was more than just one of the highest-ranking major generals in the Confederate army; he also had a solid record as a dependable, assertive leader. He executed orders with flair and enthusiasm, and he fought with imagination. Indeed, he had come to be regarded as brilliant by many— particularly those who had witnessed firsthand his mental celerity on the battlefield, his mouth straining through a litany of profanities to clearly elucidate the visionary plans hatching beneath his shining pate. Old Baldy was colorful, popular, and deeply respected. Jackson himself, in a letter to Lee, admitted that he would gladly follow Ewell in a descent on Washington. That's no ordinary compliment.

Jackson's greatest effort on behalf of his old protégé, however, was a bit graver—literally. His death from wounds incurred at Chancellorsville inspired Lee to shake up the command structure of the Army of Northern Virginia. And to Dick Ewell went the vaunted Second Corps. This was natural; after all, Ewell had been a central part of the Confederate martyr's most successful accomplishments. The decision was largely cheered by the officers and men. But was Ewell, scarred by such a savage battle wound, up to it?

Those who wondered had their answer soon enough. Nine months after receiving his wound, Old Baldy was back in action. And though he had lost a limb, he'd gained a wife. Lizinka Campbell Brown was Ewell's first cousin, a widow whose first match had made her one of the wealthiest women in the South. A longtime recipient of Ewell's affections, Lizinka was a prize—a prize, as he would eventually learn, that came with a price. But in the spring of 1863, exciting things were in the air. Fortified by the love of a good woman, General Ewell strapped on his wooden leg and headed out in search of his destiny. It was a propitious time to do so: The Army of Northern Virginia was ambling for Pennsylvania in the second of Lee's attempts to take the war to the enemy. And Ewell's Second Corps was slated to lead the way.

To many observers, the new corps commander looked sickly, frail, or worse. He mounted his horse with difficulty (one can hardly fault him) and the color always seemed absent from his face. The old flame remained, however, as Ewell proved soon enough. Charged with clearing the Federals out of northern Virginia to make way for Lee's invasion plans, Dick orchestrated a truly brilliant descent on Winchester, a Union stronghold, capturing well over three thousand of the enemy and routing the rest. It was a Federal disaster and Ewell's finest hour—an elegantly simple plan that was cunningly conceived and thoroughly executed. The whole affair had been swift, neat, and merciless. From the privates in his corps to the newspapers in Richmond, everyone sang Ewell's praises.

Thus ensured of immortality, the general was on to Pennsylvania, the vanguard of an invading army in high spirits and encouraged by the real possibility of dealing a blow that could precipitate the war's conclusion. Ewell would find himself at a crossroads in history. And he would take the wrong road.

The Battle of Gettysburg was an accidental fracas that evolved, rather quickly, into a scramble for high ground. The first round went to Ewell's Confederates, who—working in concert with elements of A. P. Hill's corps— found the enemy, trounced him, and took the town (along with a horde of prisoners). But the beaten Federals weren't simply flying to the four winds; instead, they made a fighting retreat south to the high ground that dominated Gettysburg and its environs. The prominence in question was Cemetery Hill, where the bluecoats commenced preparations to receive an assault that they were sure was coming fast.

And they weren't the only ones who had made this assumption. Indeed, an assault on the demoralized defenders of Cemetery Hill was taken as a virtual fact by men and officers on both sides. Ewell, however, wasn't so sure. To begin with, he had arrived in the area of Gettysburg with the standing injunction from Lee not to bring on a general engagement until the rest of the army had joined him. That had not yet happened. While Ewell was chewing this over, he received further instructions from Lee that seemed to give him permission to take the position if he thought it was prudent to do so (Lee made it clear that Ewell's corps would not receive any support in the action). But did Ewell have enough fresh men on hand? He wasn't at all sure. Nor was he sure whether the position on Cemetery Hill was being reinforced with fresh enemy troops (it was—eventually). And while all this back-and-forthing was going on inside Ewell's head, his officers were gritting their teeth at the realization that every lost moment gave the blue bellies on the hill more time to improve their defensive works.

All of which is to say that Ewell was displaying a degree of caution that, though controversial, wasn't necessarily inappropriate. But there was another overriding factor at work: Jackson would have gone up that hill immediately. Of this there can be no doubt. And Ewell, already viewed as Stonewall's de facto successor, had stepped into a moment that served most keenly to highlight their differences—a moment pregnant with significance.

The high ground south of Gettysburg would stay in Union hands, despite two more days of battle. And while Ewell hadn't lost the battle all by himself, many thought he'd done his share. For Robert E. Lee, the lieutenant generals that commanded his three corps were the primary weapons in his arsenal—the men whose expertise and character were called upon to transfer Lee's discretionary orders to the needs of the moment. As such, they had to exhibit a large degree of independence. Ewell had some trouble with this. Though he had made an invaluable division commander, his performance at Gettysburg seemed to lack the assertive dynamism that Lee required in a corps-level leader.

It wasn't enough to get him sacked, of course. But Lee had his eye on him and began to develop doubts. Ewell led the Second Corps ably right up through the Battle of the Wilderness in May 1864. But that same month, in the carnage of Spotsylvania, his bad judgment harvested a frightful crop of corpses and essentially gutted one of his divisions. Evidence suggests that this was the final straw for Lee, whose gentlemanly sense of protocol required an excuse to ease the blow. A searing bout of diarrhea came to the rescue, crippling Old Baldy and compelling Lee to put Jubal Early, whose fighting abilities he increasingly admired, at the head of the Second Corps. Ewell did everything short of riding a bucking bronco to prove his recovery, but to no avail. Lee had lost his faith in the gallant hero of Winchester.

So what had happened? Was it the stump? Some contemporaries blamed Ewell's erratic performance on the severe wound he received at Groveton. But those closest to the general blamed his wife. Since his return to duty after the loss of his leg, Lizinka had assumed an increasingly important role in Ewell's life—too important, according to some observers. In fact, Dick openly conferred with her over military decisions, especially crucial personnel choices such as promotions. "Petticoat government," his staff called it. And whether or not they were exaggerating, one thing's for sure: Ewell himself failed to hit the issue head-on, allowing it to fester and create divisions that would otherwise not have been there.

At any rate, the Second Corps was no longer his. Jubal Early shared Dick's love of drink, cynicism, and profanity, and had long been a friend to whom he turned for advice. Now "Old Jubilee" had taken his unit, souring the relationship and leaving Ewell without a job. Or at least a job he could be proud of. In June the one-legged warrior was put in charge of the defenses of Richmond, a post that—to a man who had raced along the Shenandoah Valley with Stonewall's "foot cavalry" and stormed the forts around Winchester—was more like a punch in the kidney than a transfer of responsibility. Nevertheless, Ewell was still one of the most valuable military leaders in the Confederacy, and the capital at Richmond was no backwater. Here was a defensive effort worthy of a man with Dick's talents.

But that was not Ewell's legacy in Richmond. When Ulysses Grant's final offensive came crashing toward the Rebel capital, Ewell was given an order by the secretary of war that he was loath to carry out: burn Richmond's vast warehouses full of cotton and tobacco. Though he fought the idea and was only obeying orders, Ewell was blamed by antagonists from the North and South for much of the destruction that left Richmond a smoking wreck. He led his troops westward in Lee's general retreat and was captured at Sayler's Creek along with nearly all the men under his command.

Ultimately, Dick Ewell died as a man keen on growing things rather than killing them. After spending time in a Boston Harbor prison following the war, he returned to his wife and commenced devoting his time to something that had fascinated him since his days in the Southwest: agriculture. Spring Hill, Lizinka's principal property in Tennessee, was developed into an extraordinarily successful stock farm. Ewell also managed properties in Mississippi. When he died in 1872 from a frightful wave of pneumonia that also claimed his wife, he had done his best to become a loyal citizen of the nation whose government he had once fought against—and to put behind him the nightmarish war that had done its damnedest to kill him.

SEE DICK CUSS. CUSS, DICK, CUSS.

Early in the war, during the Battle of Fairfax Courthouse, Ewell—still a colonel—took a bullet in the shoulder. When a nearby soldier inquired after his health, the colonel spat back that it was none of his damned business and to get back in the ranks. It was vintage Dick Ewell: irascible and vulgar. According to one man who knew him in the old army, Ewell could "swear the scalp off an Apache." A soldier who fought under the general during the Civil War called him "the most violently and elaborately profane man I ever knew" whose oaths "seemed the result of careful study and long practice." Old Baldy himself is believed to have remarked that, with his swearing and Jackson's praying, the pair could whip the devil himself.

Interestingly enough, it was Stonewall's piety that inspired Ewell to take a more religious course in his personal affairs, which meant taking the profanity down a notch or two. But that was easier said than done—particularly at such moments when an expletive seemed all but irresistible. At Spotsylvania, Ewell taunted his routed soldiers by screaming, "Run, goddamn you, run!" and beating them with the flat of his sword. Lee saw the display, which played a role in the commanding general's decision to bump Ewell permanently from the Second Corps.

THE SINCEREST FORM OF FLATTERY

In May 1862, Stonewall Jackson sent Ewell a message that "with the help of divine Providence," he had captured much of Union general Robert Milroy's wagon train. An exasperated Ewell shouted, "What has Providence to do with Milroy's wagon train?!" It was an excellent reminder of the gulf that divided Ewell, earthy and indelicate, from his churchy comrade-in-arms. They were an odd pair, to be sure, and their success in the Shenandoah Valley belied a vast difference in temperament. But in time Ewell came to view the old VMI professor as an uncanny virtuoso and stopped his practice of asking fellow officers if they had considered the possibility that Jackson was actually insane.

A longtime lightweight in spiritual matters, Ewell is said to have witnessed the spectacle of Jackson praying one night alone in his tent and walked away with a newfound eagerness to embrace the faith.

Ewell never did make a very believable pilgrim. But he did share some other curious characteristics with Jackson—stomach troubles, for one. Dyspepsia was a constant irritant for Ewell, and he adopted a diet that Jackson would've appreciated: bland oatmeal gruel, bread, tea, fruit. Breakfast often consisted of lettuce and cucumbers washed down with coffee. He even adopted some of Jackson's curatives, including cold water for neuralgia and avoiding pepper because it was theoretically so bad for the legs. When it came to alcohol, however, Ewell couldn't have been more different from Stonewall. Ewell loved the stuff, especially Madeira wine, which he credited with playing a major role in helping him recover from his amputation.

OLD BALDY

Dick Ewell was never accused of being a good-looking man. With bulging eyes, a beaklike nose, and a habit of cocking his head to one side, he seemed like some hapless avian spy who remained unaware that his shoddy human costume was giving him away. In fact, so many witnesses compared him to a woodcock that one suspects they had all gathered at some point and come to a consensus on the description. Capping his fowl physiognomy was Ewell's most distinguishing physical characteristic: a gloriously hairless head as smooth as a magpie's crown. Unburdened by functioning follicles almost since its owner's West Point days, Ewell's dome made him stand out at a considerable distance, even through the chaos of a battlefield. When he grew a full beard as if to compensate, someone asked him about the contrast. He replied that the condition resulted from the fact that he used his head more than he did his jaws.

WOODEN YA KNOW?

True to form, Ewell proved difficult to rescue in the frantic moment after his grievous wounding at Groveton. Hoisted by Alabama soldiers hoping to carry the wounded general to safety, he demanded that they put him down, pay him no more attention than any other wounded soldier, and get back to killing enemy troops. He was no more accommodating to the surgeon whose saw had an appointment with his leg the following day. "Tell the #@%$ doctor that I'll be #@%$ if it shall be cut off, and that these are the last words of Ewell," growled the distressed patient. But the wooden leg that ended up replacing his amputated one proved more than adequate. At the Battle of Gettysburg, a sniper's round struck Ewell in his prosthesis. He later instructed a fellow officer on the merits of going into battle with a fake limb. "You see how much better fixed for a fight I am than you are." He would use the peg years later on his Spring Hill farm when challenged by an especially aggressive Angora billy goat. After being knocked to the ground by the animal, Ewell fended off further attacks with his prosthesis until help arrived.

CALL PETA!

Though Ewell suffered three wounds during the war, including the one that cost him his leg, his mounts fared much worse. Ewell had five horses shot from under him by the end of the conflict.

20 AMBROSE POWELL
HILL

November 9, 1825–April 2, 1865

HIGHEST RANK:

Confederate General

ASTROLOGICAL SIGN:

Scorpio

NICKNAME:

Little Powell

WORDS TO REMEMBER:

"If the Union is dissolved I shall make tracks for home, and offer my services to the governor, and intimate my modest desire for a brigade at least. I've been a sub long enough, and wish now to seek the bubble reputation at the cannon's mouth."

Of all Robert E. Lee's principal lieutenants, A. P. Hill remains the most enigmatic. James Longstreet was the old warhorse, "Stonewall" Jackson the pious eccentric, Dick Ewell the bird-faced whiner, etc. Hill, on the other hand, was the little guy who was always ill, who fought brilliantly and made spectacular mistakes, who boasted an aristocrat's breeding but favored calico shirts with the sleeves rolled up. He was proud and humble, careful and rash, robust and sickly, solicitous and quarrelsome—an illustrious and deeply flawed hero who seemed to personify the star-crossed rebellion for which he gave his life. His death at the Confederacy's eleventh hour couldn't have been more fitting.

A. P. Hill's good luck charm was a ham bone that he received from his mother as a keepsake. He carried it for most of his life and was rumored to be without it on the day he died.

Descended from a martial lineage that included Revolutionary War heroes and an Indian fighter named Ambrose Powell who rubbed shoulders

with James Madison, "Powell," as his family called him, was born in Culpeper County, Virginia, to landed wealth. His good education prepared him well for West Point, but debilitating sickness led to prolonged absences, and he graduated a year late in 1847. Bouts of infirmity that robbed him of his full physical and psychological ability throughout his life would only intensify late in the Civil War. Though the precise nature of his ailment was a mystery for years, biographer James I. Robertson drew on the input of medical experts to confirm a popular theory: Powell's suffering began with a case of gonorrhea contracted in 1844 during a stop in New York City, leading to recurring inflammation of the prostate that was as incurable as it was painful. Until his dying day, Hill had to live with intermittent breakouts of prostatitis.

The condition was with him during the war in Mexico, to which he arrived late but in plenty of time to catch a nearly lethal case of typhoid fever. And it blossomed brutally in Florida, adding to the interminable misery of boredom, humidity, insects, and yellow fever that made the notion of dying at the hands of a Seminole war party seem positively delightful by comparison. From the lawless wastes of south Texas to the sublime isolation of Key West, Powell Hill did his time on the nation's frontier and then some, often numbing his pain with drink. With a slight build and unsteady constitution, it is hardly surprising that he took a much safer job in Washington at the Coast Survey in 1855. He quickly became popular in capital social circles, where his wit, eloquence, and obvious good breeding endeared him to officers and civilians alike. In the summer of 1859, he married a widow named Kitty Morgan McClung, sister of future Confederate celebrity John Hunt Morgan. It was a perfect, loving match, and Hill would take extraordinary pains to be with "Dolly," as he called her, even during the harrowing months of war.

The arrival of war in 1861 was greeted by Hill with ferocious enthusiasm. Though opposed to slavery, he was appalled by the willingness of the federal government to take up arms against his beloved Virginia. But just as important, he saw an opportunity to write his chapter in history. Through years of service in lousy locales, he'd hungered in vain for promotion, and he knew his time had come. Self-assured and passionate, Hill took the bit in his teeth and, during the blood-soaked years that followed, he rarely let it go. Like Stonewall Jackson, against whom he would bitterly quarrel, he seemed transformed by military action, as if the cacophonous, mutilating maelstrom of the battlefield were somehow his natural environment. Quick, decisive action—some would say "impetuosity"—became his hallmark.

But that lay in the future. For now he had to settle for a colonel's commission in the new Confederate army, a regiment of fellow Virginians to command, and an irritating lack of action. In fact, 1861 was a pretty underwhelming year for Hill. To his extreme dismay, he and his troops even missed the war's first great clash at Bull Run when they were shunted off to a quiet sector of the front as soon as they showed up. He impressed his superiors as an officer of quality who saw to the efficiency and welfare of his men, and he was rewarded with a brigadier general's rank. But just as telling was the Richmond newspaper that reported the promotion of "A. P. Hall of North Carolina."

All that would change during the Peninsula campaign of 1862. Leading a brigade in Longstreet's division, Hill made his mark where he knew he would: under enemy fire. At the Battle of Williamsburg, while opposing ranks separated by less than fifty yards unleashed gales of lead into each other under a drenching rain, Hill could be seen walking the battle line, his eyes flashing beneath a soaked felt hat and his voice hoarse with commands. He led with guts and intelligence, and he led from the front. Promotion soon followed as the Army of Northern Virginia struggled to fit hordes of new recruits into a coherent command structure. By the end of May, Hill had become the youngest major general in the Rebel army—at the head, oddly enough, of the largest division. With conspicuous irony, he christened it the "Light Division," and a legend was born.

What followed were the glory days of "Little Powell" and the Confederacy. But the Army of Northern Virginia first had to do some maturing, as did the Light Division, and Lee's offensive of the Seven Days' Battles offered more than enough opportunity. The growing pains, however, were horrific. At Mechanicsville, Stonewall Jackson's tardiness conspired with

Hill's own impulsiveness to conjure a bloodbath: the Light Division, hurled against unassailable defensive ground, was decimated by relentless musketry and artillery fire. It was even worse the following day at Gaines' Mill, costing Hill's division a grisly 2,600 killed and wounded. Throughout the Seven Days' Battles, Little Powell displayed some trouble making the transition from brigade to division command and occasionally erred on the side of recklessness. But he proved himself as a tough frontline fighter.

He also proved just how peevish he could be, when a squabble sparked by the Richmond press over proper credit for winning the Battle of Frayser's Farm mushroomed into a full-blown feud with his superior, James Longstreet. Things got so bad between the two that Longstreet had the waspish Virginian placed under arrest; Hill responded with an absurd request to settle the matter with a duel, which, thanks to the intercession of Robert E. Lee, never took place. But all this was nothing compared with the battle royal that erupted with Jackson, now overseeing the Light Division. Hill, who had rebelled against his mother's Baptist fervor as a young man, found Jackson's odor of sanctity a little cloying. The thing that really bugged him, however, was Stonewall's . . . well, stonewalling. Jackson, flinty and detached, had the maddening habit of withholding vital information from his subordinates, a trait that mixed poorly with Hill's penchant for rash decision-making. Nevertheless, throughout the campaign that climaxed in the Second Battle of Bull Run, from Cedar Mountain to Chantilly, Hill and Jackson manhandled their Union adversaries even as they increasingly loathed each other. Things between them finally snapped just as Robert E. Lee was commencing his daring invasion of Maryland in September 1862. Hill, infuriated by Jackson's habit of issuing orders to Light Division officers without going through him first, vented weeks of pent-up frustration at Jackson, who was already fuming over Hill's inability to get his men up and marching on schedule. And suddenly—for the second time in less than three months—Little Powell found himself under arrest.

Incredibly, the hostility between Hill and Jackson would not truly end until the latter's death. It lived on in hotheaded correspondence that proved at least two things: Stonewall Jackson often abused his rank like a tyrant, and A. P. Hill could be a prima donna.

But in September 1862, much more pressing matters occupied them both. At Antietam Creek, Maryland, George McClellan had the greatest chance he was ever going to get to utterly destroy the Army of Northern Virginia. With A. P. Hill guarding Harpers Ferry miles to the south, Lee found himself without the Light Division, facing a much larger force, with the Potomac River barring any hope of retreat to his west or south. Riding from flank to flank, furiously filling gaps in the line by moving troops to the most hotly contested areas, Lee began to wonder if it all might end then and there. As if in answer to his prayers, dust clouds to the south announced the arrival of Little Powell. Hill, having been alerted by messenger to the situation, had driven his men on one of the most celebrated forced marches of the Civil War, all the while exhorting them with shouts of "General Lee is in trouble, and he needs you!" His arrival could not have been timed better by a Hollywood director. The famously reserved Lee even broke down and hugged him. Coming up from the south, elements of Hill's exhausted division drove into the flank of Ambrose Burnside's Federals, starting a retreat that spread like wildfire. Hill had saved the Army of Northern Virginia with fewer than three thousand men—the other half of his division had yet to arrive.

If Antietam was the bloodiest day in American history, it was also the greatest day in A. P. Hill's life. He even delivered an encore performance at Boteler's Ford on the Potomac: While bringing up the rear of Lee's withdrawal into Virginia, Hill turned around and trounced a force of pursuing Federals. This guy had become the Army of Northern Virginia's trump card.

One can only hope that he savored the feeling, for it was not to last. Back in August, at the Second Battle of Bull Run, Hill had made a bizarre and pronounced blunder by leaving a gap between two of his brigades big enough for assaulting bluecoats to pour through. The Rebels had still carried the day, but the debacle was indicative of Hill's capacity to slip in the unlikeliest of circumstances. Now, in December, he did it again at Fredericksburg, allowing a veritable chasm of six hundred yards to yawn ominously between two of his brigades on his part of the front line. It was an invitation the enemy couldn't refuse. In fact, the only appreciable gains the Union army made on that day of defeat were made precisely at that point, throwing Hill's men into a flurry of desperate activity and costing no small number of lives. Worst of all, Hill wasn't even there to fix his mistake—he had established his headquarters at the far left end of his sector and was nowhere to be found when all hell broke loose.

His poor performance at Fredericksburg (often attributed to the loss of his daughter Netty to diphtheria just before the battle) notwithstanding, Hill was probably the finest division commander in the Army of Northern Virginia. Naturally, he was promoted to lieutenant general and given an entire corps to command—a mistake, as events would prove soon enough. The origins of that decision lay in the chaos of Chancellorsville, on the evening of Jackson's great flanking maneuver. Little Powell was riding with Stonewall when a sheet of friendly fire grievously wounded the hallowed Second Corps commander. Hill was one of the few in the party to escape mauling in that unfortunate incident, but he caught a piece of shrapnel in the leg not long afterward. Command of Jackson's corps then fell temporarily to Jeb Stuart. But in the reorganization of Lee's army that followed, Hill—once he recovered from his wound—was considered a natural to replace the great Stonewall (ironic, perhaps, considering the enmity that had divided them). And while Lee ended up giving the Second Corps to Dick Ewell, he had a Third Corps created especially for the hero of Antietam.

Call it the Peter Principle, call it whatever you like, but Hill proved much more adept at leading smaller units "at the cannon's mouth," as he liked to say, than he did at orchestrating the big picture from a corps commander's perspective. When the Army of Northern Virginia invaded Pennsylvania in the summer of 1863, Hill, while in Cashtown, sent a division east to forage for supplies and shoes in Gettysburg. Though guided by Lee's directive not to bring on a general engagement (he had yet to concentrate his entire army), the division got ensnared in a fight with Union forces and managed to bring on a general engagement anyway. Hill has often been blamed for starting the Battle of Gettysburg by sending a division on a reconnaissance that should have been conducted by a smaller force—one that wouldn't have invited a major fight. Whatever the truth, virtually every one of the Army of Northern Virginia's commanding generals blew it at the epic three-day struggle that ensued. Lost in the transition between division and corps command, Little Powell seemed nonplussed at best. On the second day, with one of his divisions slated to support Longstreet's poorly executed assault on the Union left, Hill, listless and possibly confused, failed to galvanize his men for their part of the plan. And, though commanded by Longstreet, the epic tragedy known as "Pickett's Charge" on the third day included two of Hill's divisions—responsibility for which fell through the cracks that existed between the two incommunicative corps commanders. Hill had become more a spectator of war than a participant in it.

For the Third Corps, the dreadful pain of Gettysburg was followed in October by the unmitigated disaster of Bristoe Station. Having stumbled upon a corps of hapless Federals, the ever-impetuous Hill decided to bag them then and there, before they could get into battle formation. Prudent reconnaissance would have revealed another Union corps waiting behind an embankment to the southeast, but Hill wasn't in a prudent mood. When the trap was sprung on the division that he had sent rolling forward, slaughter ensued. It may well have been the nadir of Hill's career.

His old nemesis, prostatitis, returned with a vengeance the following winter, adding considerably to the burdens of his command. Through much of the battles at the Wilderness and Spotsylvania in 1864, Hill confined himself to an ambulance because mounting a horse was so painful. He feigned recovery long enough to direct an abortive assault against tough Federal positions at the North Anna River toward the end of May and to savor the victory at Cold Harbor days later. Once the war settled into the protracted siege of Petersburg, Hill and his Third Corps sallied from the trenches on numerous occasions to prove they could still deal out the damage—not least at the celebrated victory of Reams Station, where the great Winfield Scott Hancock's Union corps essentially flew the coop. And Hill was sick as a dog through the whole thing.

By April 1865, he was as wan and fatigued as the thin gray line that guarded Petersburg from imminent Federal attack. When the storm did break, Hill became the most prominent victim of its suddenness and chaos: Riding with a courier in search of his retreating troops, he found himself amidst the enemy and was shot from his horse. Given his ardor for a South that was even then beginning to disappear, it is perhaps good that he didn't live long enough to watch the finale.

HIDING IN PLAIN SIGHT

Powell Hill had a thing for calico shirts, including a red one that became his trademark on the battlefield. But such plain apparel could lead to confusion. On the march to Antietam, for instance, Hill berated a teamster in the wagon train who was beating his stubborn mules and was promptly and gruffly told to mind his own business. The fellow didn't even recognize the commander of the Light Division (and was struck by the flat of Hill's sword for his mistake). In fact, Little Powell's homespun appearance saved his life on at least two occasions. In 1863, while personally reconnoitering fords in the Rappahannock on the eve of the Gettysburg campaign, he led his horse briefly into the river to get a better look at the opposite bank, where Federal pickets stood guard. After he left, a Rebel called out across the water, asking the Yankees why they hadn't taken a shot at General Hill, who'd been sitting on his horse in the river plain as day just a moment ago. They shouted back that they thought he was the officer of the guard and not worth the trouble. An even closer shave occurred during the nightmarish inferno of the Wilderness in 1864. Hill and some of his staff arrived at a farm, where the cleared land offered an opportunity to study the surrounding topography. Quite suddenly, Federals appeared at the edge of the woods behind them and began dismantling a fence that stood in their line of march. They were perhaps a hundred yards away. With impressive composure, Hill and his companions slowly and casually walked their horses away from the enemy soldiers and back into the concealment of the forest. Only later did they discover from a prisoner that the bluecoats at the fence thought Hill and his fellows were local farmers.

Below the Belt

One of Ambrose Powell Hill's closest friends at West Point was a brilliant bantam from Philadelphia named George McClellan. The Civil War would test that friendship, of course. But another, smaller conflict made trouble for the relationship long before that. And it had a name: Ellen Mary Marcy, the woman who would ultimately become Mrs. McClellan. In the winter of 1855–1856, McClellan—anointed by the Marcys to be their daughter's future husband—was thousands of miles away observing the Crimean War. Hill entered Ellen's life around this time and quickly captured her heart. In seemingly no time at all, he had proposed and she had accepted. Convinced that Hill was beneath Ellen's station, Mr. Marcy was beside himself with disappointment and pleaded with his daughter to end the thing. It was Mrs. Marcy, however, who took the gloves off. After doing a bit of digging, she came upon evidence of Hill's bouts with venereal disease and leaked the information to those in the Marcy circle. The fall-out not only destroyed Hill's engagement with Ellen; it also began a testy feud between Mrs. Marcy and George McClellan, who had long since returned to America, conferred with his old buddy, and bowed out of his association with Ellen like the gentleman he was. But Mrs. Marcy had tagged him as the one who'd fingered her as the cur who had spilt the incriminating information about Hill, a fact that McClellan adamantly denied. At any rate, it seems that everybody had come out of this mess with a bruising—except Powell's sister, Lucy, to whom he ended up giving the engagement ring that Ellen returned to him.

LUCK BE SOME GRAVY TONIGHT

Of all the things that Powell Hill took with him to West Point, the strangest—and most indispensable—was a ham bone, bestowed to him by his mother,

Fannie, as a keepsake. He kept it with him the rest of his life as a good-luck charm and is rumored to have been without it the day he was killed.

SOME FINAL THOUGHTS

A. P. Hill was buried three times. His first resting place was in the private cemetery of the Winston family in Chesterfield County, Virginia, largely because the location was relatively close at the time of his death. His remains were moved in 1867 to a plot in Richmond's Hollywood Cemetery to rest with other heroes of the Confederacy. Finally, in 1891, he was relocated to rest beneath the monument to his memory that was erected at the intersection of Laburnum Avenue and Hermitage Road in Richmond. Fittingly for the irreverent Hill, not one of the interments was accompanied by a religious ceremony of any sort.

But Hill had another distinction after life, and one that has become legendary: His was the only name that both Stonewall Jackson and Robert E. Lee mentioned in their deathbed deliriums. "Order A. P. Hill to prepare for action!" cried Stonewall just before his death. "Pass the infantry to the front immediately!" Lee cried simply, "Tell Hill he must come up!" Whatever Hill's merits as a commander of troops, it cannot be denied that occupying a place of prominence in the minds of the Southern Confederacy's two greatest heroes while in their death throes ain't bad.

21 BRAXTON BRAGG

March 22, 1817–
September 27, 1876

HIGHEST RANK:

Confederate General

ASTROLOGICAL SIGN:

Aries

WORDS TO REMEMBER:

"In many efforts, I believe I never made but one successful speech—and that was, in a few words, when I courted my wife—the result then being due less to any merit either in the speech or the speaker than to an unfortunate habit with young ladies of deciding more from impulse than reason, by which, as in my case, they are too apt to be unfortunate."

Of all the Americans who acquired national fame in the Mexican War, few emerged with a greater reputation than Braxton Bragg. A stickler for drill, detail, and discipline, he had earned a reputation as something of a martinet. But on February 23, 1847, he got a chance to show the world that he was also one hell of an officer.

On that day, near a hacienda named Buena Vista, General Zachary Taylor's ambition got him into trouble. Irate over the fact that the Polk administration had stripped his units to build up Winfield Scott's army for the climactic march on Mexico City, Taylor—ordered to sit on his hands at Monterey—decided instead to march his much-depleted force south to scare up a fight. He got one in spades at Buena Vista, where a much larger force of Mexicans prepared to cut his little command to ribbons. In the spirited clash that followed, Bragg moved his "flying battery" of horse artillery with an alacrity that few, except him, thought possible. After racing all the way to the far left from his position on the far right, Bragg helped defeat a determined Mexican flanking attack. He then unlimbered all but the essentials and ran his battery toward the center of the front line where another Mexican attack appeared imminent. There, deprived of infantry support and looking at a determined mass of enemy

troops bearing down on him, Captain Bragg calmly instructed his men to load and fire their guns as quickly as they were able, using deadly canister to decimate the enemy ranks. With remarkable self-control, they waited until the Mexican infantry was practically within spitting range before opening up on them. From there they kept up a destructive tempo, savaging their assailants and completely blunting the attack with but three pieces of field artillery. It was an unforgettable spectacle of sheer nerve.

> During the War with Mexico, an irate colleague placed an eight-inch shell under Braxton Bragg's bunk—and then ignited the shell with a trail of gunpowder. The mattress was destroyed, but Bragg walked away without a scratch.

A legendary exchange was purported to have taken place between Bragg and his superior, Taylor. After asking for support, Bragg is supposed to have been told by Old Zach that there was none to give and that he should "double shot your guns and give 'em hell!" For reasons that are lost to history, Taylor's rustic command was twisted by the popular press and imagination into "Give them a little more grape, Captain Bragg," a phrase that was not only inaccurate but disturbingly affected for a guy whose nickname was "Old Rough 'n' Ready." Other accounts insist that Taylor shouted simply, "Stand to your guns and give 'em hell!" Still another asserts that an adjutant delivered the message from Taylor, which was "Tell him to give 'em hell, God damn him!" (This option, with a maximum of mild vulgarity, is probably correct, given Zachary Taylor's penchant for colorful speech.)

In fact, it is entirely possible that no such exchange occurred at all. But it helped determine the fortunes of the two men involved. Zachary Taylor, an apolitical soldier who nevertheless opposed the regime of President Polk and General Winfield Scott, rode into the White House partly because voters have a soft spot for leather-faced war heroes who shout stuff like "hell," "Goddam," and "double-shot." And as for Bragg: well, it wasn't long at all before parties back home were toasting the man who had dashed those Mexican devils with "a little more grape"—parties that relied on wine to provide a double entendre that was impossible to resist.

The most celebratory of those fetes were thrown in his hometown of Warrenton, North Carolina. And that was a little awkward, because the society folks of Warrenton had never looked favorably upon the Braggs, who were widely dismissed as lowborn trash. Braxton Bragg, the son of a carpenter, had come home a virtual Caesar to be lauded by the aristocratic jackasses who used to laugh at him. In fact, he was better educated than most of them. Schooled at the excellent local academy for the entirety of his youth, he received his free education at West Point and graduated fifth in a class of fifty. Stationed in Florida during the Seminole Wars, Bragg went on to a series of frontier postings before finding fame, and three brevets, in the War with Mexico. Bragg exerted himself in the postwar army as a supreme disciplinarian and malcontent—a man whose adherence to the book, and disputatiousness on its behalf, earned as many foes as it did admirers. This, unfortunately, was to become a major part of his legacy.

But not until the nation tore itself apart. Long before then, Bragg—now a married man—left the army for richer pursuits. He became a sugar planter in Louisiana and managed to secure the position of commissioner of public works for the state. But like so many who left the army for brighter pursuits in those days, he was on a hiatus without knowing it.

In the mounting sectional crisis, Louisiana, in which Bragg lived and did business, understood his worth as a soldier in case of war. In January 1861, Bragg, appointed a major general of state troops, accepted the surrender of the Baton Rouge armory—his first bit of official business as a secession-ist officer. By September 1861, he was a major general in the Confederate army, placed in charge of the Department of Alabama and West Florida. There he exercised what was his greatest gift: an ability to turn recruits into soldiers through adherence to discipline and endless drilling. By the time he left the department, his troops were easily some of the finest in the Rebel army.

They would have to be, too, because they were headed for some of the toughest fighting of the war. Bragg led them up to Mississippi, where Confederate forces were strung out and divided under a confusing command structure that would never get much better and that would essentially doom Rebel efforts in the West. At Corinth, Bragg contributed his excellent troops to the army gathering under Albert Sidney Johnston for a strike at Pittsburg Landing, where forty thousand of Ulysses Grant's troops were waiting to be joined by reinforcements. Johnston, determined to bring structure to his hodgepodge host, made P. G. T. Beauregard his second-in-command. Bragg, appointed chief of staff and given command of a corps, set about training, equipping, and organizing Johnston's army, a Herculean task for which, all agreed, he was ideally suited. Time was of the essence, however, and the army marched toward the enemy before Bragg was able to complete the job to his satisfaction. Now in charge of his corps, he would fight the ensuing battle at Shiloh as a combat general, not as chief of staff. And if he excelled at administrative responsibilities, he was adequate at best at tactics. While Bragg and his fellow commanders managed to whip the Yankees on the first day of the struggle, their overtaxed and disorganized troops were shoved back off the battlefield the following day by Grant. Relying on outdated frontal assaults (Bragg, like many of his contemporaries in both armies, maintained a glassy-eyed love affair with the bayonet), the Confederate commanders had thrown away many of the men Bragg had toiled so hard to turn into soldiers. The Rebels, having finally massed their disparate armies for a concentrated strike, had blown it.

They had also lost Albert Sidney Johnston. Beauregard took his place, but wilted from a bout of interminable illness. The Confederates soon lost Corinth and Beauregard as well—he went on sick leave without permission and brought down the wrath of President Davis. Bragg, having already been promoted to full general, was now in charge.

Starting off with a bang in August 1862, Bragg invaded Kentucky to draw Union attention away from Western Tennessee, to get his army fat on the bounty of the bluegrass state, and to recruit all the pro-South men he was convinced awaited him there. After capturing a Union force at Munfordville and moving on to Bardstown, Bragg watched with pride as Richard Hawes was inaugurated the provisional Confederate governor of Kentucky.

Then things started going south—literally. Turned back by Federals under Buell at the Battle of Perryville, Bragg was compelled to retreat back into Tennessee. There, the following December, he fought a larger force under William Rosecrans at Murfreesboro in what could have been a stunning victory. But ill-advised assaults and the mishandling of troops by Bragg and his subordinates resulted in a bloodbath for both sides that achieved little except to convince Bragg that he should withdraw again. The Kentucky dream was dashed.

And so was confidence in Braxton Bragg. From newspaper editors to government officials to officers and men in the Army of Tennessee itself, derision was heaped on the man who had become a symbol of Rebel failure in the Western theater. One of his division commanders, Franklin Cheatham, vowed he would never serve under Bragg again, while at least two of his corps commanders begged the president himself to replace Bragg. General John Breckinridge, former vice president of the United States and now one of Bragg's principal subordinates, came close to challenging Bragg to a duel. Stunned by the widespread acrimony, Bragg formally asked his staff and corps commanders to give their honest opinions on whether or not he should be relieved. Almost to a man, they agreed that he should.

How had things come to such a pass? To be sure, Bragg's Kentucky campaign and its aftermath had been poorly directed. Many in the Confederacy believed that neither Perryville nor Murfreesboro were bad enough to retreat from; indeed, both were widely regarded as tactical victories that Bragg had simply thrown away. And he continued to use battle tactics that were simplistic, outdated, and unwise by turns. But plenty of his subordinates had made mistakes as well.

In fact, it wasn't just Bragg's leadership failures that were driving everyone nuts. It was also his personal failures. Bragg was a disputatious, curmudgeonly, irritable tyrant—qualities that seemed to find physical manifestation in the black, bushy eyebrows that met seamlessly atop his merciless gaze. He could not learn to set aside feelings for those he didn't like, and he lacked the charisma to secure the loyalty of those he did. His temper was legendary, as was his insistence on doing everything by the book, a supremely impractical trait when leading an army of citizen volunteers. He led by forcing, shoving, and yelling, rather than by example. He was devoid of the personal touch, and the widening gap between him and his subordinates served only to make him harsher and more difficult to get along with. When added to a growing belief that the general lacked imagination and grit in the face of the enemy, it is hardly surprising that Bragg's command was in a lather.

But he wasn't going anywhere, at least not yet. General Joseph Johnston, sent by President Davis to investigate the Army of Tennessee, did not conclude that its commander should be replaced, despite the fact that several of Bragg's lieutenants begged Johnston to take his place. William Rosecrans came after him again, driving him from Tullahoma to Chattanooga and ultimately to Georgia. By this time some of Bragg's subordinates simply began ignoring his orders, making his subsequent triumph at Chickamauga the following September a minor miracle. Reinforced by troops under James Longstreet, Bragg whipped "Old Rosey" in two days of hard fighting, forcing the Federals back into the confines of Chattanooga. Bragg, having determined to take the city at all costs, invested it and settled into a siege.

That was probably a bad idea. His increasingly worn-out army was in no position to force the Federals to do anything, especially after sending part of it away with Longstreet to lay siege to Knoxville. Flagrant disobedience amongst his officers had grown to outrageous levels. Besides, Ulysses Grant soon showed up and began turning the Chattanooga forces around. He struck in November, breaking Bragg's siege—and his army—in a series of brilliant strikes. The Army of Tennessee was a mess.

Even Davis, who had stood by Bragg for so long, had had enough. As for Bragg himself, he was finished as a commanding general. Always more sensitive than he let on, he was exhausted—emotionally and physically—from the hostility toward him that he struggled to understand and ameliorate. After tendering his resignation (which Davis accepted with disturbing rapidity), the irascible North Carolinian went into temporary retirement, and then was brought back to Richmond in a classic example of being "kicked upstairs." There he acted as the president's military advisor, much as Robert E. Lee had once done. Though certainly a better position for Bragg than that of army commander, it did little to better the man's reputation. Bragg tackled the government's embattled supply, recruitment, and administrative systems, but with mixed results. Ineffectual in the face of circumstances that made the government's cause seem increasingly hopeless, Bragg was reassigned to a series of field commands, from Virginia to Georgia to the Carolinas.

His professional fortunes were soon as bad as those of the country he served. In the summer of 1864, Bragg, as Davis's advisor, had sacked Joseph Johnston, the general who had replaced him as commander of the Army of Tennessee. Now back in the field, Bragg found himself coming under the jurisdiction of Johnston, whom Robert E. Lee, newly appointed general in chief of all the Rebel armies, had put back at the head of the Army of Tennessee (or, to be precise, what remained of it). Such turns of fate would be humiliating to anyone. But to a haughty fellow like Bragg, they cut to the bone. He was back with Davis and the government for the flight south and exile, then, with his wife, took a separate course. They were caught in Georgia on May 10.

Bragg went on to better, if not bigger, things in the wake of the war that had annihilated his reputation and nearly destroyed his health. He served as superintendent of the New Orleans waterworks and secured the post of chief engineer of the state of Alabama. Bitter and argumentative, Bragg never forgave either side in the war: the North for doing what it did, and the South for letting it happen. "The war is over, but there is no peace, and never can be between two such people." Not long after moving to Galveston, Texas, he fell dead in the street while walking with an associate. He was just fifty-nine years old, though he looked much, much older.

JAILBIRD

According to biographer Grady McWhiney, Braxton Bragg never mentioned his mother once in all the countless letters of his that have survived. Perhaps it's because she did time in a North Carolina prison for murder. While pregnant with Braxton, Mrs. Bragg was convicted of killing a free African American. It is not known how long she spent behind bars—indeed, some sources contend that Braxton was born in jail, though it seems likely that his mother was released just in time to give birth. At any rate, Braxton—already conscious of his lower-class standing in the Warrenton community—must not have appreciated the added infamy of a mother who had been an imprisoned killer.

STICK THAT IN YOUR SUGGESTION BOX

While stationed outside Monterey during the War with Mexico, Braxton Bragg was left in charge of the camp by his superior, who preferred to stay in the city. As commander, Bragg soon galvanized his reputation as the finest disciplinarian in the army—a distinction that earned him at least as many detractors as supporters. "I am somewhat obnoxious to a few," he wrote in a letter, a dramatic understatement. That someone was willing to bring his reign of terror to an end was brought violently home when two attempts were made on Bragg's life. Though little is known about the first, the second was certainly dramatic, if nothing else. Someone managed to place an eight-inch shell underneath the authoritarian's bed while he was asleep, then set if off by way of a trail of power that led out the door. The ensuing explosion, though tremendous, did more damage to Bragg's mattress than anything else. Incredibly, he walked away from the incident with little more than a ringing in his ear.

Nobody was ever caught for the crime. And as for Bragg, he never lost his ardent belief in stern discipline.

SICK AND TIRED OF BEING SICK AND TIRED

In 1837 Bragg was stationed in Florida to fight Seminole Indians. Within a very short time he was requesting sick leave, having succumbed to the prolific climate and its numerous pathogens. Worse, he never actually recovered. Bragg's ill health seemed a physical manifestation of his sour, spiteful personality. The two fed on each other; in fact, his biographers assert that his symptoms may have been psychosomatic. If some people wore their heart on their sleeves, Bragg seemed to wear his on his skin, temples, joints, and stomach. From boils to migraines, dyspepsia to rheumatism, Bragg sank with time into a vicious round-robin of ailments, a cycle that always increased in intensity when the burdens of his command became greatest. By 1863 he looked like a veritable ghoul. "He is very thin," reported one observer. "He stoops, and has a sickly, cadaverous, haggard appearance." And with doctors prescribing mercury and opium as palliatives, Bragg was likelier to feel worse than better. Under these circumstances, it is hardly surprising that some of his officers and men spoke of Bragg's habit of getting muddle-headed in combat.

22 JAMES EWELL BROWN
STUART

February 6, 1833–May 12, 1864

HIGHEST RANK:

Confederate General

ASTROLOGICAL SIGN:

Aquarius

NICKNAMES:

Beauty, Flower of Cavaliers,
Jeb, Knight of the Golden Spurs

WORDS TO REMEMBER:

"As to being laughed at about
your husband's fondness for
society and the ladies. All I can
say is that you are better off in
that than you would be if I were
fonder of some other things,
that excite no remark in others.
The society of ladies will never
injure your husband and ought
to receive your encouragement"
(in a letter to his wife).

Urbana, Maryland, was an unlikely spot for revelers the night of September 8, 1862. Especially those of a Confederate bent. But here, in the midst of Unionist territory, young warriors in their finest gray made merry by candlelight with a bevy of local ladies, breathing life into a great cold hall that, before the intervention of war, had housed an academy of learning. Then the rumble of distant guns upset the rhythm of the quadrille, and a delicious tension fell upon the place. As riders brought news of enemy action at an outpost, the men dashed away to their waiting saddles with more than the usual pluck. Courage, after all, loves an audience. By midnight, the horsemen had dispatched their adversaries, chased them as far as their galloping mounts would allow, and returned in triumph. The music struck up once again and women dizzy with battle musk pressed their young suitors for tales of derring-do.

The wounding truth, unfortunately, intruded. As injured soldiers from the clash began to be helped through the academy's entrance, ladies started swooning for a very different reason, throwing a decidedly pallid patina over the festivities. Musicians put away their instruments, dancers tended

to the dying, and the familiar rhythm of blood-red reality returned.

All in a night's work for Jeb Stuart and his merry band. The ball had been his idea—jump-starting the social season was his standard modus operandi when settling into new headquarters. Simply put, war was a pageant to Stuart. Though unprecedented in scope, mechanization, and slaughter, the American Civil War was also a reflection of the Victorian age through which it sliced, producing no small number of hotspurs for whom national disintegration was an opening to chivalric distinction. And none of them could hold a candle to the cavalry general from Virginia who called himself "Knight of the Golden Spurs."

Known as the "Flower of Cavaliers," the handsome Jeb Stuart was often swarmed by admiring Southern belles and would happily surrender to their requests for kisses. Mrs. Stuart was not pleased.

Stuart had another nickname, as well: "Beauty," an ironic sobriquet he picked up at West Point because he wasn't much to look at. Unfortunately, he was also easily offended, a combination of traits that got him into one scrape after another. Proud and envious of power, he wore his bruises proudly and resolved to make himself into somebody that people admired—especially women. By the time he graduated from the academy in 1854, he had already fallen for one: A probable proposal to his cousin Bettie Hairston, whom Stuart got to know during his furlough in 1852, was turned down.

The next time he proposed to a woman, in the summer of 1855, he got an answer in the affirmative. Her name was Flora Cooke, the smart, hard-riding daughter of a colonel of dragoons. The couple had met and fallen in love at the romantic lovers' getaway of Fort Leavenworth, Kansas, where Stuart was trying to make a name for himself after a stint on the west Texas frontier. Fort Leavenworth had more than its fair share of trouble, as the army attempted to keep pro- and antislavery militants from cutting each other to pieces (mostly in vain). With the issue over slavery in Kansas left to settlers, the territory, predictably, fell prey to an increasingly volcanic guerrilla conflict. Fights with the Cheyenne were no picnic either—in 1857 Stuart was shot in the chest at close range during a battle with hostiles, nearly ending his life.

But Stuart wasn't just another faceless officer doing time on the prairie (there were no shortage of those). He had stuck with the army because, unlike so many of his fellow West Point graduates, he genuinely liked the rough life, the hard beds, and the moldering food. Enduring it all was a distinction of sorts. But more important, the army was a means of affirmation, a catalyst for his burning need to turn heads in his direction. Outwardly disdainful of the power elite whose ranks he inwardly craved to join, his background nevertheless offered connections to it. Elizabeth, his termagant of a mother, had exacted from him an oath never to touch liquor. But his father had bestowed something of genuine worth: political connections. Archibald Stuart had been an officer during the War of 1812 and a popular figure in state and national politics. The Stuart name was familiar and liked in Virginia. Beauty's greatest asset, however, had been secured at West Point: the Lee family. Custis Lee, a fellow graduate, was one of his best friends, and Custis's father, Robert E., the academy's superintendent between 1852 and 1855, had welcomed the young Stuart into his home as a close acquaintance. All these factors came together in 1859 to decide Beauty's fate.

It began with a stroke of creative genius. Stuart, a consummate horseman (he had often jibed Yankees at the Point for their clumsy equestrian skills), invented a "saber hook" to be attached to a cavalryman's saber belt; it allowed a rider to quickly hang his sword on the saddle, freeing him to dismount with ease. Duly impressed, the government gave Stuart six months' leave to go to Washington and secure a patent for his inspired creation. He was in the offices of the War Department on October 17 when word arrived of the raid on Harpers Ferry. Having appointed Colonel Robert E. Lee to do something about it, the secretary of war awarded an eager Stuart the task of fetching Lee, who was on leave across the river at his Arlington estate. When Lee traveled to Harpers Ferry that evening, his young protégé was with him—and the following day, Stuart found himself standing before the heavy doors of a fire engine house in which a partisan called "Smith" was holed up with his associates and some hostages, his plan to start a slave rebellion having foundered. Stuart held Lee's ultimatum in his hand, and after getting the raiders to open the door under a flag of truce, he beheld the face of the abolitionist who called himself Smith. Immediately, the lieutenant recognized the fellow as none other than John Brown—an unsparing militant he had once met back in "Bloody Kansas." After negotiations went nowhere, Stuart stepped away from the door and waved his hat in the air, giving the signal to Lee and the marines under his command that the time for talk had ended. Later, when the dust had settled and the insurgents were in custody, Stuart, the only person present who had ever met John Brown, was able to positively identify him. All in all, the young officer had performed well, prominently lending his nerve and knowledge to the resolution of an incident that had the whole country talking. Things were looking pretty good for Stuart—he'd even earned $5,000 for the patent of his hook.

Though he was back in Kansas when Abraham Lincoln's election was causing much gnashing of teeth, his name was already on the lips of those in the South who were anticipating a war. Pledging to "go with Virginia," Stuart packed up and took his family back east upon hearing of his native state's secession, resigning his commission in the United States Army. The Confederates already thought better of him than his erstwhile employers: En route to his new lieutenant colonelcy in the Provisional Army of Virginia, he received word that the U.S. Army had planned to give him a promotion of their own—to captain. Pshaw.

It's a wonderful irony that the Civil War's preeminent cavalier began the conflict with a commission in the infantry. (No cavalry openings were available at the time.) But Thomas Jackson, soon to be known to the world as "Stonewall," wasn't going to let that stop him. He gave Stuart a cavalry command, a decision for which virtually everyone in the South would soon be grateful. In skirmishing with Union forces in the northern Shenandoah Valley, Stuart proved uncannily gifted not only at confusing his foes, but also

JAMES EWELL BROWN STUART

at passing his tactical expertise on to the un-blooded civilians under his leadership. After Joseph Johnston assumed command over the forces around Winchester, Stuart screened the army's withdrawal from the Valley, then caught up with it on the road to Bull Run. There, in the war's first major engagement, he led his men in a charge that broke up a unit of Zouaves. But more important, the knowledge of the field gained by his swift horsemen allowed him to guide Jubal Early's infantry to where it was needed most, where it routed the Union right.

Such speed and agility—the ability to be at so many places at once and, when necessary, to seem to be—defined the cavalry; and nobody understood or made use of this as well as Stuart did in the first two years of the war. Tireless, aggressive ("when in doubt, attack"), and to the saddle born, Stuart drew on the South's equestrian culture to forge mounted units that, with his charismatic leadership, made fools of their Union adversaries. His secret weapon, simply enough, was concentration: While Federal troopers were being spread thin across every theater, the Confederacy was pooling its cavalry assets so as to overwhelm the enemy at every encounter. It all meant that Stuart could do things his enemies couldn't. And some of those things were spectacular.

In September 1861, Stuart was given six regiments of horsemen and the rank of brigadier general. By June of the following year, Richmond was being threatened by McClellan's inexorable advance during the Peninsula campaign, Stuart's cavalry was busy screening the Rebel army's retreat toward the capital, and Joseph Johnston was wounded badly enough to be replaced by a new commander. That replacement, of course, was Robert E. Lee. Stuart himself could not have made a more congenial choice.

Jeb Stuart had a case of "the Lees." The new chief of the Army of Northern Virginia was like a father to him, but that was just the beginning. Two of Stuart's regimental commanders were Lees: Robert's son William "Rooney" Lee led the Ninth Virginia Cavalry, while Fitzhugh Lee, a nephew of the elder Lee, rode at the head of the First Virginia. Jeb was still close to his old chum Custis, considered Mrs. Robert E. Lee a sort of second mother, and carried on a correspondence with Lee's daughter, Mary, a friend since his time at West Point. At any rate, Stuart needed no introduction to his new superior. And the two quickly developed a working relationship that any military officer, in any age, would envy.

Lee had to stop McClellan's advance and throw the huge Northern army, already uncomfortably close to Richmond, back down the Peninsula from whence it came. But Lee (being Lee) wanted to do more than that—he wanted to destroy the larger foe, piecemeal. And his dashing young cavalry czar would help him do it. Beauty was charged with making a reconnaissance north of the Chickahominy River, where torrential rains had separated parts of McClellan's army from the rest, inviting their extermination. Stuart did that and went one better. In a move of singular hubris, he drove his 1,200 carefully chosen horsemen on a one-hundred-mile circuit of McClellan's entire army, burning, looting, and confusing as he went. Sure, Lee's intelligence requirements were met: Stuart discovered just how vulnerable those stranded Federal elements were north of the river, paving the way for Lee's advance of the Seven Days' Battles. But Stuart's most significant accomplishment, though less tangible, was incalculably greater. He had turned the Confederacy's dark hour into a bloody good lark, playing "Marco Polo" with the biggest army yet seen in American history. On the eve of an attack like the one Lee was about to unleash, such shenanigans had an unnerving effect—an abusive bit of effrontery that shattered Union delusions of control.

It was merely the first of Stuart's headline-making raids. In late August 1862, he led a descent on Catlett's Station, Virginia, catching the camp of Union general John Pope off guard and grabbing tons of loot, thousands of Yankee greenbacks, and invaluable correspondence that alerted Lee to his enemy's intentions. In October, Stuart went in search of horses at Chambersburg, Pennsylvania, and found more than a thousand of them—in the course of which he once again rode right around McClellan's army and destroyed all manner of matériel. The raid on Dumfries, in December 1862, caught hundreds of prisoners and horses and gave Stuart an opportunity to snipe at Federal quartermaster general Montgomery Meigs, to whom Stuart wired a complaint about the low quality of Northern mules with which he was forced to haul his booty back home. (To add insult to injury, he sent the message from Burke's Station, which Washington believed at the time was still under Union control.)

Stuart had become a legend in his own time. The papers sang his praises. Poets scribbled verses about him. To his countrymen, he was the bold and dashing knight with the devil-may-care style and a real pair of golden spurs to match—sent to him by an admiring Baltimore woman. And to the Union he was a bona fide bogeyman who appeared whenever and wherever he wished, offering battle only when he wanted to and then disappearing after trouncing his opponents.

Who the hell would take this lying down? Nobody—not even the Federals. When Northern cavalry under William Averell came in force across the Rappahannock at Kelly's Ford in March 1863, they were gunning for Stuart himself. It was an unpleasant reminder that the blue-coated students of Jeb Stuart's school of cavalry hard knocks had been paying attention in class. Stuart's men fought them to a draw, but were hard-pressed and dis-comfited by the attack, which was unprecedented in scale, ferocity, and intent. Worst of all, Stuart's beloved artillery chief, John Pelham, was killed in the action. During the Chancellorsville campaign that followed, Joe Hooker offered more of the same—throngs of cavalry, rather than the old dribs and drabs, in numbers only the North could produce. Stuart did well against them under the circumstances and even got an opportunity to com-mand Stonewall's corps after the great Jackson was mortally wounded. Though he lobbied to make the position permanent, Lee gave him an even better prize: an expanded cavalry command, bringing Stuart's force to around ten thousand riders.

He would need them. On June 9, Union general Alfred Pleasanton crossed the Rappahannock with a force that made Averell's effort at Kelly's Ford look like a wine tasting. In the battle near Brandy Station that fol-lowed—the largest cavalry clash in North American history—Pleasanton managed to catch Stuart with his pants down, though his men were compelled in the end to withdraw. Nevertheless, Stuart's days as mounted master of Virginia were over.

Stuart himself, however, didn't seem to notice. In the Gettysburg campaign that followed, it was like the old days—ranging across a supine Pennsylvania countryside that bowed before his quickening wrath, yielding up its riches. Lots of riches. But while he was lugging around well over a hundred wagons full of captured supplies and provisions, the Army of Northern Virginia was groping forward like a great blinded beast. Stuart's cavalry, effectively the army's eyes, was off gallivanting. And when Lee bumped into the enemy, beginning the three-day Battle of Gettysburg, it was in a place not of his choosing, against an enemy whose strength had to be guessed. Stuart showed up the second day, too late to do more than take up the far left wing of the army and, on the third day, launch a futile assault around the Rummel farm that would reap a pile of bodies and little else.

Nobody's perfect. But Stuart had failed to perform what was essentially Cavalry 101: screen the infantry in enemy territory and scout for details about the enemy's strength and whereabouts. The spectators back home reacted accordingly, angrily stripping him of the laurels he'd won in sunnier days. Newspaper editorials began popping up throughout the Confederacy— had been, in fact, since Brandy Station—in which the Knight of the Golden Spurs was dismissed as "indolent" and even "weak-minded." And it wasn't just the folks back home who were pissed off. Wade Hampton, one of Stuart's most able subordinates, had been seething for quite some time over what he believed was Stuart's preferential treatment of Virginians at the expense of South Carolinians like himself. Thomas Rosser, a colonel in Stuart's command, pretty much hated his superior for his conceit and duplicity—a fact of which Stuart remained completely ignorant. Then there's the notorious "Grumble" Jones, who'd been griping about Stuart virtually since the moment he was assigned to his command. Officers like these bore witness to the other Jeb Stuart, the guy who knew he looked great in the saddle with his high boots, French sword, and black plume; who could hold up the progress of a raid just to get smothered in kisses by admiring damsels; who loved the reviewing stand at least as much as he loved victory; and whose conspicuous need for affirmation made it uncomfortably obvious that the adoration of the ladies was the cause he fought for.

After months of increasing Federal strength, it is hardly surprising how Beauty met his end. He had always said, "All I ask of fate is that I may be killed leading a cavalry charge." But by May 1864, circumstances were such that he was more likely to be on the receiving end of a cavalry charge. And that, more or less, is what happened. When Phil Sheridan came trotting south while infantry of both sides were mauling each other at Spotsylvania, it was with the intention of doing what none of his predecessors could: finish the Stuart legend. Sheridan came at the head of hard, ruthless officers who led huge numbers of troopers with a surfeit of repeating rifles, well-fed mounts, and confidence. When Stuart deployed at Yellow Tavern to stop them, it was with the understanding that he was confronting a foe whose goal was Richmond. Sheridan, however, wanted Stuart. And he got him. Or, more precisely, a private from the Fifth Michigan named John Huff got him while running past Stuart, who sat on his horse squeezing off shots from his LeMat at a swarm of onrushing Federals as if it were the most natural thing in the world. He died from the wound the following day.

A HOUSE DIVIDED

"He will regret it but once," said Stuart about his father-in-law's decision to fight for the Union, "and that will be continuously." Stuart's in-laws, the Cookes, hailed from Virginia and went with the Confederacy—with two exceptions. Philip St. George Cooke, Flora's father, never doubted that his primary allegiance was to his country, rather than his state. (The other was Flora's sister.) To Cooke, the fact that he wore blue during the War Between the States while his son and son-in-law wore gray was more a reflection of their treason than his lack of clan loyalty. Jeb, for his part, believed that Cooke's decision was evil and unforgivable—a stain on the family honor that no amount of time could remove. But this furious attitude posed a difficult problem for Stuart: his son had been named after the elder Cooke. Stuart solved the problem by convincing Flora to rename the little tyke. His new identity? James Ewell Brown Stuart Jr., a.k.a. "Jimmy."

Facing and killing his father-in-law on the field of battle remained Stuart's principal fantasy through much of the war, but it never came to pass. Philip Cooke died in 1895.

War-drobe

Very early in the morning of August 18, 1862, Stuart and his staff barely escaped capture by Union cavalry at Verdiersville, Virginia. It was such a close-run attack that Stuart had no time to grab his hat, gauntlets, or cloak before vaulting into his saddle and getting the hell out of town. (He had been sleeping on a porch when word arrived that enemy horsemen were nearby.) For a fellow like Stuart, who prided himself on getting the drop on the enemy rather than the reverse, the capture of his personal clothing was no small slight. "Where's your hat?" was the all-too-common greeting he received throughout the Army of Northern Virginia. And though he was the "jolly cavalier," celebrated for his sense of humor and good fun, enough was enough.

Which is why the raid at Catlett's Station just four days later was so important to him. In addition to sensitive documents and lots of booty, the raid produced the uniform of Union general John Pope himself—the guy whose horsemen had stolen Stuart's hat. Beauty made the most of his revenge by sending Pope a request for an exchange: his hat for Pope's uniform. But Pope's duds were destined for greater things. Stuart ultimately sent the clothes to Virginia governor John Letcher, who had the cloak displayed in the state library in Richmond like the war trophy that it was.

THE "PRICE" OF CELEBRITY

Stuart spared no effort to make the mood at his headquarters, wherever it might be, as lighthearted as possible. Feuds of any sort amongst his principal subordinates made him very uneasy, and he hastened to smooth them over. He openly favored those of a jolly disposition, and his sense of humor was legendary—indeed, he was probably the only man in the entire Confederacy who could get a laugh out of both Stonewall Jackson and Robert E. Lee, two notoriously stern fellows. A fan of extraordinary, even exotic people, he attracted some unusual types to his HQ, including a hulking, ferocious, unusually hairy corporal named Hagan and a 250-pound Prussian soldier of fortune named Heros von Borcke (who, despite—or perhaps partly because of—his clumsy English, would become one of Stuart's closest associates).

Not everyone in Stuart's circle bought into the convivial atmosphere, of course. Tom Price, an engineer on Stuart's staff, wrote in his diary of Stuart's boastful, "garrulous" behavior in camp, where he often "prattled on" and indulged in "over-acting." A portrait emerges of a commanding officer who's trying too hard and who loves to hear himself recount his own heroics. Unfortunately for both Stuart and Price, the diary was captured by Federals during the Chancellorsville campaign and was ultimately excerpted in the *New York Times*. Price transferred out of Stuart's command soon after.

BAND OF BROTHERS

Stuart, who dabbled in poetry and loved to sing (he had an excellent voice), made music a fundamental element of camp life. His retinue nearly always featured musicians, including a servant of his named Bob, who played the bones and the violin. But by far the most celebrated minstrel in Jeb's coterie was Sam Sweeney. The younger brother of Joel Sweeney, who is credited with popularizing the banjo, Sam could hold an audience spellbound or set them to dancing up a storm. And the song he was most often asked by Stuart to play was "Jine the Cavalry," which recounted Stuart's exploits and whose opening chorus boomed, "If you want to catch the Devil, if you want to have fun/If you want to smell Hell, jine the cavalry!" Needless to say, it was Stuart's favorite song.

Sweeney died from smallpox in January 1864, taking much of the brio out of Stuart's celebrated soirees.

REMEMBER THE LADIES

It seems nearly certain that Jeb Stuart never committed an act of adultery. But in all fairness, it couldn't have been easy to be the wife of the "Flower of Cavaliers." Late in the war, Flora began to tire of the pernicious rumors of her husband's fondness for female admirers. Stuart got defensive about it, confirming the chasm that existed between their respective notions of proper behavior. His flirtations—though innocent enough—were so numerous as to beg the question: What was their purpose? He was once swarmed by admiring belles in Middleburg, Virginia, happily surrendering to their requests for "kisses." And his association with Richmond socialites Constance and Hetty Cary spawned plenty of gossip—Stuart once asked Hetty at a charades party to spend some time with him alone in a closet. It's as if Stuart was reaping the ultimate affirmation for a Victorian practitioner of courtly love—a reminder, through the attentions of women, that he was everything the newspapers said he was.

A final, touching tragedy was perhaps emblematic of Stuart's relationship with his wife. After receiving word of his wounding at Yellow Tavern, Flora rushed with all available speed to be at his side. But she arrived too late to say farewell. On his deathbed, Stuart asked for her on several occasions. He also conferred with his aide, Major Henry McClellan (a first cousin of the renowned Union general George McClellan), about the disposition of his personal effects: his sword, to be given to his son; his spurs, to Mrs. Lilly Lee, a friend and war widow; and, folded within his hat, a small Confederate flag that McClellan did not know existed—to be sent to a woman in Columbus, South Carolina.

23 JUBAL ANDERSON EARLY

November 3, 1816–March 2, 1894

HIGHEST RANK:

Confederate Officer

ASTROLOGICAL SIGN:

Scorpio

NICKNAMES:

Old Jube, Old Jubilee

WORDS TO REMEMBER:

"We haven't taken Washington, but we've scared Abe Lincoln like hell!" (regarding his appearance on the outskirts of Washington, D.C., in 1864)

The afternoon of March 2, 1865, was frigid and gloomy in the upper Shenandoah Valley. There, just west of Waynesboro, some two thousand ragged men in gray and butternut stood wearily in the cold drizzle, their numbers stretched thin along three-quarters of a mile of low ridgeline. At around 3:00, they watched in horror as throngs of cavalry troopers in mud-spattered blue came charging and screaming and shooting their way toward them from directly ahead and on the left flank. Outnumbered and outmaneuvered, the hungry, threadbare Rebels knew a really bad thing when they saw it, and they began falling back to a pair of bridges that crossed the South River behind them. Most of them didn't make it and were either cut down or captured by the pursuing Federals.

Jubal Early was given to frequent outbursts of profanity—even on the rare occasions when he set foot inside a church.

Perched on a vulnerable piece of ground, its flanks left hanging without proper protection, the defensive position at Waynesboro must have been chosen by an amateur or an idiot. But the Confederate officer in question, Lieutenant General Jubal Early, was neither. He was, however,

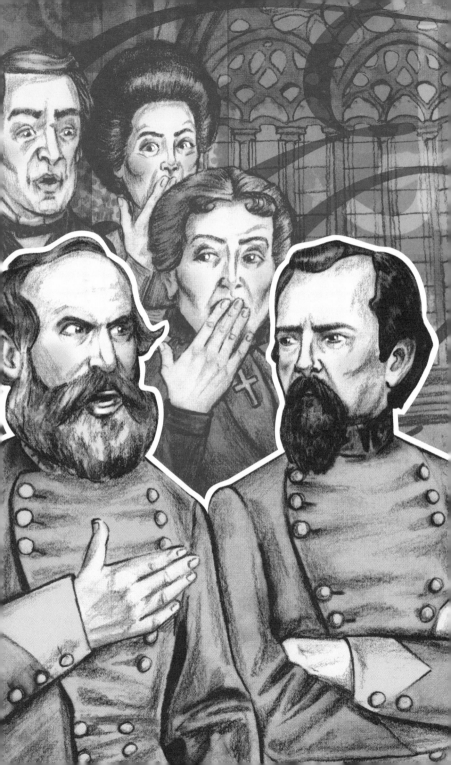

disillusioned by fighting against outrageous odds with little to no resources and men who looked more like scarecrows than soldiers. Since its spectacular reverse at the Battle of Cedar Creek the previous October, his once glorious Army of the Valley had been living on borrowed time, its ranks inexorably thinned by hunger, desertion, and Robert E. Lee, who needed every man he could muster for the desperate campaign around Petersburg. Early was, to put it simply, psychologically played out, and Waynesboro proved it. It was to be his last battle during the Civil War—but not, interestingly enough, his last fight on behalf of the Confederacy.

Jubal Anderson Early had grown to manhood in Franklin County, Virginia, surrounded by the comfort and ease of the tobacco-growing caste. His unusual first name was the result of an old Early family custom of bestowing names that began with the letter J. According to the Book of Genesis, Jubal, a descendant of Cain and brother of Jabel, was the "forerunner of those who play the harp and the flute." He entered West Point in 1833, where he distinguished himself by consistently ranking near the bottom of his class in the conduct department and for having a plate broken over his head by Lewis Armistead, who would fall in battle years later during Pickett's Charge at Gettysburg. Though pissing off his fellow cadets and racking up demerits seemed to come naturally, so did classwork, and he graduated with high academic marks. He was sent to fight Seminole Indians in the wilds of Florida, where American soldiers were suffering more from the lacerations of saw palmetto than they were from an enemy who had perfected the art of evasion. For the impatient Early, the drudgery of Florida was enough to set his mind on a career change. He resigned his commission and, after a period of intense study, began practicing law in Rocky Mount, Virginia, and got himself elected to the state legislature.

When war broke out with Mexico, Early's unpleasant memories of Florida faded behind a resurgent patriotism. He joined the Virginia regiment as a major and set off, like so many of his fellow gringos, in search of battlefield glory.

He didn't find any. But he did make a name for himself as the military governor of Monterrey, a post he'd been given by General Zachary Taylor himself. In addition to establishing law and order, Early drilled the troops under his command to perfection—a skill that would serve him well in years to come. Despite this considerable accomplishment, Early's Mexico experience did nothing to alleviate his abiding ambivalence to army life. He had seen no action, and the only physical danger he'd encountered was from arthritis—a gift from the Mexican campaign that remained with him for the rest of his days. Disenchanted and as cynical as ever, he went back to Virginia a civilian.

Early couldn't have known it at the time, but his return to civilian life was, once again, to be temporary. As a lawyer, his talents lay principally in his unadorned honesty, perseverance, and penchant for thinking ill of others, which tended to galvanize his legal confrontations. Bereft of the oily charm typical of courtroom solicitors, he did much of his work in the confines of his office and stuck to the small stuff. But when he was elected to his state's secession delegation, he waded into some very big stuff and didn't hold back. Jubal Early was levelheaded, patriotic, and dismissive of what he considered Southern hubris. Few Virginians were as adamantly pro-Union in those days as he was. Not even Abraham Lincoln's inaugural speech—interpreted as insufferably aggressive throughout much of Dixie—could change Early's mind. Right up until the vote to secede, the scrappy lawyer from Rocky Mount did his darnedest to sway his fellow delegates from a course he considered tantamount to madness.

Still, like many of his countrymen with military experience, he put aside his political views once the Confederacy became a reality, and he ran to the defense of his homeland—the local soil to which his blood was bound. "Whether we have the right of secession or revolution," he solemnly proclaimed, "I want to see my state triumphant." It was a statement that accurately summed up the beliefs of many.

He began the Civil War as a colonel, but that didn't last long. At the First Battle of Bull Run, Early marched his brigade from its original position on the far right of the Confederate line all the way to the left flank, where his troops played a crucial role in routing the enemy. It was a six-mile march, completed in just three hours—a performance made possible by Early's ability to quickly whip untried civilians into passable soldiers, which earned him a promotion to brigadier general. In time he became one of the most estimable fighting generals in the Army of Northern Virginia, a crotchety, rumpled oddball who knew his business and got results from his men. His élan could verge on recklessness: In May 1862, during the Battle of Williamsburg, his hastily arranged assault on a Union redoubt was brave, costly, and pointless; Early himself got a bullet in the shoulder. But mishaps like this were the exception rather than the rule.

He was a virtuoso of maneuver under fire, as he proved at the Battle of Antietam. In the hellish action of that bloodiest of days, Early took over the division when his superiors were wounded and proceeded to blunt a potentially decisive Northern attack by changing fronts twice and delivering the fire of his troops where it was needed most, to devastating effect. Later that year at Fredericksburg, he saved Stonewall Jackson's end of the line by foiling a Union stab that had thrown the whole wing into disarray. In January 1863, he was promoted to major general and given his own division in Richard Ewell's corps. He would lead his division at such important engagements as Chancellorsville, where he covered the far Confederate right near Fredericksburg; the Second Battle of Winchester, where his men helped to rout and capture much of the Union garrison; and Gettysburg, where, after helping to sweep the town of enemy forces, he made a daring assault against the Union right that ultimately came to nothing for lack of reinforcement.

Repulsed at Gettysburg, the Army of Northern Virginia took a breather, then once again began dueling with George Meade's Army of the Potomac. In November, at the Battle of Rappahannock Station, Early's men found themselves pinned against the Rappahannock River by an overwhelming Union force. Early, who called the debacle "the first serious disaster that had befallen any of my immediate commands . . . since the commencement of the war," had the ignominious fate of watching his routed soldiers brave the bone-chilling waters of the river rather than suffer capture by the enemy.

Meade's advance was stopped a few weeks later at Mine Run, where Early found himself in temporary command of the Second Corps while the perpetually ailing Ewell was on sick leave. The two armies settled back into the positions they had occupied just two months before.

The high-water mark of the Confederacy had passed, and few felt it as acutely as Jubal Early. By the winter of 1863–1864, the curmudgeonly Virginian had become even more irritable than usual, throwing accusatory invective at his fellow officers with disturbing recklessness. Even Ewell, his friend and superior, felt Early's lash, and their relationship soured. "Old Jubilee" had acquired a well-earned reputation for detesting things: officers who brought their wives on campaign, civilians who didn't know how to march like troops, unruly soldiers who plundered and burned without orders to do so, and—most notoriously—cavalry. Dismissed by Early as "buttermilk rangers," his cavalry officers were constantly being blamed for any and every reverse. At least one of them, John Imboden, felt compelled to seek redress through official channels, though the confrontation ulti- mately fizzled. In February 1864, a thoroughly nettled Early wrote Robert E. Lee for a leave of absence to assuage a growing "lukewarmness in the cause." It was granted.

In fact, Early may not have returned to duty at all had it not been for the thing he detested most of all: Yankees. "I wish they were all dead," he had said after the Battle of Fredericksburg, during which Federals had brutishly ransacked the town. "I not only wish them all dead but I wish them all in Hell." And he did his utmost to facilitate their journey. Having begun the war as a reluctant military professional who openly ridiculed secession, Early had since formed the opinion—based on personal experience of the enemy's ruthlessness—that Northerners were the filth of humanity. And his fury would only grow.

Shortly before the Battle of Cold Harbor, he once again assumed com- mand of Ewell's corps, a post that remained permanent this time—Lee made it official by promoting Early to lieutenant general. Having already acquired corps-command experience (in addition to substituting for Ewell, he had assumed control of A. P. Hill's corps during the Battle of Spotsylvania Court House in early May), Old Jube eased into the role in which he was destined to make history.

Jubal Early had been one of Stonewall Jackson's favorite protégés. Now, in the Shenandoah Valley that had made Stonewall an icon, Early was to write his own legend and nearly outdo his deceased mentor. It all began when Ulysses Grant sent Major General David Hunter into the valley as the right hook of a great pincer intended to squeeze the Confederacy to death once and for all. A holdover from the appointments that served to highlight Abraham Lincoln's early ineptitude at choosing generals, "Black Dave" Hunter was an abstemious zealot with a penchant for punitive warfare, ersatz martial law, and arson—precisely the sort of sanctimonious Yankee brigand that made Jubal Early's heart fibrillate with spleen. Hunter fell upon the Confederacy's breadbasket like the self-appointed Second Horseman of the Apocalypse, razing and burning as he went. During a four-day visit to Lexington, he set the Virginia Military Institute and Washington College on fire and destroyed former governor John Letcher's home for good measure. Then he headed for Lynchburg.

Waiting for him there was Jubal Early, sent racing westward by Lee with the Second Corps to defend the town and do something about Hunter. After halting the oncoming Federals at Lynchburg on June 17, Early pushed the despised Hunter back down the valley and into the mountains of West Virginia. And that was just for starters. With virtually the whole valley to himself, Early made his way northward, going over to the offensive down an avenue of invasion that opened onto the vitals of the enemy. Time for a little payback.

Brushing aside the meager resistance it met, the Army of the Valley came rolling out of the Shenandoah Valley like a fierce and sudden storm on a sunny day. Early's secret weapon was speed, made possible by a ruthless paring of kit and baggage. After crossing the Potomac, he swept into Maryland and extorted $20,000 from the terrified folks of Hagerstown. Frederick coughed up an impressive $200,000. But while Early was busy holding up civilians, desperate preparations were being made to meet the obvious threat he posed to Washington, D.C. Moving southeast toward the Union capital, Early came up short before a hastily assembled enemy host on the Monocacy River led by Lew Wallace—the future author of *Ben-Hur*. Early's hardened veterans (many of whom had fought under Jackson) butchered Wallace's brave greenhorns, but at a remarkable price: one whole day of a very tight schedule. The Rebels went on to the suburbs of the capital on July 11, causing a stir the likes of which Washingtonians had not seen since the bad old days of 1861. The district's militia was called up, stupefied government clerks had firearms thrust into their sweating hands, and gleeful Democrats began whooping it up in anticipation of Lincoln's defeat at the polls.

All for naught. Though Early was within sight of the nearly completed Capitol dome, he could also see the extraordinary defensive works that stood between him and his precious prize. Washington, D.C., was some of the best defended real estate in the western hemisphere. And while the trenches had been manned by the Union army's dregs just days prior, they were now full of men from the Sixth and Nineteenth Corps—gnarled veterans who didn't need the elaborate fortifications of Washington to give Early and his crew trouble. Lew Wallace had bought enough time at the Monocacy for the Northern high command to race seasoned troops into the defenses around the capital.

But Early had done his job as well. When Lee sent him into the Shenandoah, it was with the hopes of creating enough of a mess to draw Union forces away from the Army of the Potomac that was pressing down on Richmond. He had done that and more. As his marauding army made its way toward Washington, newspapers throughout the North—and, more significantly, the world—reflected the belief that Jefferson Davis's Confederacy was anything but dying. Perhaps, if nothing else, Jubal's adventure held out the hope of igniting intervention from a reluctant Europe.

That never happened, of course. Early's raid was like swinging a stick at a hornet's nest—in addition to sending units from around Washington in pursuit of Early's force, Grant unleashed Hunter into the Shenandoah Valley once again with the instruction to strip it of food "so that crows flying over it, for the balance of this season, will have to carry their provender with them." He might as well have ordered a fish to go swimming. But as Black Dave set about his familiar deleterious tactics with renewed gusto, Early, ever the opportunist, was awaiting another chance to strike. He got it when much of the pursuing Union force from Washington was pulled back, freeing him to go on the offensive again. Moving north, Early struck the Federals at Kernstown on July 24 and sent them retreating across the Potomac, leaving him once more in control of the Shenandoah Valley. And this time the payback was to be more spectacular.

Determined to cover the mounting cost of Hunter's excesses by bringing the war to the other side, Early sent troopers up to Pennsylvania on a little errand. They were to give the good people of Chambersburg a choice: scare up $100,000 in gold or watch their tidy hamlet go up like kindling. Refusing to be intimidated, the townspeople called the Confederates' bluff—and watched their town burn to the ground.

The destruction of Chambersburg was controversial, even to some of the officers on Early's staff. He himself always assumed full responsibility for the affair and never admitted so much as a twinge of guilt. After all, anyone who doubted whether the war had entered an implacable new phase needed only to look at the Shenandoah Valley itself, where bluecoats had been destroying property for weeks. Besides, the bursting Northern economy could afford such depredations; Early's Confederacy could not. It is significant to note that one of the reasons Chambersburg's citizens failed to take their occupiers very seriously is that they hardly looked the part: By this time, even Jubal Early's vaunted veterans looked like shoeless vagabonds.

And they weren't going to get any prettier. To put it simply, Old Jubilee's salad days were behind him. For months he had made a mockery of Northern military might, pushing around an enemy that always outnumbered him and tweaking the nose of the Lincoln administration itself. To Grant in particular, the recent high jinks in the Shenandoah were a very, very bad joke that had to go away. It was against this background that he loosed one of his favorite dogs of war upon the wily Early: Phil Sheridan. With overwhelming force and some of the toughest cavalry on the continent at his disposal, Sheridan grappled with the Army of the Valley at Winchester and routed it completely at Fisher's Hill. Early showed his age at the Battle of Cedar Creek in October by making a truly spectacular breakthrough against superior numbers and inexplicably failing to complete the job; the predictable Union counterattack blew his army to smithereens. The hangers-on were defeated the following March at Waynesboro. And so passed Lieutenant General Jubal Early's illustrious Army of the Valley.

When things started to go badly for Early, the Confederacy on whose behalf Old Jube had fought so hard let him down, blaming his reverses on rumored drunkenness. The stupendous indignity at Cedar Creek, in particular, drew irrational anger from the newspapers. Robert E. Lee stood by him until the clamor in civilian and military circles became too loud to handle; Early then found his forces gradually relocated for more pressing service around Richmond, relegating his command to a sort of formality. As for Early himself, he just got meaner and meaner. While riding past his ragged men one day and hearing them chant, "Give us something to eat," Old Jubilee responded scornfully by throwing their recent defeat in their faces: "Fisher's Hill! Fisher's Hill, damn you!"

Ironically, for this one-time opponent of secession, defeat at the hands of the Union was simply intolerable. In the wake of Lee's surrender at Appomattox, he armed himself and fled to Mexico, where his attempt to get the French-backed emperor Maximilian to declare war on the United States came to nothing. By 1866, he was in Canada, from which he watched the unfolding Southern Reconstruction with horrified fascination. Not until 1869 did he find it in himself to give life in Virginia another go. During the 1870s, he began supporting himself as a drawing supervisor, with fellow unreconstructed veteran P. G. T. Beauregard of the Louisiana State Lottery Company, which freed him to devote time to what became his obsession: creating the cult of the "Lost Cause." As president of the Southern Historical Society, Early did more than anyone else to paint the War Between the States as a tableau of naked aggression by a vast, mongrelized horde of laborers upon a race of nobility whose leaders—particularly Robert E. Lee, the only human Early never bitched about—were manliness personified. His scapegoat to explain the South's defeat at the hands of such an unworthy opponent was James Longstreet, whose dilatory performance on the second day of Gettysburg was nothing less than a betrayal that undermined any chance of victory in that critical battle. Interestingly, the war of words ignited by Early against Longstreet—whose postwar conversion to the Republican Party was seen as the ultimate apostasy and proof of his guilt—essentially demolished the latter's reputation as one of Robert E. Lee's most trusted lieutenants, giving Early the final and, perhaps, most enduring victory of his career as a Confederate partisan.

In the end, it seems that friction defined Jubal Early's life—right up to its end in March 1894 from injuries incurred during a fall down the steps of the Lynchburg post office. To Robert E. Lee, he had been "my bad old man." But the local newspaper's obituary editor probably hit the nail on the head when he referred to the deceased as "a rough diamond . . . [with] an exclusive and repellent exterior."

SOUTHERN COMFORT

For a man feared by the enemy for his aggressive generalship, Jubal Early wasn't much to look at. Beneath a white slouch hat with a black plume feather that became his hallmark, he often preferred the comfortable clothes of a common civilian. In winter he was known to wrap his head and extremities in cloth and don a duster that fell to his ankles. But it was the man himself, more than the packaging, that tended to shock. Stooped and aged beyond his years by arthritis, constantly spewing vulgarities in a shrill voice through a spray of saliva stained umber by an ever-present tobacco plug, he gave the appearance more of an eccentric barnyard fool than a sharp-minded lawyer and leader of armies. Little wonder that one of his aides described him as "decidedly a character . . . with some peculiarities that render him very amusing."

SURLY EARLY

In April 1864, Richard Ewell placed Jubal Early under arrest for insubordination. Though the precise nature of the offense remains lost to history (Ewell was dissuaded from carrying through with the affair by Robert E. Lee), it is hardly surprising, given Early's capacity for intemperate behavior. While stationed in Virginia at the very beginning of the Mexican War, Early got kicked out of his quarters for fighting with the assistant adjutant general. His anti-secession outbursts on the eve of civil war got him into hot water with many of his fellow Virginia delegates, including his friend John Goode—with whom Early very nearly got into a duel. The outbreak of war only made him more waspish, as he proved during the winter of 1861 during a celebratory assemblage of prominent Confederate officers. After a toast was offered to three fallen heroes of Bull Run (Francis Bartow, Barnard Bee, and C. F. Fisher), Early flatly refused to drink because no Virginians had been mentioned—a needless peccadillo that got everyone yelling, inspired the Virginia delegation to get up and leave, and drove Early into a drink-inspired funk that left him dozing in the woods against a tree for the duration of the night.

Not surprisingly, he didn't make a very tolerant butt of other people's jokes. In the summer of 1864, his men once noticed that a passing staff officer bore a stunning resemblance in dress to Old Jube. After the men began chanting "Jube's brother, Jube's brother!" for a time, one of them suggested that Early go and "kiss his brother." The general rode over to the ranks in a fit of pique and shouted that he was going to do his best to create a battle especially for their benefit, so "that every one of them would be killed and burn in hell through all eternity."

DAMN THE CONSEQUENCES

Jubal Early never married. He did, however, father four children by fellow Rocky Mount resident Julia McNealey, with whom he carried on a very cordial relationship for nearly twenty years. She married another man in 1871. True to form, Early cared not a whit about public censure, passing his surname on to all four of his kids.

He's a Soul Man

Jubal Early was infamously irreligious, though he was known to attend church on rare occasions, if only to buttress the morale of his more pious troops. But as Charles Osborne recounts in his book *Jubal*, not even the sacred confines of a church could compel Early to keep his peace when his blood was up. While attending services toward the end of the war, Early and his staff heard a sermon in which the minister posed a question about the Resurrection: "What would be your feelings," he asked the congregation, "at seeing those gallant ones who have given up their lives for their beloved country, rising in their thousands and marching in solemn procession?" The general shocked his fellow churchgoers by shouting out an answer: "I would conscript every damned one of them!"

NATHAN BEDFORD FORREST

July 13, 1821–October 29, 1877

HIGHEST RANK:

Confederate General

ASTROLOGICAL SIGN:

Cancer

NICKNAME:

Wizard of the Saddle

WORDS TO REMEMBER:

"War means fighting, and fighting means killing."

The war in the West was unusually mean. Fought by hard men who'd been raised on the frontier, across great swaths of scrub, swamp, and forest that were often denuded of forage or supplies, it had a desperate edge to it that set it apart from the conflict in Maryland, Pennsylvania, and Virginia. But what happened at Fort Pillow, Tennessee, on April 12, 1864, was hard even by western standards. A strongpoint that overlooked the Mississippi River some forty miles above Memphis, the fort enclosed a small Union garrison of fewer than six hundred soldiers, roughly half of whom were black. That afternoon, after a demand to surrender was turned down by the fort's garrison, some 1,500 Rebel troopers stormed the works, easily overwhelming the smaller force within. What happened next has been the subject of heated debate ever since. Either the defenders were cut down during a fighting retreat to the river, or they were slaughtered like sheep after surrendering. Or both. Whatever the truth, the results were shocking: thirty-five percent of the white defenders lay dead. The black mortality rate stood at a staggering sixty-six percent.

The weight of evidence leans toward a massacre, as recent scholarly accounts have pointed out. Nevertheless, we shall probably never know for sure. Certainly a surfeit of killing had occurred (66 percent?!), but what about the Rebel commander? Did he order a fight without quarter?

Nathan Bedford Forrest was already a legend in his own time before Fort Pillow became good copy for Northern newspapers looking to stir up a

cause célèbre. To him, Fort Pillow was a significant triumph—nothing more, nothing less. The Federal presence there had threatened his control of western Tennessee, which he had been using as a source of supplies and recruits. After sending the cavalry troopers ahead under a subordinate to invest the works, he showed up himself the day of the assault and, true to form, conducted an unusually thorough reconnaissance of the place on horseback, allowing him to deploy his troops in such a way that took advantage of the terrain, undermined the firepower of the defenders, and even rendered a Union gunboat moored in the Mississippi superfluous. He was thorough and incredibly resolute. And his surrender demand to the commander of the garrison concluded with a threat that, though a favorite of his, had never been stated quite this way before: "Should my demand be refused, I cannot be responsible for the fate of your command."

Responsible indeed. Whether or not this dark little chapter of the Civil War can be laid at his feet is a question that has endured precisely because

> **Of all the men you wouldn't want to meet on a Civil War battlefield, few were more ferocious than Nathan Bedford Forrest—a general who personally killed some thirty men.**

Bedford Forrest was the sort of man who could believably have done such a thing. In a way, he was emblematic of the western theater he so brilliantly dominated: extreme, tough, and at his best when he was breaking the rules. Long before the end of the war, such qualities—and a few others that don't lend themselves so easily to description—had made him arguably the greatest cavalry virtuoso that America, Union or Confederate, had ever produced. Not for capricious fate was he the only man on either side to enter the war as a private and end it as a lieutenant general. This guy was a breed apart.

He was born in Bedford County, Tennessee, into a family that would eventually become quite large. Raised to help his mother deal with his siblings and make ends meet, he grew into a canny administrator with a sense for the practical and the profitable. He became the quintessential self-made man of the South, making a considerable fortune in Tennessee and Mississippi as a cotton planter, livestock breeder, and slave trader—all with less than six months' worth of education. He served as a Memphis alderman, paid for his siblings' schooling, and became respected as a man of importance.

Such credentials were enough for many rich men to buy themselves into the officer caste at the outbreak of civil war. Forrest demurred, however, and joined a Tennessee unit as a private. After all, his military experience added up to nil. But pressure from prominent Memphians and the governor himself convinced the man to raise and equip a cavalry battalion of his own. They obviously understood Forrest's abilities better than Forrest did, for it was the beginning of an astounding military career. The new colonel of cavalry gave some idea of the sort of man he was in February 1862 when he refused to surrender with the rest of the Confederates who had been trapped by Grant at Fort Donelson, surreptitiously leading his troopers to safety without a shot being fired at them. Forrest had come to fight, not surrender.

And fight he did. In April, after the Battle of Shiloh, he staged a profoundly daring rearguard action to protect retreating Confederates, bringing William T. Sherman's pursuit to a halt with just three hundred hard-fighting troopers. The following July, the month he was made a brigadier, he captured Murfreesboro and its much larger garrison, securing a treasure trove of supplies. It was the first in a long series of remarkable triumphs as one of the South's preeminent raiders. Often saddled with green recruits, he nevertheless managed to fly across the countryside like a ghost, making trouble wherever he went and moving too quickly to be caught. He wreaked havoc with Grant's supply lines, crippling the advance on Vicksburg, and chased a column of Union raiders through Alabama and Georgia like a relentless bloodhound, bagging hundreds of prisoners toward the end of spring. At the Battle of Chickamauga, he threw his dismounted cavalry into the fight like infantry, proving the versatility of his command. Following the battle, in the midst of arguments over whether or not to recapture

Chattanooga, Forrest blew his lid with his superior, Braxton Bragg (hardly an unusual thing for Bragg), and—after threatening to kill him if they ever met again—demanded another assignment in northern Mississippi and western Tennessee. He continued to burn his name into Northern nightmares with the controversial victory at Fort Pillow and, in June 1864, the astonishing clash at Brice's Cross Roads, Mississippi. There Forrest performed one of his classic double envelopments, slashing both of his enemy's flanks at once, allowing him to defeat more than 7,500 Federals with a force less than half as large. Sherman, whose designs on Atlanta were now hampered by such Rebel exploits, began referring to "that devil Forrest." Indeed, his praise went further, insisting that the infernal raider from Tennessee should be "hunted down and killed if it costs 10,000 lives and bankrupts the treasury."

Fortunately for Sherman and his superiors in Washington, it didn't come to that. But clearly Forrest wasn't going down without a very nasty fight. How had he come to be such a martial phenomenon? It certainly wasn't because of his education—Bedford Forrest was no West Point man, and he had no trouble saying so. Rather, he came to cavalry fighting as if it lay in his genes behind a glass sign reading, "Break in time of war." He was a natural, blending bold imagination with good ol' common sense. Subterfuge was a favored weapon. In 1861, after recruiting his first unit of cavalry rangers, he camped his men along the Louisville & Nashville Railroad, swelling their ranks with wives, friends, and kinsmen, all gathered beneath a great Rebel flag. The intention was to impress passengers riding past with the size of his host, knowing full well that they would take the information south to the Union force waiting for him, scaring it into withdrawal. The ruse worked.

Such trickery came naturally to Forrest, who understood that the psychological elements of war were decisive. Hence his penchant for issuing the "surrender or be put to the sword" ultimatum to enemies, many of whom outnumbered him (and nearly all of whom accepted the offer). War wasn't all mind games, however. By the end of the war, Bedford Forrest would personally kill an estimated thirty enemy combatants; more than twenty-five horses died while bearing him into battle. He not only led from the front—he hacked from the front, eagerly drawing his saber in a melee once his pair of "navy sixes" had been emptied. More than a few witnesses attested to his wild-eyed, red-faced aspect in battle, like a six-foot-two-inch brute who had come to vent his rage. "So fierce did his passion become that he was almost equally dangerous to friend or foe," penned one of his officers. This was not the way of Virginia's chivalric finest, those well-bred gentlemen back east who wooed the British press and dazzled the ladies with their sub-tlety and wit. Jeb Stuart may have prided himself on romantic flummery and circuitous steeplechases around McClellan's army, but Forrest staked his reputation on something altogether different: violence, rapid and gory. Toward this end, his men were tools to be cared for. Unless on a forced march, they were given every small luxury that circumstance would allow. In battle, however, they were expected to obey instantly and fight like furies—to turn the battlefield into a hell unsuitable for any sane enemy. "Shoot any man who won't fight," he was fond of telling his subordinates. Like the grim ultimatums he gave his enemies, he meant it. And his soldiers knew it.

Almost from the beginning, this unlearned planter-turned-ravager employed maneuvers taught at the military academy whose pedagogical titles he had never heard of. Combined with his instinct for conjuring chaos and flouting convention, they made him formidable. Nevertheless, it couldn't last. Serving in Tennessee during the final months of 1864, he found himself at the head of all the theater's cavalry and was promoted to lieutenant gen-eral the following February. But no amount of daring or duplicity or sheer luck could save him from the reckoning that Northern forces, now irre-sistible, were arranging. He surrendered at Gainesville, Alabama, in May 1865, his legendary command having shrunk to a husk of its former self.

Not surprisingly, the war had destroyed his fortune. Forrest attempted to resurrect his long-gone finances through cotton farming, which he knew well, and then as an insurance agent and a railroad baron. Nothing worked. Nevertheless, he was a man of immense stature—a hero (in the South) who had pulled off some of the most dazzling achievements of the rebellion. His name meant something—especially to the Ku Klux Klan. Originally a sort of foolish gentleman's club established by bored racists in Pulaski, Tennessee, the Klan developed popularity amongst the small-minded who felt threatened by Reconstruction. It eventually swallowed up other groups with a similar bent and became a force to be reckoned with. Forrest, taken with their aggressive rejection of the new order, fell in with the cult and became their first grand wizard—a title created, so the story goes, because of Forrest's "Wizard of the Saddle" moniker. At any rate, it was a decision he came to regret. Already excoriated throughout the North as the butcher of Fort Pillow, his association with the white-hooded riders of the night became a grisly sensation—like a man adding insult to his own injury.

Time heals all wounds, so it is said. And Bedford Forrest morphed into old age like a man trying to forget old injuries. In his waning years the man who'd become a symbol of the KKK distanced himself from the organization's rampant, sadistic violence. Indeed, he became one of the Klan's sincerest critics and an outspoken supporter of programs for freedmen that he once viewed as a hallmark of Republican intrusion. But by that time, the South had gone back to its antebellum ways, and the Klan's goals of returning blacks to political and social bankruptcy had been secured. Against this background, it can hardly be surprising that the uncompromising fighter called Forrest should remain one of the most controversial—and divisive—figures in American history.

GETTING PHYSICAL

In the sensational charge that Forrest made to buy time for the withdrawing Confederates after Shiloh, he found himself in the midst of enemy infantry, completely surrounded and alone. Wheeling around with the intention of fighting his way out of the trap, he was shot in the left side. He remained in the saddle, and is said to have scooped up one of his assailants and used him as a shield while galloping back to safety. The story would seem nearly impossible to believe if it weren't for the fact that Forrest was always getting into scrapes. Indeed, he seemed entirely at ease in physical confrontations.

In the spring of 1845, he got into a street fight in Hernando, Mississippi, that ended up making the newspapers. It seems that his uncle, Jonathan Forrest, got into a heated argument with some fellows named Matlock and one of their employees, an overseer. The younger Forrest intervened, insults were exchanged, and one of the Matlock brothers drew a weapon—probably a gun, but perhaps a stick. Bedford drew a revolver of his own, but fired off only two shots before the thing clicked empty, whereupon somebody threw him a large knife, with which he finished his handiwork. Though Forrest walked away from the scuffle wounded, his uncle was killed.

Forrest received four wounds during the war—one of which was from his own subordinate. Lieutenant A. W. Gould, who received word that Forrest was transferring him to another command, confronted the latter for an explanation. During their heated exchange, Gould, insisting that a transfer might be construed as an indictment of his courage, decided to avenge his wounded honor by drawing a pistol from his duster. He got off one shot before Forrest, now wounded in the hip, grabbed his assailant's pistol hand, held it, opened the blade of a penknife with his teeth, and thrust it into Gould's side. (Forrest had been using the knife to pick his teeth before being rudely interrupted.) The two bleeding contestants now staggered away from each other—Gould, to be helped into a tailor shop, where he was examined by a doctor; and Forrest, to the office of another physician, who determined that his gunshot wound might be fatal. Now convinced that he would soon be dead, Forrest snatched up a brace of revolvers and set out for the tailor shop to finish off his murderer. Gould, seeing him coming, got up off the table on which he was being examined and stumbled out the back door, trailing blood the whole way. Forrest fired a shot at the fleeing target but missed. (The ricocheting bullet, incidentally, struck an innocent bystander in the leg.) After seeing Gould crumple in a patch of weeds behind the shop, Forrest, satisfied, got some more medical attention. When it was discovered that he had incurred merely a flesh wound, he was overcome with remorse for his treatment of Gould and ordered his doctors to go and save him. They were unable to, however. Within two weeks the lieutenant was dead.

SO MUCH FOR THE COMPETITION

Even Forrest's marriage began with a series of bullying standoffs. He first met Mary Ann Montgomery in 1845 in a creek bed: The carriage carrying her and her mother to church was stuck in the mud. As a slave wrestled to free the wheel himself, two dandies who didn't want to sully their Sunday clothes sat their horses off to the side and watched. When Forrest came along, he waded out to the wagon, carried the women over to the dry bank, and helped the slave free their carriage. He then made a point of confronting the two male witnesses, calling them useless and threatening to kick the crap out of them if they didn't immediately make themselves scarce. Deciding to court the young lady, Forrest showed up at the Montgomery residence a few days later, only to discover two other callers waiting on the porch. Recognizing them as the two boneheads from the creek, he again threatened them with bodily harm, literally chasing them off the grounds. Forrest was wed to Mary Ann before the year was out.

DELUSIONS OF GRANDEUR

A few years after the war, Forrest—not unlike many former Confederate officers—found himself staring failure and boredom in the face. Ennui set in, and he couldn't help waxing nostalgic for the glory days. According to some of his associates, Forrest hatched a plan that can only be called outrageous. It involved recruiting an army of former Rebels and buying or stealing enough rifles to arm them—say, twenty thousand. At the head of such a host, he would descend on Mexico, conquering the entire country in just six months. After confiscating all the church property (Forrest was never a very pious fellow), he would establish himself as king and open the borders to immigration. He was convinced that 200,000 Southerners, easily, would flock south to escape Reconstruction. Needless to say, the world would never find out if he was right. Forrest eventually came to his senses and apparently abandoned the scheme.

"BURP!"

The Fort Pillow "massacre" remains a deeply controversial topic to this day, and rightly so—whatever the truthful details, such things should never be forgotten. As for Bedford Forrest, he was never allowed to forget. One story has it that he was gruffly challenged one morning in a hotel by a formidable-looking woman with a Bible in her hand. After establishing that he was in fact the "Rebel General Forrest," she demanded to know if it was indeed true that he had "murdered those dear colored people at Fort Pillow." "Yes, madam," he replied. "I killed the men and women for my soldiers' dinner and ate the babies myself for breakfast."

25 WILLIAM CLARKE
QUANTRILL

July 31, 1837–June 6, 1865

HIGHEST RANK:
Confederate Guerrilla Leader

ASTROLOGICAL SIGN:
Leo

A.K.A.:
Charley Hart

WORDS TO REMEMBER:
"Kill! Kill and you will make no mistake! Lawrence should be thoroughly cleansed, and the only way to cleanse it is to kill! Kill!"

In 1854, Congress passed the Kansas-Nebraska Act and lit the fuse of civil war. Until then, the northern limit to slavery in the territories had been drawn at the latitude 36°30′ north, as established by the Missouri Compromise of 1820. But Stephen Douglas, the Democratic senator from Illinois, wanted to lay the groundwork for a transcontinental railroad running west from Chicago and needed Southern support to make it happen. The result, sponsored by Douglas, was the Kansas-Nebraska Act, which stipulated that slavery could exist north of the 36°30′ line if settlers there voted for it—a rather harmless-sounding concept dubbed "popular sovereignty."

Harmless it definitely wasn't. The act led directly to the creation of the Republican Party, which dedicated itself to containing the further spread of slavery and ultimately sent Lincoln to the White House. But just as important, slavery wasn't the sort of issue that people calmly debated and decided at the polls like diligent citizens, especially on the frontier. The immediate effect of Douglas's pet project was to turn the Kansas Territory into a literal battleground. Homesteaders from neighboring slave states came pouring over the border to swell the ranks of pro-South men, while Northern "emigration societies" sent a flood of settlers into Kansas to buttress the free-soil camp. "Bushwhackers," pro-slavery partisans, fought bloody battles with free-soil fighters known as "jayhawkers" in a wrathful guerrilla war of assault and

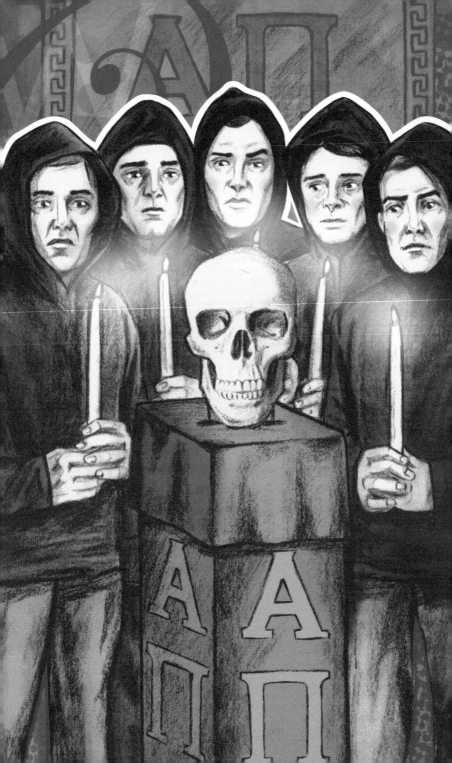

retaliation that held a horrified nation enthralled. It looked very much . . . well, like a civil war.

Which it was. For more than six long years before the shelling of Fort Sumter, Kansas shuddered with sectional violence. From 1854 to the end of the wider conflict that began after Lincoln's election, the plains would produce no small number of dubious celebrities: John Brown, who would take his holy mission all the way to Harpers Ferry and the gallows; Jacob Herd, ruthless scourge of the Underground Railroad; John Stewart, the "Fighting Preacher," a part-time Methodist minister and full-time jayhawker; James Lane, called "The Grim Chieftain of Kansas," a senator, brigand, and notorious bane of slaveholders; "Doc" Jennison, abolitionist and cattle thief; "Bloody Bill" Anderson, collector of Yankee scalps; the Younger brothers, driven to brutality by their father's murder at the hands of jayhawkers; and Frank and Jesse James, bushwhackers and future bank robbers extraordinaire.

> From 1905 to 1942, the skull of guerilla leader William Quantrill was used in a mysterious fraternity initiation ritual. Fraternity brothers nicknamed the prop "Jake."

Dominating this rogue's gallery was a figure who continues to personify the maelstrom that was "Bleeding Kansas." William Clark Quantrill arrived late on the scene—folks had been shooting and stabbing and burning each other along the Kansas-Missouri border for more than five years by the time he chose to join the fray. But in time his name would be as celebrated and reviled as any in the annals of the Civil War.

He had an unlikely background for a desperado. Born the son of a tinker in Dover, Ohio, he was a pretty good student who graduated from high school and became a teacher. In time he grew bored and eager to make something more of himself, and—like so many of his generation—journeyed west to find his fortune.

It proved elusive. Quantrill ended up doing all manner of things for money—he tried a bit of farming, sold copies of a book his father wrote on tinsmithing, shot prairie chickens for petty change, gambled a lot, tried prospecting in Colorado, and even slung hash and drove a wagon for the army. But nothing put real distance between him and the poverty that seemed ever to stalk him.

There were, of course, other ways of making money. And most of them were illegal. Having gotten a job as a teamster hauling army supplies out of Fort Leavenworth, Kansas, he came under the influence of pro-South border ruffians who introduced him to the wide world of bushwhacking. Since arriving in the territory, Quantrill—who had begun using the alias "Charley Hart"—had essentially abandoned the antislavery stance he'd acquired in his Ohio upbringing and come to look upon abolitionists with suspicion and even disgust. To the men he now associated with, jayhawkers had brought violence upon themselves by killing and burning for their cause. Bushwhackers were only returning the favor and defending their own. It was an idea that both sides could've argued. But by 1860, Quantrill had harnessed his fortunes to the South-leaning side.

And, conveniently, he had found himself a job: for in Kansas, being a partisan was as much a vocation as an ideological struggle. If Quantrill now threw himself into the strife of Bleeding Kansas, it was because it offered hard material reward as well as participation in the Cause. In 1860, he rode with a bunch of fellow bushwhackers, making a decent amount of money by hitting stations on the Underground Railroad. They would hold up the operators at gunpoint, kidnap whatever fugitive slaves happened to be there, and collect reward money from the masters who were eager to get their slaves back. Other ways of making ends meet included kidnapping, extortion, robbery, and cattle rustling.

In 1861, however, everything changed. For one thing, a Republican had made it to the White House. For another, Kansas was formally made a state in January—a free state. And, last but not least, civil war broke over the country like a long-anticipated deluge. Now a Confederate, Quantrill rode for a while with a unit of pro-South Cherokees, then enlisted in General Sterling Price's army after the Battle of Wilson's Creek in August, enlisting as a private. It was the extent of his regular army career—the following autumn he fell in with a band of Missouri bushwhackers and soon became their leader.

Considering himself a legitimate Confederate combatant, Quantrill tried to behave as one, whether parolling captured Union officers or offering terms to defeated foes. This didn't last long, however, and for several reasons. First, the environment that produced him and the men he attracted to his group had long since been inured to savagery and the expectation of savagery. Second, the Union authorities immediately outlawed bushwhackers like Quantrill's raiders as illegal combatants who were not subject to the established rules of war, a fact that Quantrill took to heart. And third . . . well, perhaps Quantrill himself was affected by the desperate clash to which he'd attached his fate.

Operating along the border that separated Kansas and Missouri, Quantrill's band of bushwhackers became embroiled in the ruthless tit for tat that had been going on since 1854. A bold, brutal, and lucky guerrilla leader, Quantrill earned a reputation that made him one of the most wanted men in the West. In April 1862, the Confederate government passed the Partisan Rangers Act, legitimizing (and, hopefully, bringing under control) the numerous irregular raiders who terrorized Unionists throughout the long frontier that separated North and South. The following August, Quantrill helped capture Independence, Missouri, and was soon given a captain's commission in the Confederate army. His raiders held up stagecoaches, robbed prominent Unionist households, harried Federal camps and their supply lines, rode down and murdered enemy soldiers, and generally shot their way into newspaper headlines. Quantrill had embraced a war without quarter, becoming a horror on horseback that sowed fear throughout the countryside and profited from his depredations.

Of course, lots of unscrupulous malefactors were doing that in Kansas and Missouri—it was all the rage, in fact. But Quantrill was in a class by himself, as he proved the following year. In November 1862, he traveled to Richmond and perhaps acquired a colonel's commission, though this remains in dispute to this day. The following August, however, he undertook the "operation" that would forever link his name to atrocity.

Lawrence, Kansas, was the center of Northern and abolitionist activity in the state. The home of Jim Lane and other anti-South partisans, it had long been a jayhawker sanctuary and, since 1861, a center of Union recruitment. To William Quantrill, it was the holy grail of targets—a fat hog waiting to be shot, cleaned, butchered, and smoked. For weeks the guerrilla leader reconnoitered his target, familiarizing himself with its schedules and geography. Then he struck. On the morning of August 21, he and his men hit Lawrence like a biblical plague, setting as much as they could to the torch and looting everything in sight. Drinking, ransacking, they sentenced every male inhabitant they came across to death—by the end of the nightmare, some 150 men and boys would be hauled out into the street and shot before their screaming womenfolk. (Jim Lane, a choice target, managed to escape.) Their horses laden with booty, the marauders left behind a scene of mass murder and smoldering devastation.

Even in a state accustomed to crimes of ideological passion, the Lawrence massacre was a shock. Union authorities reacted with equivalent insensitivity: Identifying Missouri as the hive from which Quantrill's raiders flew to do their dastardly deeds, the Federals issued General Order Number 11, which actually commanded all inhabitants of several Missouri counties bordering Kansas to get out. The area was soon depopulated, all because of Quantrill's audacious barbarity—a stunning example of Unionist excess that, ironically, filled Quantrill's ranks with more recruits.

Federal units did their best to catch him in the weeks that followed, but to no avail. Deciding to winter in Texas, Quantrill led his men south in October and ran into a hundred Federals escorting the headquarters of Major General James Blunt to Fort Smith. Surprising the bluecoats at Baxter Springs, Kansas, Quantrill's raiders slaughtered the majority of them, plundered the column's unusually large store of liquor, and sat about getting drunk amongst the charred and mutilated corpses. (Though Blunt managed to escape the massacre, he would later go insane and die in an asylum in

1881.) Deposed at gunpoint by one of his own, a bushwhacker named George Todd, Quantrill was back in Missouri the following spring. Times were changing, and not for the better: Toward the end of 1864, the Confederate cause was finished in Missouri, and Quantrill, accompanied by thirty or so diehards, made for Kentucky.

Armed with stolen Federal uniforms, the band had a high old time getting the drop on enemy soldiers, then robbing and executing them. But the end was closer than Quantrill knew. In January 1865, a shady character named Edwin Terrell was hired by Union authorities in Kentucky to hunt down Quantrill. Terrell finally caught up to his quarry on May 10, shooting him in the back as the infamous raider ran for his life. Quantrill, paralyzed, lingered for weeks until dying on June 6.

Throughout his career, the destroyer of Lawrence had ridden with—and commanded the respect of—some of the era's most storied bushwhackers, including Bill Anderson, Cole Younger, and both Frank and Jesse James. Such credentials speak for themselves. Hardened by a conflict in which both sides dramatically lowered the bar of established conduct, Quantrill's hands were some of the bloodiest in a very bloody struggle. As one contemporary wrote, Quantrill's "mode of warfare" was "little, if at all, removed from that of the wildest savage . . . [an] inhuman warfare, in which men are to be shot down like dogs, after throwing down their arms and holding up their hands supplicating for mercy." The author of these words? Brigadier General Henry McCulloch—the regular army officer who, while Quantrill's raiders were wintering in Texas, was technically their direct superior.

BUTCHWHACKER

Before the war, William Quantrill fell hard for Anna Walker, the beautiful daughter of a large Missouri slave owner named Morgan Walker. Though the feeling was mutual, the relationship did not last. (Anna's taste in men stayed more or the less the same—she ended up hooking up with George Todd, the bushwhacker who deposed Quantrill, and went on to marry Joe

Vaughan, also a **Quantrill** raider.) The true love of **Quantrill's** life, however, was Sarah "Kate" King of Jackson County, Missouri. The two probably met sometime in 1863, though Kate was soon forbidden by her father to keep seeing the famous guerrilla. In spite of his efforts, the romance blossomed in secret, and Kate and William may even have married—a topic that historians continue to debate. Whether or not she actually married **Quantrill**, Kate took "Clarke" as an alias last name to further conceal her connection to her infamous lover.

But of all the women in **Quantrill's** life (and there were probably many), the oddest has to be Sue Mundy. Called the "Wild Woman Guerrilla," Sue rode with **Quantrill** in Kentucky in 1865. And she wasn't a woman at all. Her—his—real name was Marcellus Jerome Clark, a former Confederate artilleryman with unusually smooth facial skin. Many stories circulated as to how Jerome came to be called Sue, including the one told by Clark himself: that a female horse thief named Sue Mundy blamed her crime on Clark, and it stuck. At any rate, Clark's colorful career as a Kentucky terror came to a grisly end. In March 1865, he was publicly hanged for his crimes, but dropped a distance that was too short to snap his neck. He thrashed for what seemed an eternity before succumbing to asphyxiation.

UNLUCKY HORSESHOE

Quantrill's demise began, strangely enough, with a horseshoe. His treasured horse, Old Charley, was known for his speed and coolness under fire and had gotten Quantrill out of numerous scrapes. He also didn't like being handled by anyone except his owner. So when one of Quantrill's men attempted to change Old Charley's shoe, the animal reared testily and injured himelf. A vexed Quantrill had no choice but to procure another mount.

The mishap proved deadly when Terrell and his fellow riders caught Quantrill's men napping in a barn on the morning of May 10, 1865. As Quantrill attempted to mount his horse, the beast—who had never before smelled gunpowder or experienced the chaos of battle—bucked wildly amidst the hiss of bullets, preventing his desperate rider from mounting him. Quantrill was forced to give up and simply run as fast as he could behind his galloping men. Just moments later, as he was attempting to mount another horse, Quantrill took a bullet in the left shoulder that ended up lodging near his spine. He fell into the mud, incapable of moving his stricken body. The end had come.

The Headless Horseman

Upon his death in 1865, William Quantrill—who converted to Catholicism on his deathbed—was buried in a Catholic cemetery in Louisville, Kentucky. But that is hardly the end of the story. In 1887, his mother, Caroline Clarke Quantrill, enlisted the help of an Ohio publisher named William Scott to track down her son's bones and bring them back to Dover. Scott, however, proved unscrupulous in his dealings with the widow: Instructed to bring the remains home and bury them in the Quantrill family plot, the publisher did that and more—he buried some and kept the rest in his office to be peddled for money.

Among the bones he decided to keep was Quantrill's skull, though Scott was never able to sell it. He died in 1902. Not long afterward, Scott's son gave or sold the skull to a local fraternity, who used it for years as the featured prop in their initiation ceremonies. (As Quantrill biographer Edward E. Leslie relates, the brothers dubbed the thing "Jake.") In the early 1970s, a trustee of the fraternity handed the relic over to the Dover Historical Society, who used it to fashion a wax likeness of the infamous bushwhacker. Not until 1992 was Quantrill's head reunited with the rest (or at least part of the rest) of its body. In October of that year, the skull—enclosed in a child's coffin—was lowered into the plot that contained the bones Scott had buried more than a century before. Less than a week earlier, the Missouri division of the Sons of Confederate Veterans had buried five of Quantrill's bones in the Confederate Memorial Cemetery in Higginsville. Some six hundred mourners and curiosity seekers had attended the ceremony.

26 ROSE O'NEALE
GREENHOW

1817–October 1, 1864

HIGHEST RANK:

Confederate Spy

ASTROLOGICAL SIGN:

Unknown

NICKNAMES:

Wild Rose, Rebel Rose

WORDS TO REMEMBER:

"The fate of the slave rests with his Southern Master—as the Masters with God! But will you free him? Never, either extermination or eternal slavery is his lot according to the lights before me."

Just before dawn on October 1, 1864, a dark shape with three funnels churned through the waters off the North Carolina coast. It was the side-wheel steamer *Condor*, using the last hours of night to conceal her approach to Wilmington. Defended by Fort Fisher, the port city offered the only surviving sanctuary for *Condor* and her ilk: Confederate blockade-runners slipping through the garrote of Union warships that was slowly strangling the South to death. Suddenly the steamer's pilot, fooled by a beached wreck that looked like an enemy vessel, veered rashly and slid up on the shoals, helpless as a fish out of water. Union ships were already circling for the kill, but the skipper assured his passengers that Fort Fisher's rifled guns would offer protection until the high tide lifted their steamer off the bar.

Being placed under house arrest didn't stop Rose O'Neale Greenhow from being one of the Confederacy's most effective spies. She simply sneaked notes and coded messages to her daughter, who would slip them past the Union guards.

Several passengers weren't so sure. One of them, Rose Greenhow, had been a prisoner before and had no wish to reacquaint herself with Yankee

hospitality. With a formidable persuasiveness that had duped senators, snared lovers, and charmed royalty, Mrs. Greenhow convinced the captain to let her make a run for shore in one of his lifeboats—to brave the windswept waters in twilight rather than the humiliation of capture. He reluctantly complied, allowing the determined woman to be lowered, along with several other passengers, into a dinghy that was to whisk them to safety. The sea, however, had other plans for the hapless party, sending a breaker over the shoal to strike the boat broadside. In the chaos that ensued, all the passengers swam to safety save one: Rose Greenhow disappeared with the foam, never to be seen alive again.

It was a storybook end to a storybook life. Though born in Montgomery County, Maryland, to a rather ordinary drunk who would leave his Catholic family little money, Rose O'Neale ended up securing a privileged place in the country's most powerful circles. Alluring, brilliant, and spirited, she became one of the great provocateurs of the age and a celebrated heroine of her country, driven by a defiant patriotism that was matched only by her scorching race hatred. She has to be one of the most fascinating women in American history.

She certainly was fascinating to her contemporaries. Indeed, the detectives who tracked her movements in 1861 referred to her in their messages as the "fascinating widow." Rose had become such an engaging character by growing up in one of the most colorful cities in the country. Her mother, stuck with a dead husband and too many mouths to feed, had sent Rose and her sister to live in Washington when they were still teenagers. There they lived with Aunt Maria and her husband, Henry Hill, at Hill's Boarding House, a popular location for Southern politicians to call home while Congress was in session. After her older sister married into a prominent Georgetown family, Rose found herself attending the same social events as Andrew Jackson and Daniel Webster. She was getting an intimate education in the many-layered world of capital power broking and glad-handing. Moreover, she was doing so from the vantage point of a very attractive young lady of breeding whose long, dark hair and stimulating conversation could make the most seasoned debaters stumble over their words. Through her sister Ellen, she met and befriended the great Dolley Madison, ageless arbiter of capital society, and developed an unabashed preoccupation with John C. Calhoun, presidential pretender, states' rights sanctifier, and slavery defender. In time, she would grow close to this ferociously eloquent Southern icon—close enough to tend to him while he lay on his deathbed in 1850.

By that time another man had captured much more than her admiration. Dr. Robert Greenhow, a physician by training and a State Department official by trade (he spoke several foreign languages fluently), met Rose at the altar in 1835 in a Catholic ceremony officiated by the Reverend William Matthews, the first American to be ordained a Catholic priest in the United States. Theirs was a typically worldly Washington match, complete with a diplomatic posting to Mexico City. But in 1854, Robert died after a fall in San Francisco. It was more than just a devastating blow emotionally: For the second time in her life, Rose found herself facing an uncertain future—and this time she had a family to raise.

If she didn't have lots of money, she at least had lots of friends. Important friends. One of them was James Buchanan, the perpetually womanless Washington operator from Pennsylvania who assumed the presidency in 1857. Few in the city were as close to the Keystone State's most famous bachelor, and Rose assumed an importance in capital schmoozing that Dolley Madison herself would've envied. Stunning in her forties, with an air of seductive mystery and a whiplike retort for every politically volatile observation offered within earshot, the incomparable Widow Greenhow had become as venerated a capital fixture as Lafayette Square. It was under such circumstances that Rose, an earnest student of the Calhoun school of pro-slavery, anti-centralization politics, became a prisoner in her own city.

The Republicans had come to town. Like a rabble of nouveaux riches, they lorded over their secessionist and Democratic opponents, opening the capital gates to all manner of abolitionist filth and their opportunistic lackeys. Such was Rose Greenhow's view of the 1860 revolution. That shameless "Black Republican" beanpole Lincoln had ruined what had been a most civilized place to live. The good ol' days of the Buchanan regime were quite over. Warned by her Southern circle to get out of town while the getting was good, Rose stayed. Her daughter Gertrude, racked by typhoid fever, could not be moved. But another reason seemed to compel this most Southern of belles to stay put.

This was her city. Her home. There may have been a changing of the guard, but she wasn't going to let that intimidate her. When Gertrude died, it marked the fifth child that Rose had to bury. Anchored by long experience and deep emotion, the Widow Greenhow wasn't going anywhere.

Which is why Thomas Jordan paid her a visit early in 1861. A captain in the regular army, Jordan planned on defecting to the Confederacy and revealed to Rose his plans for building a spy network in Washington itself. She was an ideal addition to his grandiose plans: poised, connected, established. Presented with an opportunity to play a vital role in the struggle against "Black Republicanism," she responded with enthusiasm. Jordan gave her a cipher code to be used in her messages to him and to other agents in the network, and she committed it to memory. Before long she had recruited a small cabal of fellow spies who reported back to her on military developments in and around the capital, of which there were many indeed. And she herself excelled at seducing information out of contacts in the government, not least of whom was a man who signed his love letters with the letter "H"— probably Massachusetts senator Henry Wilson, though H's identity continues to inspire debate.

But as important as all this information was, it was nothing compared to the bold stroke that Rose contributed to the Rebel cause in July 1861. Upon learning that Union general Irvin McDowell was heading out to advance on P. G. T. Beauregard's Rebels at Manassas Junction, Rose sent an accomplice, Betty Duvall, out across the Chain Bridge that linked the capital with Virginia. Duvall, dressed as a simple farm girl, carried a ciphered message in her hair that had been composed by Rose, detailing McDowell's plan. Beauregard acted on the intelligence by alerting Joseph Johnston, his colleague in the Shenandoah Valley, who proceeded to quickly transfer his troops to Manassas by rail. By the time McDowell arrived at Bull Run, he was facing a much larger force than anticipated. The ensuing Union rout was made possible by the Confederates' ability to concentrate their forces.

Whether or not Rose Greenhow is responsible for thwarting an early Federal advance on Richmond and ensuring that the rebellion would extend into a four-year bloodfest of catastrophic proportions is debated to this day. General Beauregard, however, was certainly thankful. And Rose's neighbors, most of whom were pro-Union, did not doubt that she was up to something nefarious. After all, the woman had plenty of male callers, many of whom were in uniform—a very suspicious thing indeed for a house that was openly pro-South. The capital was a lousy place to keep secrets, as Rose herself used to her advantage. And so, alerted by suspicious citizens, the assistant secretary of war called on an old colleague to keep an eye on "Rebel Rose": Allan Pinkerton.

Pinkerton, the Scottish-born head of the secret service, went about the assignment with his usual aplomb. Despite his formidable reputation, he wasn't the greatest detective around—indeed, his later intelligence gathering for the Army of the Potomac would prove outrageously inaccurate. Nor were his tactics very original. (In an attempt to gather evidence that Laurel and Hardy would've considered ideal material, he once stood bootless and precariously perched on the shoulders of two fellow agents in a Washington downpour while clumsily attempting to peer into the parlor window of the Greenhow residence.) Nevertheless, he was tenacious and resourceful. And Rebel Rose wasn't exactly the most tactful spy in Washington. In about a month, the intrepid sleuth had enough evidence to move on his quarry. On August 23, 1861, Pinkerton, accompanied by several colleagues, made his move, arresting Greenhow on the street before her residence. "I have no power to resist you," she sniped upon hearing of her fate, "but had I been inside of my house, I would have killed one of you before I submitted to this illegal process."

The authorities searched her house, confiscated any and all papers they came across, and put the grande dame under house arrest—which, it soon turned out, proved about as effective as containing a bad stench by enclosing it in chicken wire. Rose continued her clandestine activities right under the noses of her captors. She encoded the needlework she gave to friends, encrypted her conversations with visitors, wrote letters with cleverly worded messages in the clear that not even her censors could detect, and—most effectively—used her eight-year-old daughter, Little Rose, as a go-between. For their part, the authorities added insult to injury by using "Fort Greenhow," as the house came to be called, as a prison for other female felons, most of whom weren't the sort of people Rose would've associated with willingly. The spy mistress seethed.

Catching on to her activities, the government moved her to Old Capitol Prison, which—in a cruel bit of irony—used to be the boardinghouse in which she grew up with her sister. In fact, Rose was held for a time within the very room in which she nursed Calhoun during his final days over a decade before. Little Rose was incarcerated along with her mother, and the two became heroines throughout the South. Though a trial was arranged, it proved more trouble than it was worth—an opportunity for this spirited beauty to vent her secessionist views and become a martyr. As Lincoln did with many folks who became irritating to his administration, he banished her to the South to let her fellow traitors deal with her.

And deal with her they did. Welcomed as a celebrity, the Widow Greenhow met with President Jeff Davis, whose government gave her $2,500 as a reward for services rendered. In time they would call on her services once again, this time in a much more significant capacity. A year later, in August 1863, Rose Greenhow boarded a famously swift Confederate vessel appropriately named *Phantom* that was to deliver her safely to Europe. Once there she was charged with pulling off what the Rebel government had hitherto failed to do: convince Great Britain and France that it was in their best interests to actively support the struggling Confederacy. After a three-week stopover in Bermuda (where she noted that "the Negroes are lazy, vicious and insubordinate"), Rose and her daughter were delivered to England, where her most significant accomplishments were the publication of her memoir (*My Imprisonment and the First Year of Abolition Rule at Washington*), a journey across the channel to meet with French emperor Napoleon III and to enroll Little Rose in Catholic school, and a romantic affair with an unknown Englishman. Her diplomatic efforts, however, were a failure. In short, Rose was too late: By the middle of 1863, the European powers had all but ruled out the possibility of joining the fracas in America. Though feted as a daring and intelligent emissary of Southern culture, her hosts across the Atlantic were loath to do more than enjoy her engaging company. And her unfortunate habit of hotly defending the institution of slavery did nothing for her cause.

And so it was back to her beloved South aboard the *Condor*, having left her daughter behind to be educated in Europe. When the waters claimed Rose in 1864 off the coast of North Carolina, they were aided by the weight of gold—four hundred British sovereigns, to be exact, worth more than $2,000. The treasure, profits from her memoir, was kept in a bag she had attached to a chain around her neck. It might just as well have been a noose.

SEEING THE LIGHT

House arrest was genuinely humiliating for Rose Greenhow, and not just because she was held prisoner in her own home. The soldiers assigned to guard her weren't exactly the flower of Union manhood. In fact, some of them were slobs. She wasn't allowed to lie down for a nap without one of them sitting nearby. And when dressing, she was required to keep the doors open, offering a perfect opportunity for the guard to sate his prurient curiosity. Such conditions would have been hard on anyone, but for a woman as proud as Rose Greenhow, they were almost debilitating. Inherently defiant, she was hardly a demure inmate. Later, while incarcerated in Old Capitol Prison, she lighted a candle one night while rummaging through her belongings. Ordered to put it out, Rose fired up another just to piss off the guards. One of them shouted from the yard that he would fire into her room, but it only inspired her to gather up more candles, light them, and place them all defiantly on her windowsill. When another guard, yelling at her for sending signals from her window, pounded on the door to get her to stop, she simply threatened to shoot the fellow with a pistol. It wasn't loaded, but nobody knew that. (The prison staff deprived her of the weapon the next morning.)

Enemy Mine

Few people hated Abraham Lincoln more than Rose Greenhow. And yet Stephen Douglas, the "Little Giant" who debated Lincoln so famously in 1858, was her nephew—a nephew who, much to her chagrin, became closer to Lincoln in the months leading up to the latter's inauguration. In fact, Douglas literally stood at the president-elect's side and held his hat while Lincoln was sworn in.

As galling as this was to Rebel Rose, it couldn't have hurt as much as the relationship she had with her own son-in-law. Tredwell Moore, Florence Greenhow's husband, was a soldier stationed out west when the war began. Though he and Florence expressed sympathy for the South, they were strict Unionists, a fact Florence never failed to mention in her letters to her fire-eating mother back in Washington. Moore hated being stuck in Nevada as the country blew apart and wanted more than anything to become an officer in the Ohio volunteers to fight secessionists. Like everyone else who wanted to secure a commission, he turned to someone with influence—in this case, his mother-in-law. Rose soon found herself in the unlikely situation of writing a letter to Secretary of the Treasury Salmon Chase—a radical Republican—to ask that Tredwell be given the posting and promotion he needed to come east and kill those on whose behalf she was risking her life in acts of espionage. Civil wars are hell.

Moore did end up getting into the war. But his mother-in-law's precarious financial situation compelled him to send her money on a regular basis—a total of $10,000, according to him, which he and Florence attempted (unsuccessfully) to reclaim from the settlement of Rose's estate after her death.

SELECTED BIBLIOGRAPHY

Blackman, Ann. *Wild Rose: Rose O'Neale Greenhow, Civil War Spy*. New York: Random House, 2005.

Blanton, DeAnne, and Lauren M. Cook. *They Fought Like Demons: Women Soldiers in the Civil War*. Baton Rouge: Louisiana State University Press, 2002.

Boatner III, Mark M. *The Civil War Dictionary*. New York: Random House, 1988.

Catton, Bruce. *The Army of the Potomac: A Stillness at Appomattox*. Garden City, New York: Doubleday, 1953.

———. *The Army of the Potomac: Glory Road*. Garden City, New York: Doubleday, 1952.

———. *The Army of the Potomac: Mr. Lincoln's Army*. Garden City, New York: Doubleday, 1962.

Clinton, Catherine. *Harriet Tubman: The Road to Freedom*. New York: Little, Brown and Company, 2004.

Davis, Burke. *The Civil War: Strange and Fascinating Facts*. New York: Random House, 1996.

Davis, William C. *Jefferson Davis: The Man and His Hour*. New York: HarperCollins, 1991.

Donald, David Herbert. *Lincoln*. New York: Simon and Schuster, 1995.

Foote, Shelby. *The Civil War: A Narrative*. (Three Vols.) New York: Vintage Books, 1986.

Freeman, Douglas Southall. *Lee*. New York: Scribner, 1961.

Gallman, Matthew J., ed. *The Civil War Chronicle*. New York: Gramercy Books, 2000.

Gansler, Laura Leedy. *The Mysterious Private Thompson: The Double Life of Sarah Emma Edmonds, Civil War Soldier*. New York: Free Press, 2005.

Garrison, Webb. *Civil War Curiosities: Strange Stories, Oddities, Events, and Coincidences*. Nashville, Tennessee: Rutledge Hill Press, 1994.

———. *Civil War Trivia and Fact Book*. Nashville, Tennessee: Rutledge Hill Press, 1992.

———. *More Civil War Curiosities: Fascinating Tales, Infamous Characters, and Strange Coincidences*. Nashville, Tennessee: Rutledge Hill Press, 1995.

Hallock, Judith Lee. *Braxton Bragg and Confederate Defeat*. Volume Two. Tuscaloosa, Alabama: University of Alabama Press, 1991.

Hebert, Walter H. *Fighting Joe Hooker*. Indianapolis: Bobbs-Merrill, 1944.

Hirshson, Stanley P. *The White Tecumseh: A Biography of William T. Sherman*. New York: John Wiley & Sons, 1997.

Hurst, Jack. *Nathan Bedford Forest: A Biography*. New York: Alfred A. Knopf, 1993.

Jennison, Keith W. *The Humorous Mr. Lincoln*. New York: Bonanza Books, 1965.

Keneally, Thomas. *American Scoundrel: The Life of the Notorious Civil War General Dan Sickles*. New York: Doubleday, 2002.

Larson, Kate Clifford. *Bound for the Promised Land: Harriet Tubman, Portrait of an American Hero*. New York: Ballantine, 2004.

Leslie, Edward E. *The Devil Knows How to Ride: The True Story of William Clarke Quantrill and His Confederate Raiders*. New York: Random House, 1996.

Long, E. B., and Barbara Long. *The Civil War Day by Day: An Almanac, 1861–1865*. Garden City, New York: Doubleday, 1971.

Marszalek, John F. *Commander of All Lincoln's Armies: A Life of General Henry W. Halleck*. Cambridge, Massachusetts: Harvard University Press, 2004.

Marvel, William. *Burnside*. Chapel Hill: University of North Carolina Press, 1991.

McFeely, William S. *Frederick Douglass*. New York: W. W. Norton and Company, 1991.

McPherson, James M. *Battle Cry of Freedom: The Civil War Era*. New York: Oxford University Press, 1988.

McWhiney, Grady. *Braxton Bragg and Confederate Defeat: Volume I: Field Command*. New York: Columbia University Press, 1969.

Morris, Roy Jr. *Sheridan: The Life and Wars of General Phil Sheridan*. New York: Crown Publishers, 1992.

Osborne, Charles C. *Jubal: The Life and Times of General Jubal A. Early, CSA, Defender of the Lost Cause*. Chapel Hill: Algonquin Books, 1992.

Pfanz, Donald C. *Richard S. Ewell: A Soldier's Life*. Chapel Hill: University of North Carolina Press, 1998.

Piston, William Garrett. *Lee's Tarnished Lieutenant: James Longstreet and His Place in Southern History*. Athens: University of Georgia Press, 1987.

Robertson, James I. Jr. *General A. P. Hill: The Story of a Confederate Warrior*. New York: Random House, 1987.

———. *Stonewall Jackson: The Man, the Soldier, the Legend*. New York: Macmillan, 1997.

Ross, Ishbel. *First Lady of the South: The Life of Mrs. Jefferson Davis*. Westport, Connecticut: Greenwood Press, 1973.

Sears, Stephen W. *George B. McClellan: The Young Napoleon*. New York: Ticknor & Fields, 1988.

Sifakis, Stewart. *Who Was Who in the Civil War*. New York: Facts on File Publications, 1988.

Smith, Gene. *Lee and Grant*. New York: Penguin Group, 1984.

Smith, Jean Edward. *Grant*. New York: Simon & Schuster, 2001.

Styple, William B., ed. *Generals in Bronze: Interviewing the Commanders of the Civil War*. Kearny, New Jersey: Bell Grove, 2005.

Thomas, Emory M. *Bold Dragoon: The Life of J. E. B. Stuart*. New York: Harper and Row, 1986.

Wagner, Margaret E., Gary W. Gallagher, and Paul Finkelman, eds. *The Library of Congress Civil War Desk Reference*. New York: Simon and Schuster, 2002.

Warner, Ezra. *Generals in Blue: Lives of the Union Commanders*. Baton Rouge: Louisiana State University Press, 1964.

———. *Generals in Gray: Lives of the Confederate Commanders*. Baton Rouge: Louisiana State University Press, 1959.

Wert, Jeffry D. *General James Longstreet: The Confederacy's Most Controversial Soldier*. New York: Simon & Schuster, 1993.

Woodward, Stephen E., and Kenneth J. Winkle. *Oxford Atlas of the Civil War*. New York: Oxford University Press, 2004.

INDEX

ACKNOWLEDGMENTS

My heartfelt gratitude goes out to the people at Quirk who made this possible. I would especially like to thank Jason Rekulak, my editor and a man of inexhaustible patience, and Jon Barthmus, who did a splendid job designing the pages and coping with a harried schedule. I am also grateful to Monica Suteski for her extraordinary illustrations (as always!); Robert Romagnoli for the exquisite map on pages 14–15; Jennifer Shenk for doing such a thorough job with her fact checking and copyediting; Faatima Qureshi and Nick Volo for their help with the research; and Lauren Beck for her understanding and . . . other things.